'It is to Mark Doyle's considerable c[...] in making the Kinks's records, these h[...] era, seem brand new, fresh and rele[...] the past . . . I know these records inside out, but Doyle sent me back to them with fresh insights and enthusiasm . . . There are more straight-forward accounts of the Kinks's career available, including some by members of the group, but few are as eloquent, persuasive or fully engaged as *Songs of the Semi-detached*.' – ANDY MILLER, *The Spectator*

'Doyle is less a fanboy, more inclined to trace the psychogeography of Ray Davies's immaculate lyricism, drawing a ley line from Fortis Green to all things Carnabetian . . . As an example of critical rather than academic investigation, *Songs of the Semi-detached* nails Davies's observational cynicism and class-consciousness, revealing his many masks.' – *Classic Rock Magazine*

'Mark Doyle's excellent *The Kinks: Songs of the Semi-Detached* . . . traces the band's music from their formation in Muswell Hill, North London, in 1964 to 1971's *Muswell Hillbillies* . . . His book is a welcome piece of historically informed criticism that situates the Kinks in their proper milieu – postwar, working-class North London – and their cultural moment: the British music explosion of the 1960s.' – WESLEY STACE, *Wall Street Journal*

'As a piece of rock criticism this is a masterful text, and as an examination of social change in 20th Century Blighty, it is as illuminating as it's possible to get. Doyle unravels the Kinks' relationship to working class England in a variety of ways, casting a light on Ray Davies' genius for creating immediately identifiable characters as vehicles for social commentary . . . Davies' own love affair with London and its people is brought to life through the author's exhaustive research and his commen-surate skill in both contextualising the songs and celebrating the "apartness" of their creator. A compelling read for anyone even remotely interested in the band and its music.' – *Shindig!*

'Doyle finds the world of postwar Britain, rapidly changing yet also nostalgic, endlessly fascinating. He sees class and social attitudes through the eyes of an outside observer, and places Davies in the company of Betjeman, Auden and Larkin as a chronicler of suburbia . . . *The Kinks* is thoughtful and readable.' – *Literary Review*

The REVERB series looks at the connections between music, artists and performers, musical cultures and places. It explores how our cultural and historical understanding of times and places may help us to appreciate a wide variety of music, and vice versa.

reverb-series.co.uk
SERIES EDITOR: JOHN SCANLAN

Already published

THE
KINKS

SONGS OF THE
SEMI-DETACHED

MARK DOYLE

REAKTION BOOKS

For Joey

Published by Reaktion Books Ltd
Unit 32, Waterside
44–48 Wharf Road
London N1 7UX, UK
www.reaktionbooks.co.uk

First published 2020, reprinted 2020
Copyright © Mark Doyle 2020

Printed and bound in Great Britain by
TJ International, Padstow, Cornwall

A catalogue record for this book is available from the British Library
ISBN 978 1 78914 230 3

Contents

The author's Ray Davies doll: Cuban heels, red hunting jacket
and a characteristic smirk.

Introduction: A Face in the Crowd

'Perhaps you can only express your feeling in your music',
said Shrieve. 'I've always thought that the really great artists
wrote and painted and so on with such marvellous conviction
because they were somehow detached from everyone else,
and could only express their love by indirect means.'

Julian Mitchell, *The White Father* (1964)

On a bookshelf in my house there's a small, crude Ray Davies doll dating from 1964 or 1965. It's made of two pieces of coarse cloth stitched together and stuffed with cotton, with a two-colour heat-transfer image of the Kinks' lead singer and songwriter on one side. You can tell that he's from 1964 or '65 because he's wearing a red hunting jacket, tight black trousers and spiked Cuban heels – the iconic Kinks costume during the first year of their success – and you can tell that it's Ray because his right eyebrow is cocked and the left corner of his mouth is turned up in a characteristic smirk. Presumably there are matching dolls of the other three Kinks somewhere in the world, but this one, which my wife plucked from an online curiosity shop a few years ago, has been separated from his bandmates and the long-forgotten teen marketing machine that produced him. So there he stands, alone on a shelf, detached and decontextualized. His expression seems to say that he always knew it would come to this.

That smirk is the Kinks in a nutshell. The jazz musician and cultural critic George Melly once summarized the Kinks' relationship to their era thus:

They stood aside watching, with sardonic amusement, the pop world chasing its own tail, and they turned out some of the most quirky intelligent grown-up and totally personal records in the history of British pop. Their trouble (or perhaps their strength would be more accurate) was their non-conformism, their refusal to join the club. They were and are hugely underrated as a consequence.[1]

This was true of the Kinks from about mid-1965 onwards, but it is not quite true of the first phase of their career, which began nearly two years earlier. In the early days, despite the weird costumes, they did not look or sound all that different from most other British beat groups, and if they were rated less highly than the others, there probably were good reasons for that. But even in the early days it was evident that Ray Davies, at least, was keeping himself one or two steps removed from the pop world in which he was entangled. You can see it in many of the group photos of the period. Dave Davies, Ray's younger brother and the group's lead guitarist, was a much more carefree character: in photographs you can usually identify him by a twinkling eye or a careless grin. Mick Avory, the drummer, has the solid and slightly impatient look that drummers often have, and bassist Pete Quaife tends to pout moodily in a way that makes him look either surly or sleepy. But Ray, ostensibly the front man of the group, usually looks like he'd rather be anywhere other than where he is. He rarely smiles, and when he does it is always with his lips sealed in a crooked grin. Whether he thinks he's above all of this pop silliness or simply uncomfortable in front of the camera, you can see that his mind is elsewhere, that he's not really playing the same game as everybody else. He is both inside and outside the frame, wary and abstracted, observing the foolishness even while he acts the fool. He is mostly detached, but not completely: he is, as it were, semi-detached.

The Kinks in 1964: (L–R) Dave Davies, Ray Davies, Pete Quaife and Mick Avory.

This book is neither a comprehensive history of the Kinks nor a love letter to Ray Davies and his bandmates. The world has more than enough biographies, memoirs, magazine profiles, documentaries and gossipy chronicles of the group's three-decade career to satisfy even the most ardent fan.[2] Rather, this is an exercise in what I have decided to call historically informed rock criticism. I am interested in the artistry embedded within the Kinks' songs – usually, though not always, written by Ray Davies – and to understand that artistry I will do what we historians are trained to do: situate the object of analysis within its historical context. But what interests me is not the context itself so much as the odd angle from which Davies viewed his world. Although he and the other Kinks had deep roots in a particular social milieu (post-war, working-class north London) and participated in a distinctive cultural moment (the British pop explosion of the 1960s), they were never fully a part of either world. This book is an attempt to explain both why this was so and how this position of partial (but never total) detachment shaped their art.

'Art', the German art historian Max Raphael once wrote, 'is an interplay, an equation of three factors – the artist, the world and the means of figuration.'[3] Most of what has been written about the Kinks concerns the first part of this equation, that is, the life of the artist(s): the early inspirations, the initial rush to fame, the hedonism, the fights, the hits, the four-year ban from America, the commercial ups and downs, the quarrels with managers and publishers, the ambitious but abortive theatrical projects, the over-ambitious theatrical projects that should have been aborted (but weren't) and the eventual conquering of America as an arena rock band in the late 1970s and 1980s. It is not my purpose here to rehash these stories or to offer any stunning new revelations about the life of Ray Davies and his fellow Kinks. Nor will I have much to say about the third factor in Raphael's equation, 'the means of figuration'. This refers to the medium in which artists create their art, which in this case is the musical raw material – the arrangements, the instrumentation, the melodic structures and so forth – that went into constructing the Kinks' songs. I will touch upon these elements from time to time, but for the most part I leave it to the professional musicians and theorists to explain what makes a song like 'Autumn Almanac', say, such a satisfying aural experience.

Raphael's second factor, 'the world', is where most of our attention will be focused. What kind of world did the Kinks inhabit, and how did they turn that world into art? The Kinks are a natural choice for such an approach, for few other rock bands have subjected their world to such relentless, sometimes pitiless, interrogation. Indeed, sometimes it seems that you can hardly write about the Kinks without taking their historical context into account: even the most superficial biographies usually end up speaking at some length about the social and political changes the Kinks were responding to in their songs. For historians, Davies's lyrics offer useful primary-source information about the changes Britain underwent in the 1960s, shedding light on such diverse subjects as working-class affluence, popular attitudes towards the welfare state and changing ideas about sexuality. Academics of a more literary bent, meanwhile, have subjected Davies's songs to detailed textual and thematic analyses, identifying the affinities between his work and that of the Romantic poets, for example, or tracing the role of humour, food, home and other big themes across his entire body of work. Much of this academic work is valuable,[4] but it is not quite what I am doing here. My aim is essentially aesthetic, even if my technique is historical. I believe that understanding the deep historical currents upon which the Kinks' music draws – not just the immediate context in which it was produced, but the structural changes to which it was responding and the traditions of English thought upon which it was drawing – can help us appreciate their music in satisfying new ways. The idea is to understand their art by understanding their world and the unique, historically conditioned perspectives they brought to it: history in aid of musical appreciation.

So what, exactly, was the Kinks' world? Geographically, we can picture it as a series of concentric rings centred on 6 Denmark Terrace, the Davies family home in north London, in a residential area called Fortis Green between Muswell Hill and East Finchley. The first ring takes in the square mile or so around Denmark Terrace, where Ray and Dave Davies encountered their earliest musical inspirations. Within this ring were the homes of assorted Davies sisters and brothers-in-law and cousins, the home of bassist Pete Quaife, the parks the Davies brothers played in, the library from which they borrowed books by the likes of George Orwell and Alan Sillitoe, the first schools they attended and the modest semi-detached house that Ray Davies would buy in 1965 during the group's early rush to fame. The next ring swings a few miles southeast to Holloway and Barnsbury, the old working-class district of northeast London where the extended Davies clan lived before the Blitz. The Kinks would return to these streets many times over the years to check in on the past and present of working-class London, and what they found often turned up in their songs. The next ring encompasses central London: the clubs and cafés of Soho where the Kinks got their start, the boutiques of the King's Road and Carnaby Street where they bought their threads, the music publishers of Denmark Street where they signed their deals and, of course, the sunset as viewed from Waterloo Bridge. A still wider ring takes in the countryside surrounding London, the site of Sunday drives when the brothers were children and, later, of a failed experiment in rock-star living amid the commuters of the stockbroker belt. The penultimate ring encircles England itself, its history and traditions, its class system and prejudices, its ways of thinking and talking about itself. And the final ring stretches across the Atlantic to America, the source of the group's earliest inspirations and the site of their most persistent longings. All of these places (along with a few outliers like Australia and Waikiki) shaped the Kinks' music in various ways, but by far the most important were the first location and the last, which were, respectively, the sites of their earliest experiences and of their earliest dreams. For much of their career, the Kinks were a band caught in a tug of war between the familiar, quotidian world of Fortis Green and the fantastic but only dimly understood world of America. Sometimes they were pulled one way, sometimes the other, and their songs marked the progress of that struggle.

There is another way to conceptualize the Kinks' world, however, and that is to situate them not in space but in time. Here the starting point is Britain from the late 1950s to the early 1970s, an age of unprecedented affluence, irreverence and optimism. These were what we might call the Muswell Hill years, the period when the centre of the Kinks' creative universe was the small patch of suburban north London where the brothers had grown up, the home base from which they struck out into the wider world. But Ray Davies also applied his imagination to an earlier era, the era of the Blitz and the big-band dance halls, when his older sisters would go out dancing with American servicemen and the London working classes were poorer but also more cohesive and (it seemed to him) somehow happier. The time before the Second World War, a time when the suburbs were expanding and the working classes lived quite desperate lives, also informed Davies's work, as did the time of the First World War. The Edwardian and Victorian eras were also part of the Kinks' world: they showed up in a superficial way in the aristocratic hunting jackets that the group wore and the Dickensian stage names they briefly adopted, but they were more substantially present in the things the Kinks chose to sing about (the suburbs, London street life, the countryside, working-class identity) and the musical vocabulary that their songs employed. Indeed, some of the Kinks' most important themes had been the subjects of artistic depiction and contemplation well before even the Victorian era. Eighteenth-century ideas about English national identity and seventeenth-century warnings about the dangerous pleasures of London also had their echoes, however faint, in their music.

Part of my aim is to situate the Kinks' songs within these deep traditions of English art and thought, taking in such figures as William Hogarth, Edmund Burke, John Clare, Charles Dickens, George Orwell and John Betjeman. My purpose in connecting the Kinks to these deep traditions is not to undercut the band's originality but, rather, to bring their originality into sharper relief. Although I will spend a good deal of time identifying the traditions on which their music draws, I will also explain why their songs do not fit entirely comfortably within these traditions. The standard line about the Kinks is that they were a 'very English' band. They sang about village greens and afternoon teas, satirized the class system and dressed like characters from English costume dramas. Having been banned from the United States just when their star was beginning to rise, so the narrative usually goes, they 'retreated' into Englishness, settling for a few years into the rock-band equivalent of mucking about in the back garden. As we will see, there is some truth to this version of the story, but I will argue that the band's Englishness was much deeper and more complex than most fans and critics realize. For even more than they were a 'very English' band, the Kinks were a very working-class band, and this fact ensured that their variety of Englishness never quite aligned with the dominant (that is, upper- and middle-class) artistic and intellectual traditions of England – although sometimes, particularly when they were pretending to be aristocrats, they came quite close. What becomes clear when we compare their work with that of other 'very English' writers and artists, in other words, is just how working-class the Kinks really were.

The Kinks' relationship to working-class England is the central concern of this book. As we will see, as a songwriter Ray Davies had a hard time committing to one point of view for very long – his outlook could swing wildly from one song to the next, or even from one verse to the next – but his songs do show a remarkably consistent commitment to an idea of a working-class community that was probably more myth than reality, an idea of a jolly, tight-knit, homogeneous and fundamentally decent community deeply rooted in the bricks and stones of inner London. His commitment to this community was evident throughout this period, from the Kinks' earliest songs of youthful rebellion to their half-drunken hymns to working-class resilience in the early 1970s. You could hear it in their youthful rage, their class-conscious satire, their fondness for lowbrow culture and their embrace of a 'very English' sort of anti-establishment politics that was simultaneously backward looking and forward facing, regretting a lost Golden Age even as it looked ahead to a New Jerusalem. Yet even here Davies's perspective was idiosyncratic. As a suburban kid who had grown up during a period of unprecedented national affluence, he was never fully a part of the old working-class world that he regarded so fondly. Even within his own family he tended to keep himself to himself, and in the wider world in which his family was embedded he was always something of an interloper – part of the community, to be sure, but just barely, and becoming less so by the year. It is this apartness – this coming-close-but-never-quite-fitting-in-ness – that, to me, is the defining characteristic of Davies's songs, and the secret to what makes the greatest Kinks songs so great. Whatever box you try to place Davies in – peddler of nostalgia, Dickensian caricaturist, tortured artist, nineteenth-century Romantic, sneering hipster, camp entertainer, radical insurgent, small-c conservative – bits of him inevitably end up sticking out at awkward angles. He is both there and not there, travelling down well-worn paths but not always keeping to the road, a working-class kid with ideas above his station and an intellectual who can never quite shake the mud from his high-heeled boots.

Which brings us back to that smirk: 'That ragged, quizzical smile – the very incarnation of wryness, slyness and wistful melancholy', as the critic David Dalton once described it.[5] There are, I think, several ways that Ray Davies's characteristic facial expression in those early photos can help us understand the music that he made. First, it hints at the ambiguity that structures many of his songs, for what is a smirk but something like a half-smile, indicating that its wearer is half-serious and half-amused? This was the default attitude with which Davies wrote and delivered many of his songs, and it creates the fundamental dilemma for any thoughtful Kinks listener: how to untangle the serious from the comical, the heart-felt from the sarcastic. Is 'The Village Green Preservation Society' an earnest plea to preserve England's vanishing heritage or a satire on traditionalist Little Englanders? Is 'Shangri-La' an indictment of suburban conformity or an affectionate ode to suburban

Three out of four Kinks showing their teeth in 1967: (L–R) Mick Avory,
Pete Quaife, Ray Davies and Dave Davies.

contentment? Is 'Autumn Almanac' a parody or a celebration of the
working-class penchant for Blackpool holidays and Saturday football? Davies's half-smile tells us that the answer is, well, yes and yes.

This ambiguity is one of Davies's great strengths as a songwriter. Like gemstones that take on different colours depending
on the light, his best songs have a way of changing from moment
to moment; how you respond to them depends on your disposi-
tion, your stage in life, even your current mood. The literary critic
William Empson once identified 'seven types of ambiguity', which he
suggested undergird some of England's finest poetry. The seventh
type, 'the most ambiguous that can be conceived', is that which
occurs 'when the two meanings of the word, the two values of the
ambiguity, are the two opposite meanings defined by the context,
so that the total effect is to show a fundamental division in the

writer's mind'. Someone confronting art that is composed of such opposites – as, for instance, in the art of the ancient Sumerians that showed 'two beasts in exactly symmetrical attitudes of violence' – will feel 'drawn taut between the two similar impulses into the stasis of appreciation'.[6] Empson's point was that internally contradictory art generates pleasure and appreciation precisely from the sharpness with which its contradictions are drawn. Sometimes contradictions can collapse into mere muddle, but at other times they can create profound new meanings that are greater than their component parts. Many Kinks songs display such a 'fundamental division' in Davies's mind about all sorts of things, and what might have been simple indecision on his part is capable of generating quite profound responses on the part of the listener. The tension that he often sets up between a longing for the past and a rejection of such longing, for example, can lead you not only to contemplate the problematic nature of nostalgia, but to carefully weigh the various arguments in favour of either position. In this way you end up thinking, and maybe even feeling, much more than you do with a song of the 'I love my baby but she don't love me' variety (although, of course, the Kinks recorded many of these as well).

Because songs occupy a limited span of time, moreover, an ambiguous or self-contradictory song can arouse different emotions at different moments during its performance, taking you from one attitude to another over the course of several minutes. The total experience is more dynamic, more invigorating or unnerving, than a song that is uncomplicatedly joyful or sorrowful. This is the case with a song like 'Shangri-La', which in five minutes runs through at least three different moods that evoke conflicting attitudes towards the character's suburban predicament, so that by the end, if you've been listening closely, you feel a bit worn out by the experience. You might instinctively identify more with one mood than with the others, but the presence of the others can subtly undermine the one that you first identified with. There is a toppling sort of feeling to a song like this: you're never quite sure which foot you should be resting your weight on. This is not just a matter of ambiguous lyrical content: it also comes from the mismatch between the mood or attitude of the lyrics, which on 'Shangri-La' are often rather sneering, and the mood or attitude of the music, which is intermittently triumphant. 'The best pop songs', as musicologist Simon Frith has said, 'are those that can be heard as a *struggle* between verbal and musical rhetoric, between the singer and the song.'[7] As we will see, much of the Kinks' art emerges from just such a struggle.

Interestingly, members of the Kinks have often expressed their own confusion about whether their songs should be taken seriously or satirically. During an interview in 1967, journalist Keith Altham put it to Ray Davies that 'Waterloo Sunset' was rather sarcastic sounding. Davies has often described the song as one of his most personal and heartfelt, but here he admitted to Altham that his own feelings about the song might be wrong: 'I've never really thought about the lyrics being sarcastic, but I suppose they are – it's just the way I feel.'[8] A few years later *Rolling Stone* journalist Jonathan Cott, identifying something that sounded like a 'hippo groan' on the song 'Lazy Old Sun', suggested to Davies that he was afraid of sounding sincere: 'As if you're saying something real, don't want to take it seriously, so undermine it with the groan. I could be wrong.' Davies responded simply, 'But you're really right.'[9] Similarly, Dave Davies seems to have missed what is, to me, the obvious sarcasm in the song 'The Village Green Preservation Society' when it includes 'virginity' among its inventory of traditional English virtues. 'Don't know about the virginity bit', he wrote in his memoir, 'Ray's purist streak taking things a little too far'.[10] Dave has in fact often been perplexed by his brother's intentions. According to Ray, Dave once responded to the song 'She's Bought a Hat Like Princess Marina' – about a poor housewife who dresses in a manner far above her station – by declaring 'I don't know if you like these people or you hate them.'[11] If the Davies brothers themselves aren't sure whether these songs are joking or serious, then listeners can certainly be excused for wondering the same thing.

A second characteristic of Ray Davies's songs that can be glimpsed in those early group photographs is an attitude of ironic distancing, as if the singer is not entirely present in whatever situation or attitude we find him in. As George Melly recognized, the Kinks may have been a product of the supercharged pop world, but they also waged a sort of anti-pop guerrilla campaign in many of their songs. Eventually Ray Davies would write half an album's worth of songs savaging the music industry (1970's *Lola Versus Powerman and the Moneygoround, Part One*), but he fired the opening shots as early as 1965 with a string of singles satirizing the Swinging Sixties scene.

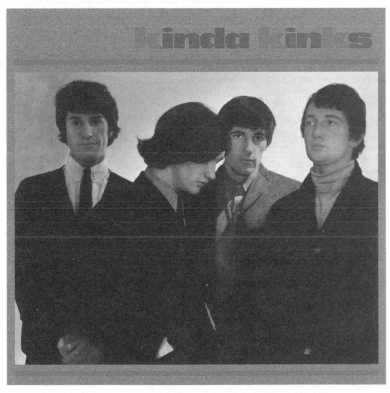

Cover of *Kinda Kinks*, the band's second album (1965).

'Dandy' poked fun at the sort of amoral lotharios who dominated the bars and clubs in which the Kinks performed. 'Dedicated Follower of Fashion' took the mickey out of the style-conscious Mods who formed the Kinks' early fan base. Even the defiantly nonconformist 'I'm Not Like Everybody Else', written by Ray but sung by Dave, can take on an ironic tone if you picture hundreds of sharply dressed Mods singing the chorus together in a Soho nightclub, fists raised in unanimous nonconformity. Yet we mustn't press this point too far. For most of this period the Kinks were still a true band, not just Ray Davies and three other guys, so it is inaccurate to see them as fully disconnected from their times. Dave, for one, was certainly much more comfortable with the go-go Sixties than his brother was, partying with the likes of Brian Jones and Eric Burdon, splashing out on drink and drugs, getting into fistfights, dressing like a peacock and maintaining a prodigious and occasionally self-destructive sex life. Dave was three years younger than Ray, world-famous from the age of seventeen, and he behaved the way that most teenage boys in his situation would. His background in working-class London had bequeathed him a certain *carpe diem* hedonism – a survival from an earlier era of hard work and deprivation, when life's few physical pleasures were best swallowed whole – and he was only too happy to indulge in the carnal perks of pop stardom. (One of my pet theories is that Ray gave Dave vocal duties on 'I'm Not Like Everybody Else' as a way of tricking his brother into an act of grandiose and uncon-scious self-satire.) Pete and Mick were more restrained than Dave but still quite taken with the fashionable world they had crashed into, and together they helped keep the Kinks grounded (if that is the word) in the clubs of Soho and the boutiques of Carnaby Street even as Ray was satirizing the scene that had birthed them.

As many critics have noted, the contrast between Ray's emo-tional detachment and Dave's passionate enthusiasm was central to the Kinks' success. Ray's lyrical and melodic gifts enabled the Kinks to become something more than just another British beat band,

and Dave's pounding guitar and high, yearning vocals provided the emotional intensity that Ray often lacked. This tension between them was as important to their sound as the tension between John Lennon and Paul McCartney or Mick Jagger and Keith Richards, even though, unlike those others, the Davies brothers almost never wrote songs together. Ray was always a loner, the thoughtful and retiring one in a large and boisterous family, and you can hear that loneliness in many of his songs. Making music was his way of elevating his natural loneliness into something meaningful; while the rest of the London pop world was out partying, he stayed in to write songs that would express his unique vision of the world. Dave was

Dave Davies draws a crowd on Carnaby Street, 1967.

The Kinks in red hunting jackets, 1964: (L–R) Pete Quaife, Mick Avory,
Ray Davies and Dave Davies.

the very opposite of his brother in many respects, reckless and gregarious where Ray was cautious and quiet, uninterested (and perhaps incapable) of being alone with his thoughts and fears, which he drowned out with his yelps and crashing chords. Without Dave, Ray would probably never have taken the plunge into pop stardom; without Ray, Dave would probably never have made music that stood out from the crowd.

The third thing that Ray's smirk can tell us has to do with self-effacement. To hear him tell it, what's really going on in all of those publicity photos is not indecision as to whether to smile or frown, nor a sign of ironic detachment, but rather a conscious effort to cover up his own insecurities. If we were actually to pry open that tight-lipped grimace, the first thing we would notice would be a sizeable gap between Davies's two front teeth, the result of a childhood accident. This physical imperfection was a source of intense embarrassment to the young Davies and something that he worked to hide as much as possible. Before the Kinks, when he was a member of the Dave Hunt Band, he got an intimation of what life as a gap-toothed pop star would be like when a girl made fun of him for it. 'She was a lot older than I was,' he told an interviewer years later, 'and after we'd finished playing I'd sing some to her and she said: "That's all very well, but as soon as you smile you mess it all up."'[12] When the Kinks started to become popular, he developed 'a technique of singing with my top lip stiffened in order to expose "the gap" as little as possible'.[13] He never quite managed to overcome the embarrassment of it. At the end of the 1960s, the rock critic and scenester Nik Cohn, in an otherwise admiring assessment, wrote, 'With his gappy teeth and his grin all twisted, he looks clownish and he seems always doubtful, unsure of himself, so that you expect him to split his pants or trip over his feet. He even wears white socks.'[14] Over the years Davies became more willing to expose 'the gap' during performances, but his reluctance to show his teeth in photographs has remained a constant. His dislike of photography is legendary. 'I've hated having my picture taken ever since I was a kid,' he recalled, 'so you can imagine how I felt when I entered a business where I had to have my picture taken on a regular basis. That's why I look so goddam miserable in pictures.'[15]

When Ray Davies is failing to smile in his photos, then, what he is really doing is hiding. This practice of creating a false front behind which to conceal his real, flawed self permeates most aspects of his art, from the characters he creates in his songs to the flamboyant, larger-than-life personas he sometimes adopts onstage. He is a bit like Bob Dylan or David Bowie in this way, trying on new identities, uttering gnomic koans to interviewers and generally wrapping himself in several layers of disguise to throw people off the scent. His autobiography *X-Ray* (1994), which he slyly subtitled 'The Unauthorized Autobiography', is a good example of this. It adopts a complicated conceit in which a young first-person narrator is hired by a nameless Corporation to interview an ageing and slightly mad rock star named Raymond Douglas, who is clearly a stand-in for Ray (Douglas is his middle name). While the book contains long reminiscences from Raymond Douglas that seem straightforwardly autobiographical, it also indulges in some weird, mystical fantasizing and dystopian prognosticating, the effect of which is to call into question whether anything in the book is actually true. What comes through the smokescreen quite clearly, however, is the overwhelming role that insecurity and occasional self-loathing have played in Davies's life. As a child, Raymond Douglas says, he had been fascinated by a hunchbacked gardener in his neighbourhood whom the local children mocked, and throughout the book he adopts the 'little hunchbacked man' as a recurring symbol of his own insecurities, the gardener's physical deformity acting as a magnified version of Davies's own shortcomings, physical and otherwise. His strategy in this book is the same as that which he adopts in many of his songs, avoiding straightforward confessional by inventing characters who may or may not share aspects of his own personality but who all

Ray Davies exposes 'the gap' in a performance on the BBC, c. 1968.

serve the purpose of protecting his vulnerability. As he admits in one of *X-Ray*'s more revealing (if typically indirect) passages, 'People who spin fantastic yarns do so because they are probably too insecure to let their true personalities surface.'[16]

Listen carefully to any Kinks record from mid-1965 onwards and you can hear the different personas come and go as Davies, an accomplished mimic, adopts different voices for his characters.

Dave reports that his brother's portentous spoken vocal on the song 'Big Sky', for example, was an impersonation of Burt Lancaster, whom Ray once jokingly told *Rolling Stone* he'd like to hear sing the song.[17] On the 1969 album *Arthur (or, The Decline and Fall of the British Empire)* Ray adopts no fewer than seven distinct voices beyond his usual singing voice, including a shell-shocked soldier, a sneering upper-class officer, a plummy denizen of the Ascot races, an Australian emigration promoter, Winston Churchill, a singer of patriotic music-hall songs and a grown son trying to communicate with his distant father. On the next album he manages at least four voices in a single song, 'Top of the Pops', which features a television promoter, a naive up-and-coming pop star, a posh agent and another posh agent with a phlegm-flecked case of rhotacism. And of course the musical theatre albums of 1973–5 are bursting with characters from the entire panoply of English life – cricketers, headmasters, vicars, accountants and so forth – who elicit from Davies a range of impersonation worthy of Spike Milligan or Peter Cook.

All of this play-acting was quite deliberate. 'Most good actors let the character consume them,' Davies once told the writer Daniel Rachel. 'One of the first books I bought after I started writing songs was Stanislavski's *An Actor Prepares*. I learnt that a lot of the rules that actors use can be applied to song writing.'[18] A bit later in the interview, when Rachel says, 'It's tempting to think the use of characters is a therapeutic device', Davies agrees. 'Yeah, it's a disguise.'[19] In another interview he confessed, 'There's an element of pretending things are happening to someone else in everything I do.'[20] Simon Frith describes this musical costume-donning as a unique feature of British popular music, one that ties 'music hall artists like Marie Lloyd and Gracie Fields to a cabaret act like Noël Coward' and on up to rock singers like Mick Jagger, Elvis Costello and Ray Davies. 'The singer is playing a part,' writes Frith, 'and what is involved is neither self-expression . . . nor critical commentary . . . but, rather, an exercise in style, an ironic – or cynical – presentation of character *as* style.'[21] There may be some self-expression involved in all of this, but it is self-expression hidden behind a cloak of plausible deniability. 'I tend to be different people when I perform,' Davies once told an interviewer. 'If I sing "I hate trees", people think it's me, but it's the character . . . Usually.'[22]

The critic Janet Maslin has noted that these multiple characters often serve a narrative function in Davies's songs. 'The many Kinks songs that set up figures in opposition – like the two sisters in the song of the same name, one a housewife and one a glamorous bachelorette, or the competing politicians in *Preservation* – aim at a notion of seesawing destinies as well as at simple dramatic conflict.'[23] This tendency can extend beyond individual songs to take in whole albums, which are often populated with characters whose conflicting outlooks and attitudes enable Davies to avoid fully committing to either a smile or a frown. *Arthur*, for instance, introduces us to characters who both love and loathe the suburban lifestyle, with Davies acting as a sort of mediator between the two, sometimes appearing to take one side, sometimes the other. There's a dialogic form to much of this that resembles the works of Plato or Galileo, who preferred to elucidate their ideas by inventing debates between imaginary characters who consider a topic from all sides, rather than propounding a single position through bludgeoning manifestos. In the Kinks' album-length dialogues, one is tempted to conclude that the 'real' Ray Davies must be hiding somewhere in there, but it is just as likely that what is 'real' about Davies changes from moment to moment, and that his shifting personas reflect his own attempts to figure out just how he really feels about things.

In fact, even in those moments when Davies drops the personas and goes for soul-bearing vulnerability, he still finds a way to hold something of himself back. Take 'Waterloo Sunset', which first appeared as a single in May 1967 and has since become the Kinks' most beloved song. According to Davies, the lyrics were so personal that he didn't share them with the rest of the band until the

Ad for the 1975 musical theatre album (*The Kinks Present*) *A Soap Opera*.

very last minute, 'Simply because I was embarrassed by how personal they were and I thought that the others would burst out laughing when they heard me sing. It was like an extract from a diary nobody was allowed to read.'[24] But of course nobody laughed, not only because it is such a touching song but also, I suspect, because it doesn't sound particularly confessional or soul-baring. The imagery is opaque enough to allow listeners to attach their own meanings to it without feeling like they're violating the singer's intent, and anyway what the singer is confessing to – finding beauty and contentment in a fleeting moment above the Thames – is something most people wouldn't find particularly embarrassing. Even if the lyric does go so far as to confess that watching the sunset from Waterloo Bridge is like being in paradise, it also says on four separate occasions that the Waterloo sunset is 'fine' – not brilliant, not heavenly, not transcendent, but 'fine'. It is as if Davies has embedded a tiny escape clause into the song, just in case somebody should come along and say that the sunset isn't so spectacular after all. Nobody said it was spectacular, he can reply; I just said it was fine.

These, then, are the angles from which Ray Davies approached his world. Half-smiling and half-earnest, half-in and half-out, the gap-toothed pop star, the hunchbacked gardener fearful of letting his flaws show: all of these attitudes and personas determined the things in the world that he would write about and the manner in which he would write about them. With one foot always planted in the working-class world from which he came, he let his other foot roam freely over the world as he found it, sometimes coming down here, at other times coming down there, but never landing terribly far from his point of origin. But before all that, before there could be a band called the Kinks or a songwriter called Ray Davies, there first had to be a jolt, something to shake Ray and his brother out of their cosy working-class world and send them hurtling off in their extraordinary arcs. That jolt, as we will see in the next chapter, came from quite a long way away, but it arrived at just the right time for a couple of working-class kids from Muswell Hill who were willing to rise to the challenge.

Houses in Onslow Gardens, Muswell Hill, London. Mike and Peggy Picker lived in an attic apartment on this street.

1

The North London Post-war Affluent Society Blues

It is a moment that will stay with him for the rest of his life. Ray Davies and his brother Dave are visiting their sister Peggy and her husband Mike Picker in their attic apartment in Onslow Gardens, a sloping street of three-storey terraces not far from Fortis Green. Mike is distrusted by some in the family because he's an Irishman, and therefore a foreigner, but he seems a decent sort on the whole. Not only has he married Peggy despite the fact that she has a daughter from a previous relationship, but he has taken her brothers under his wing, becoming something of a musical mentor to them. He has been teaching Ray the basics of classical guitar, and he has been showing Dave how to build amps and guitars. It is Mike who has introduced the brothers to the music of Buddy Holly, Hank Williams, Django Reinhardt and Earl Scruggs, teaching them how to play and sing along with the records to get the harmonies and guitar parts just right. They are quite the musical couple, Mike and Peggy, fond of performing songs together by the likes of Perry Como and Johnnie Ray: Peggy on vocals, Mike on guitar. In a few years they will take Ray and Dave to their first gig, Duane Eddy at the Finsbury Park Empire, and a few years after that Dave will grace a couple of Kinks records with the sounds of a Hawaiian guitar that he and Mike made together.[1]

Tonight, though, the brothers have made the twenty-minute walk from Denmark Terrace to Onslow Gardens to watch television.

Mike and Peggy are unusual among the Davies clan in that they own one, and it has turned their tiny apartment into a window on to worlds that few working-class Londoners have seen. It is 1958, and the programme they are watching is a collection of documentary clips presented by John Grierson called *This Wonderful World*, which tonight includes scenes from a Belgian art film starring the Chicago bluesman Big Bill Broonzy. Broonzy, who had then just recently died of throat cancer, toured Britain several times in the 1950s and even appeared on television a few times, but this is the first time the Davies brothers have seen him.

The film, *Low Light and Blue Smoke*, shows Broonzy arriving in a dimly lit club with low, curved ceilings, where a white trad jazz band are just finishing up their set. Glasses clatter and candles flicker as Broonzy sits down alone with his acoustic guitar and starts singing what he calls 'one of the old songs of America, "When Did You Leave Heaven"'. The conversations stop and a couple dance slowly while the half-lit Broonzy sings a lazy love song to an angel fallen from heaven. A lightbulb swings overhead, Broonzy takes a drag from a cigarette, and his guitar strings bend and whine as he launches into his next number, a hard-luck blues called 'Just a Dream'. There are close-ups of whiskey glasses and smoking ashtrays. A woman listens with half-lidded eyes. A mouth sucks a carbonated drink through a straw. Another woman, standing at the piano, exchanges sultry glances with the big American bluesman. Two more numbers follow, the upbeat instrumental 'Guitar Shuffle' and the lovelorn 'Saturday Night Blues', and then Broonzy picks up his guitar, puts on his hat and walks out of the club alone.[2]

Ray Davies will later describe this night at Peggy and Mike's as the moment that changed his life, 'the biggest influence on my early childhood', when Broonzy became his musical idol.[3] 'I loved the rough edges and the mistakes,' he will tell *The Guardian* in 2002, 'and it made me realise that you don't need to be a virtuoso muso to make good music.'[4] Along with several other British teenagers of the time (Eric Clapton and Keith Richards will also cite Broonzy's television appearances as a major influence), this angst-ridden, gap-toothed, introspective kid watching that impossibly sexy, mysterious scene on a flickering screen in an attic in north London feels a strong kinship with the man and his music. 'It didn't matter to me that Big Bill Broonzy was black and came from Chicago,' he will say many years later. 'What mattered was that he sounded like me. He had rough edges to his music. There was nothing really contrived about it and he sounded working class. He didn't try to be anything other than he was.'[5] Already starting to play music thanks to Mike's weekly lessons, Davies now knows the kind of music he wants to make: 'I wanted to play Big Bill Broonzy with drums.'[6] Indeed, he will spend most of the rest of his life looking for that mythical club, with its clanking glasses, ribboning smoke and mysterious American

'It was everything I felt a jazz club would be: dark, mysterious, full of great music.' Big Bill Broonzy in *Low Light and Blue Smoke* (1956).

33

bluesman singing alone with a guitar. 'It was everything I felt a jazz club would be: dark, mysterious, full of great music,' he will tell *Mojo* some sixty years later. 'To me, it created a romantic attachment.'[7]

A unique constellation of historical circumstances made that 'romantic attachment' possible. A decade earlier, there would have been almost no way that somebody like Ray Davies, the son of an East End slaughterman living in a small terrace house in the inner London suburbs, would have aspired to play the blues. A decade later, a child similarly circumstanced would be so deluged by new forms of music, American and domestic, that an obscure Belgian film about a dead American folk singer would be unlikely to leave much of an impression at all. There was something about growing up precisely at this time, precisely in this place, that enabled Big Bill Broonzy to speak to Ray Davies in such a profound way, or even to speak to him at all.

The decade before the Kinks hit it big in 1964 was an incredibly exciting, if slightly disorienting, time for working-class kids born during or just after the war, as Ray and Dave Davies were (in 1944 and 1947, respectively). Their parents, Anne and Fred, had left the bombed-out streets of Holloway, Islington, for the verdant suburbs of East Finchley and Fortis Green early in the war. Although the brothers heard plenty of stories about the old neighbourhood growing up, their world was rather different from the one in which their parents had been raised. 'East Finchley was a few stops on the bus from Holloway,' Ray would remember, 'but in its own way it was a major migration from the inner-city "projects" to the leafier suburbs. It was a critical move, and while in many ways it helped define me as a person, it also had the effect of making me feel as if my family had been cut off from its roots.'[8] Despite their uprooting, Anne and Fred had carried much of the culture of the inner city with them to their new home, which became a sort of time capsule for a way of life that was rapidly disappearing elsewhere in London.

Urban renewal, the welfare state, full employment and an America-driven consumer boom were transforming life for all Londoners, but especially for the working classes, who emerged from the depths of pre-war deprivation into a period of remarkable affluence and optimism after the war. While the Davies family certainly took full advantage of the changes as they came, they also kept one foot firmly in the past – much like the Kinks themselves would do, in time. To understand why Broonzy and the blues were able to make such an impact on the young Davies brothers, we first need to look at the way their family carried on the traditions of working-class London in their new suburban home, traditions that primed the brothers to seize upon the new ideas and possibilities that were opening up after the war.

The Davies were a large family on a small income. Fred, the son of a Welsh slaughterman and an Irish servant, worked at cattle markets in King's Cross and Smithfield, where his principal work was buying and butchering cows. He also kept an allotment for gardening, which, together with the occasional cuts of meat that he nicked from work, nicely supplemented the family's ration diet.[9] Fred and Anne had eight children, all but the youngest two of them girls, and those who had not yet married were crowded together in the family's tiny three-bedroom house next to a grocer's shop. Their house had a cracked window and a small front room, and Anne Davies maintained an open-door policy for a constantly changing cast of characters, much to the annoyance of her more buttoned-up neighbours.

The Davies' house at 6 Denmark Terrace still stands, and one of the striking things about it when you walk by is just how cramped it seems in comparison with most of the other homes in Fortis Green, which range from ornate Victorian terraces to large semi-detached houses from the early twentieth century. Then, as now, Muswell Hill, Fortis Green and East Finchley were predominately middle-class enclaves nestling gently up against the monied serenity of Highgate

The Davies family home at 6 Denmark Terrace, Fortis Green.

to the south, where a much older and wealthier Ray Davies would one day live. But in the 1950s and '60s the family's centre of gravity lay southeast, in the grittier environs of Holloway and central London, where Fred worked and much of the extended family still lived. In Fortis Green the Davies were in the suburbs but not of them, carrying on the boisterous traditions of the inner city amid streets that were quiet, inward-looking and vaguely hostile to their presence. To grasp the roots of the class consciousness (and class anxiety) that pervades many of the Kinks' songs, you could do worse than spend half an hour wandering the quiet streets of Fortis Green and marvelling at the contrast between the small house at Denmark Terrace and the spacious houses that surround it.

Large families such as the Davies' were a common feature of working-class London, as was a high degree of intimacy among family members – a consequence of so many people living in such close quarters, among other things. Scarcity of resources forced family members to develop traditions of mutual aid in everything from caring for children to helping one another find housing, and grown children normally stayed close to their parents and siblings even after moving out on their own. Sociologists Peter Willmott and Michael Young, who studied the East End community of Bethnal Green for several years in the 1950s, claimed to have found in it 'a village in the middle of London'.

> Established residents claimed to 'know everyone'. They could do so because most people were connected by kinship ties to a network of other families, and through them to a host of friends and acquaintances. Ties of blood and marriage were local ties. When they got married, couples did not usually move more than a few steps to set up a new home. They remained close to their parents, close to their brothers and sisters and close to the street markets near which they had been 'bred and born'.[10]

Postcard showing the elegant Victorian terraces of Fortis Green Road, early 20th century.

The Davies family kept up this kind of family sociability long after they left central London. When the sisters moved out of the parental home, they generally continued to live close by and kept up regular visits to Denmark Terrace; Ray and Dave's visits to Mike and Peggy were part of a larger circuit of visits and parties that encompassed siblings, aunts, uncles and grandparents. In fact, as a teenager Ray lived for a time with his sister Rose and her husband Arthur in Yeatman Road, a short block of terrace houses just across Highgate Wood from Mike and Peggy. Peggy's daughter Jackie, meanwhile, was often to be found bunking down at Davies headquarters in Denmark Terrace. Rasa, Ray's first wife, would later recall, 'It was a tiny terraced house, but the actual strength of the family bond was unbelievable. They had a good, solid, cockney London upbringing. It was amazing. I'd never experienced anything like it in my life.'[11]

In their study of Bethnal Green, Willmott and Young tell the story of Willmott's young son coming home from the local school one day (the family had moved to Bethnal Green while Willmott conducted the study) with a telling observation. 'The teacher asked us to draw pictures of our family,' young Willmott reported. 'I did one of you and Mummy and Mickey and me, but isn't it funny, the others were putting in their Nannas and aunties and uncles and all sorts of people like that.'[12] In the coming decades, Ray Davies would do exactly the same thing with the Kinks, stuffing their records with songs about nannas, aunties, uncles and much more. He would appeal to his sister Rose to return to England after she emigrated to Australia in 'Rosy Won't You Please Come Home', recall a long-dead uncle in 'Uncle Son' and base an entire album on the life of his brother-in-law Arthur, Rose's husband. He would tell of his father's difficulties with bureaucracy and unemployment in 'Get Back in the Line', his troubles with drink in 'Alcohol' and his struggles with mental illness in 'Acute Schizophrenia Paranoia Blues'. He would celebrate his sisters' love of the post-war dance halls in 'Come

Dancing' (in the video for which he would dress like his uncle Frank) and mourn his mother's passing in 'Scattered'. The Kinks are probably the only rock band in history to have released an album with back-to-back tracks inspired by their grandmother ('Here Come the People in Grey' and 'Have a Cuppa Tea' on 1971's *Muswell Hillbillies*), and of course the band's career was defined by the uniquely fraternal combination of tension and affection between Ray and Dave. Richard Hoggart, in his influential 1957 study of working-class life *The Uses of Literacy*, identified the 'core' of British working-class identity precisely here: in 'a sense of the personal, the concrete, the local: it is embodied in the idea of, first, the family and, second, the neighbourhood'.[13] Both of those elements would become core components of the Kinks' music.

Another way the inhabitants of 6 Denmark Terrace carried on the traditions of the inner city was by hosting regular sessions of group singing, often fuelled by drink, around the family piano and radiogram. These usually happened on Saturday nights, when Fred would come home from the pub with some mates and a case of beer, and whoever happened to be living there or visiting would gather in the small front room to sing the popular tunes of the day. Country music, folk songs, ballads, jazz standards, music hall – everybody had a favourite style and a theme song or two. Fred, a banjo player in his youth, now tap-danced drunkenly but expertly to Cab Calloway's 'Minnie the Moocher'. Ray sang 'Temptation', a dramatic crooner's ballad popularized by Bing Crosby and Perry Como. Sister Rene had a fondness for show tunes, and Rose and Arthur danced to Slim Whitman's 'Rose Marie' and 'Indian Love Call'. Anne's theme song was 'St Therese of the Roses', her tear-stained rendition often closing out the night after everyone else had done their piece.[14] The front room was also the celebration room, the place to bring visitors (especially the sisters' boyfriends) and mark special occasions. It was the place where the family held Rene's wake after she died of heart failure on the dance floor of the Lyceum Ballroom on Ray's thirteenth birthday. She had given Ray his first guitar a few hours before she died, and the two of them had played songs from the musical *Oklahoma!* in the front room, Rene on piano, Ray on guitar. Ray would later memorialize Rene, whose early death was in many ways the foundational grief of his life, in the song 'Oklahoma USA' (1971), which imagines his beloved sister escaping her workaday life by daydreaming about America.

The front room was not just a place for celebrations and mourning: it was also a place for dreaming – quite literally, in fact, as Ray and Dave often slept there when the house was particularly crowded. In time it became the brothers' rehearsal space, the place where they would plug in their cheap amps and play along to the records of their American heroes – Little Richard, Duane Eddy, Buddy Holly, Chuck Berry, the Shadows and the Ventures. The radiogram's speaker eventually blew out from overuse, and it was that blown-out sound that inspired Dave to take a razor blade to his little green Elpico AC55 amplifier to achieve the distorted guitar sound that gave the Kinks their first hit, 'You Really Got Me', in 1964. In this way, the front room became a direct link between the drunken singalongs of their parents' generation and the rock revolution that the Davies brothers helped to usher in. It was, in fact, one of innumerable places across London where the musical culture of the old world incubated the musical culture of the new. The brothers' earliest gigs, before they were the Kinks, were often at pubs such as the Clissold Arms and the Bald Faced Stag, where Fred Davies and his friends liked to gather for after-work pints. The brothers also played in old-style ballrooms during the intermissions between dance band performances, the kinds of venues their sisters had frequented with their servicemen boyfriends. The variety theatres – the epicentres of working-class entertainment before the war – were on their way out by the late 1950s, but Ray has memories of seeing the comedian Max Miller with his father and uncle Frank, both massive music hall fans, at the Finsbury Park Empire as a boy.[15] The Empire was also where

Ray and Dave caught their first music concert when Mike and Peggy took them to see Duane Eddy in 1960 (the year the theatre closed), and it was also where Pete Quaife and early Kinks drummer John Start saw Eddie Cochran and Gene Vincent, also in 1960.[16] Indeed, in their final years the old variety theatres hosted rock 'n' roll shows as a matter of course (Buddy Holly's 1958 tour is perhaps the most famous example); like the Davies' front room, they witnessed a torch-passing of sorts from the popular entertainers of the pre-war era to the teenage rockers who would sweep them away.[17]

These elements of pre-war working-class culture – the close bonds of extended family, the group singing, the pubs and dance halls and variety theatres – helped to make the Davies brothers receptive to the challenge that Big Bill Broonzy threw down that night in Mike and Peggy's flat. Thanks to these traditions, they knew that music was something that ordinary people like them could make, they knew who would listen to it and they knew where they could play it. Equally important in preparing the ground for

The Clissold Arms in Fortis Green. According to Dave Davies, this was the place he and Ray first performed (as the Kelly Brothers). Ray has claimed that their first gig was at the Bald Faced Stag, a pub down the road in East Finchley.

the Kinks (and other British beat bands) were the specific musical tastes of the pre-war working classes. Ever since the nineteenth century, British audiences had been fascinated by the music of black America, whether performed by white minstrels in blackface or by touring African American musicians. Despite occasionally catching the attention of the ruling classes (as the Fisk Jubilee Singers had done in the 1870s when they performed their choral renditions of Negro Spirituals for Queen Victoria), mostly it was the British working classes who came out to listen to African American performers. Ragtime and jazz, for example, had captured the imaginations of the British masses as quickly as they had anywhere: British musicians were recording ragtime as early as 1908, and the first American jazz bands toured Britain soon after the First World War.[18] In the years between the wars, black American performers were so popular that white British musicians began to fear for their livelihoods. The big American names who toured Britain in the early 1930s (Louis Armstrong, Duke Ellington, Coleman Hawkins, Cab Calloway) drew such crowds that in 1935 the British Musicians' Union prohibited American bands from touring the country, lest they steal jobs from British performers. The ban would remain in force until the mid-1950s, and in the meantime native British talent filled the gap by offering reasonably convincing imitations of the American sound. The BBC established an American-style dance orchestra, as did the Royal Air Force, and British jazz musicians such as Tommy McQuater and George Chisholm built successful careers playing in British and American bands. Even George Formby, arguably the most popular music hall performer of the interwar years (and a major influence on Ray Davies), incorporated jazz and ragtime styles into his ukulele songs about working-class English life, a sign of how deeply the music of black America had permeated the culture.[19]

Despite the embargo, African American performers still found ways to perform to British audiences during this period. In 1939

Coleman Hawkins circumvented the ban by offering 'free student concerts' to demonstrate the Selmer saxophone to invited guests, earning an exemption from the Musicians' Union on educational grounds.[20] Other American acts skirted the rules by appearing not as stand-alone performers but as part of multi-performer variety bills. In 1948, for instance, Ella Fitzgerald toured Britain on variety stages alongside British acts like Gracie Fields, singing jazz songs and pop standards to enthusiastic working-class crowds at the Glasgow Empire and London Palladium.[21] Fitzgerald's shows coincided with a wave of variety appearances just after the war by white American acts such as Danny Kaye, the Andrews Sisters, Jack Benny, Frank Sinatra and Judy Garland, all of whom were finding a large British audience despite the official ban.[22] At the same time, imported American records were slowly becoming available in the shops. Although they were generally too expensive for working-class budgets, aficionados found ways to pool their resources by hosting listening parties or forming rhythm clubs whose members would purchase and dance to the latest records.[23] American films were yet another way for British audiences to hear music directly from across the Atlantic; in the years between the end of the war and the arrival of cheap televisions – the heyday of big musical productions like *On the Town* (1949), *A Star is Born* (1954) and *Oklahoma!* (1955) – tens of millions of Britons were going to see American movies every week.

What all this points to is a working-class culture that was very much at home with American music, whether performed by real live Americans, their mechanically reproduced voices or their British imitators. Good music was good music, and as long as it could make you weep or laugh or dance, it didn't much matter who or where it came from. Black music may have been regarded with suspicion by elite tastemakers, but for many working-class people the disdain of the ruling classes only made it that much more exciting. The Davies family, with their eclectic front-room repertoire of jazz, folk, music hall, pop and show tunes, were an especially vivid example of this musical cosmopolitanism among the English working class. In their own raucous and undeliberate way, they omnivorously consumed – and reproduced – nearly the entire range of American popular music long before any of them heard a note of Big Bill Broonzy.

Yet there was also something new about the peculiar fascination that American music held for working-class teenagers of Ray and Dave's generation, and this is where the changes, rather than the continuities, of post-war Britain come into the picture. The most important change was that from the mid-1950s, Britain began to enjoy an unprecedented period of general prosperity that brought American goods and American culture more easily within reach. As the country began to shake off the grey dust of post-war auster-ity (war-time rationing finally ended in 1954), American exporters flooded Britain with alluring goods and even more alluring glimpses of a sun-drenched, carefree lifestyle, and a generation of teenagers who had no memory of the war (or the grim decade that preceded it) began to build a new youth culture that shook to a distinctly American beat. Their obsession with American culture was not new, but it was much louder than ever before.[24]

The economic underpinnings of this youth culture were full employment, rising wages and greater access to consumer goods of all kinds. London, which had an unemployment rate of 1 per cent throughout the 1950s and saw real incomes nearly double from the late 1930s to the late 1950s, was at the centre of this post-war boom, but most other parts of the country prospered as well. The changes were most dramatic in working-class communities, which benefited from a new welfare state that provided universal access to healthcare, housing, unemployment insurance and old-age pen-sions. This freed people to spend their rising wages on things like vacuum cleaners (in 81 per cent of British homes by 1965), motor cars (private vehicles quadrupled in the London area from 1945 to 1960) and, of particular importance to teenagers, records and record players.[25] The post-war boom was in many respects a leisure boom for the working classes. New labour-saving devices freed women from age-old drudgeries, giving them time to spend on more enjoyable activities. Lower airfares and package tours brought holidays abroad within the reach of the masses for the first time, and cheaper televisions (found in 85 per cent of British homes by 1965) brought the world into their homes like never before.[26] Supermarkets began to muscle aside smaller shops and provide a scale of culinary diversity that was positively dizzying after fifteen years of rationing. And the spread of the hire-purchase system and (after 1966) the credit card meant that these new, market-stimulated desires could be gratified almost instantly. It was thanks to hire-purchase that Fred Davies could afford to take twelve-year-old Dave to Selmer Musical Instruments in Charing Cross Road in 1959 to get his first guitar, a £29 Harmony Meteor, for a mere £1, 9s per week.[27] Such an extravagance would have been unthinkable for a family on a slaughterman's salary before the war.

Indeed, young people like Dave and Ray were among the chief beneficiaries of this new working-class affluence. The post-war baby boom meant that there were 22 per cent more teenagers in Britain in 1961 than in 1951, and in 1960 the termination of compulsory National Service meant that boys born after 1943 enjoyed much more liberty than even their immediate elders. For working-class teenagers in London and other big cities, jobs were abundant, pay was usually decent and there was little social pressure to continue one's education beyond the minimum necessary to get a steady wage somewhere. Flush with cash and newly liberated in sexual matters by the advent of the birth control pill (widely available by 1961), these teenagers formed a distinctive social grouping that was developing its own sets of values, priorities and tastes.[28] Surveying the state of British society in 1958, the novelist Colin MacInnes noted, 'We are in the presence, here, of an entirely new phenomenon in human history: that youth is rich. Once, the *jeunesse dorée* were a minute minority; now, all the young have gold.'[29] Before he was a pop star, Ray Davies earned his gold as a fifteen-year-old assistant in the layout department of a trade magazine, and Dave worked in the stockroom at Selmer's – the same place where he got his first guitar – when he was around the same age. The style-conscious Pete Quaife worked as an art assistant at a men's fashion magazine for about a year before the Kinks made it big, and prior to joining the band in 1964 drummer Mick Avory had done nearly every kind of manual labour under the sun, including fireplace maker, snow clearer and, at the time of becoming a Kink, paraffin deliveryman.[30] Particularly if they continued to live at home – as Dave Davies did until his mother caught him in bed with five girls sometime around 1965 – these teenagers had more disposable income than any group of working-class kids in British history. And their tastes ran towards whatever was most energetic, instantaneous, passionate and colour-ful – in a word, that which was most American.

Until the mid-1950s, getting direct access to American music was not much easier than it had been before the war. Not only did the touring embargo remain in place, but in 1949 the British gov-ernment also made it harder to get American records by placing strict limits on the importation of foreign luxury goods, a category that included records. From then until 1960, only the wealthy or well-connected could afford to buy American records – unless they happened to live in a port city like Liverpool, where it was possible to buy records from American servicemen or British seamen just back from America.[31] Overseas relatives, if you had them, might be another source: it was thanks to presents from their sister Rene, who lived for a time in Canada, that Ray and Dave became some of the first Londoners to get hold of Elvis Presley's records in 1956. The only recorded American music widely available in Britain in the 1950s was that which was being commercially released by British record companies, and until about 1956 this tended to cater to older audiences. So, too, did the music played on the radio, which was monopolized by the BBC and its philosophy of playing music that would educate, inform and (somewhat incidentally) entertain a broad swathe of the British public. Neither rock 'n' roll nor the blues normally fit this requirement, although the BBC did occasionally air educational programmes that presented the blues as interesting examples of American folk music.[32] Unless you had money to burn or were one of the fanatics who delighted in poring over the racks at speciality shops like Dobell's in Charing Cross Road (which stocked the small number of blues records issued by British labels), you were unlikely to encounter much exciting new American music in its original idiom.

These artificial restrictions meant that teenagers, in Nik Cohn's words, 'had no music of their own, no clothes or clubs, no tribal identity. Everything had to be shared with adults.'[33] With a few exceptions (Bill Haley's 'Rock Around the Clock' and 'Shake, Rattle and Roll' saw British releases in 1954), if you wanted to hear the exciting new sounds coming out of America you had either to hear imitations by British artists or to make it yourself. This was the logic behind the skiffle craze of 1956 and '57, which became the main gateway to American music for innumerable British teenagers, including the Kinks. Skiffle was a uniquely British blend of American blues, folk and country music popularized by British jazz bands when they began incorporating songs by black American bluesmen into their sets. The catalyst for the craze was a recording of 'Rock Island Line' by the British singer Lonnie Donegan, released as a single in 1956. The song was a frenetic railway folk fantasia, a sped-up version of a song Alan Lomax had recorded among Arkansas prisoners in the 1930s, which had subsequently been arranged and recorded by Lead Belly. Donegan's version appeared in the British charts shortly after the first British releases of Bill Haley's songs, and it was frequently spoken of as if it were part of the same rock 'n' roll trend.[34] But the difference was that 'Rock Island Line' – and the many other skiffle tunes that soon flooded the charts – was something that British teenagers could actually imagine themselves performing. Bill Haley had a horn section and a drummer and backing singers. He was tuneful, well-dressed and professional, and at thirty he was far older than most of the kids he was singing to. Donegan, by contrast, was breathless, unpolished and slightly awkward, doing a bad Southern accent and playing a frantic guitar with little technique or refinement. He was also British, and a few years younger than Haley, which were qualities you could hear in his voice. He was, in other words, eminently imitable.

Skiffle was something utterly new on the British cultural scene: American music that working-class teenagers could make themselves. It required neither substantial capital nor outstanding talent to form a skiffle band. A washboard, an acoustic guitar and a standing bass made out of an old tea chest and a broom handle were sufficient equipment, and familiarity with a few Lead Belly or Josh White songs was sufficient musical training. Skiffle was fast and exciting, it spoke of familiar objects (usually trains) in unfamiliar contexts (usually Chicago or the American South) and for eighteen months it was everywhere. In 1957 the skiffle musician Chas McDevitt estimated that there were 30,000 to 50,000 skiffle groups in Britain, almost all of them composed of teenagers playing their music in schools, church halls and the rapidly proliferating teenage coffee bars.[35] The Beatles, the Rolling Stones, Led Zeppelin, David Bowie and Pink Floyd all grew out of this craze. George Harrison credited skiffle with inspiring him to learn the guitar, and John Lennon's first band, the Quarrymen, was a skiffle outfit. Three of the four original Kinks (Dave, Pete and Mick) are also known to have played in skiffle bands as teenagers, and it is probably no coincidence that Ray Davies received his first guitar towards the end of the craze, in June 1957: at thirteen, he was the perfect age to become caught up in the excitement.[36] It is also likely that skiffle's DIY ethos helped to inspire Dave's technical explorations of guitars and amplifiers with his brother-in-law Mike, and it is almost certain that the craze helped to lead the Davies brothers into further explorations of American roots music. For one of the most lasting legacies of skiffle was that it inspired an enthusiastic minority of young musicians to begin seeking out the real thing. It was a short step from Lonnie Donegan to Lead Belly, and from there to other African American folk musicians such as Sonny Terry, Brownie McGhee and Big Bill Broonzy, who, as it happened, were starting to become more accessible in Britain precisely as the skiffle craze was coming to an end.

Three developments brought American roots music and R&B more readily within the grasp of British teenagers in 1957 and '58. One was the decision by the British Musicians' Union to ease restrictions on American musicians touring the country; in 1956 they struck a deal with the American Federation of Musicians (the body that would later ban the Kinks from America) to allow American acts to tour Britain in return for an equal number of British acts allowed into America. American blues musicians had long found ways to evade the ban, but now the door was open to a wider array of American musicians, including rhythm and blues acts with a harder, more contemporary sound. A second development was the decision by British record labels in the wake of the skiffle craze to release more American blues and R&B records. In 1958 Pye Records (which would later become the Kinks' label) acquired the rights to recordings by artists on the Chess and King labels in the U.S., and suddenly records by the likes of Muddy Waters, Howlin' Wolf, Bo Diddley, Chuck Berry and Sonny Boy Williamson were much more widely available, and before long other British labels were following suit.[37] A third important change, which had occurred a few years earlier, was the Television Act of 1954. This introduced commercial television to Britain for the first time, opening up the possibility of performances by rock 'n' roll and blues artists outside the restrictive format of the BBC. As independent networks like ITV began courting the youth market (for instance with its music programme *Cool for Cats*, launched in December 1956), even the

BBC was persuaded to introduce youth-oriented programmes such as *Six-five Special*, which featured live performances by rockers like Gene Vincent and Eddie Cochran.

By the end of 1957 the floodgates were open. Skiffle had come and gone, Bill Haley and Elvis Presley were on the radio (the former having toured Britain earlier in the year), television stations were finally broadcasting teenage music and record shops were filling up with American rock 'n' roll, R&B and blues records. Britain even had its own version of Elvis in the Bermondsey-born heart-throb Tommy Steele, and more imitators were to come. So what was it about Big Bill Broonzy, a middle-aged Chicago musician playing old-fashioned acoustic blues in a smoky Belgian bar, that so appealed to the young Ray Davies? Broonzy was already famous among Britain's blues cognoscenti by the time the Davies brothers saw him on television that night in 1958. Having quit the American music business in 1950 as black audiences began to gravitate towards the newer, rowdier 'jump blues', he made his first visit to Britain the following year, quickly establishing himself (in Roberta Schwartz's words) as 'Britain's ambassador of the blues, in equal parts sage, songster, teacher and touchstone to what was believed to be a fading tradition'.[38] He toured Britain several more times over the years, each time playing to larger and more enthusiastic audiences. During his final tour, in 1957, he played to a standing-room-only crowd at the Royal Festival Hall and offered after-hours masterclasses to aspiring guitarists.[39] To some extent his reputation for authenticity was a manufactured one: sensing that British audiences wanted to see him as the last of a dying tradition, he downplayed his own earlier experiments with modern sounds (he was one of the first bluesmen to use a drummer and a pianist, and he had even played an electric guitar in the early 1940s) and focused instead on the primitive stuff.[40] This was what British audiences wanted: a bluesman who could sing to them of hard times in the rural South in a style uncontaminated by the modern world.

Electric guitars and hot rhythms might have been the thing in Chicago, but they didn't really belong in what most British fans thought of as the blues.

Broonzy's old-fashioned sound was one of the reasons he caught Ray Davies's imagination. Although Davies was certainly drawn to the raucous new sound of rock 'n' roll, from quite a young age he also showed a strong nostalgic streak, a longing for the supposedly simpler times of the older generations. In a way, Broonzy perfectly combined the contradictory values that Davies would come to embrace in his own music. On the one hand he was novel, raw, passionate and exciting. He was also American, which automatically made him more thrilling than anything Britain could produce. On the other hand, Broonzy was the spokesman for a tradition that stretched back to the nineteenth century, playing an unrefined style of folk music that connected his listeners to a time before radios, televisions, amplifiers and records. His music was simultaneously old and new, organic and artificial, and from those contradictions came its power. In time, much the same would be true of the music that the Kinks created, although the folk idioms they drew from were naturally somewhat different than Broonzy's.

There were other things about the blues that appealed to working-class kids like Ray and Dave Davies. As with skiffle, the start-up costs of the blues were minimal. It might take more technical skill with a guitar to play like Big Bill Broonzy than to play like Lonnie Donegan, but it took even fewer instruments – a single guitar would do in a pinch – and the vocal techniques required little formal training. Indeed, too much refinement, too much artificial 'technique', and you would lose the point of the blues entirely. What the Davies brothers heard in Broonzy – the 'rough edges', the lack of contrivance, the working-class attitude – was what other British kids their age heard in the blues as well, and it didn't matter if you didn't hit the notes quite right. What mattered was the emotion behind the music – the longing, the passion, the angst and the joy. The point of the blues was that it rejected respectability in favour of true emotion, rebelling against, in critic Paul Garon's words, 'the degradation of language, the repressive forces of the church, the police, the family and the ruling class, against the inhibition of sexuality and aggression, against the general repugnance of everyday life'.[41] The fascination that working-class British kids felt for black American bluesmen may have been founded on an awkward analogy between their own marginalized position and the condition of blacks in the American South – John Steel of the Animals once explained that his band's background in industrial Newcastle gave them 'an instinctive emotional identification with black American blues'[42] – but it also came from a genuine identification with blues musicians as members of a despised community who found resistance and release through music. Eric Clapton put it this way: 'It was one man and his guitar versus the world . . . when it came down to it, it was one guy who was completely alone and had no options, no alternatives other than just to sing and play to erase his pains. And that echoed what I felt.'[43] But the blues were also, in Simon Frith's words, 'a means of expressing *collective* experience', and thus a suitable language for a new generation becoming conscious of its separateness from earlier generations, a vehicle for expressing 'youth's collective feelings of frustration and aggression and rebellion and lust'.[44]

Broonzy – who died in August 1958, just one month before *Low Light and Blue Smoke* first appeared on British televisions[45] – was just the beginning of the blues explosion in Britain. As the British trumpeter Humphrey Lyttleton wrote just after his death, 'Big Bill was not just a Blues singer, he was the acknowledged ambassador in chief for the whole race of folk singers . . . Almost single-handed he enlarged the audience for the Blues so that those who follow him now can be assured of a wide and enthusiastic hearing.'[46] In his wake would follow not only folk-blues musicians like Sonny Terry and Brownie McGhee, but purveyors of the harder-driving, electrified sounds of R&B and rock 'n' roll. The Kinks, the Yardbirds, the Rolling Stones, the Animals, the Beatles, Gerry and the Pacemakers and hundreds of less successful bands would start to translate those sounds into a British idiom in the early 1960s. They would do so with varying degrees of fidelity and innovation – sometimes aiming for straightforward imitation, sometimes stretching for something new – but they would all use the frustration, rebellion and lust that they heard in their first explorations of the blues to express their own emerging sense of their place in the world.

It took several years for the Davies brothers to come up with a convincing response to the challenge Big Bill Broonzy had thrown down that night in Onslow Gardens. Between 1958 and 1964, as the economy boomed and the London music scene exploded, the brothers began playing separately and together in local bars and dance halls, eventually forming a quartet with their neighbourhood friend Pete Quaife on bass and Mick Avory (from distant East Molesey, in southwest London) on drums. They experimented with blues, jazz, rock 'n' roll and R&B, recording several undistinguished covers and cycling through such names as the Ray Davies Quartet, the Pete Quaife Quartet, the Boll-Weevils and the Ravens. They finally settled on the Kinks in late 1963, and after a couple of failed singles they hit upon a winning formula in August 1964 with 'You Really Got Me', a jagged thunderclap of a song that introduced a rough new edge to the British beat movement. The song's raw, distorted guitar prefigured the sounds of heavy metal and punk and gave the Kinks a trademark sound that they continued to explore on hit singles like 'All Day and All of the Night' and 'Till the End of the Day'. Soon the Kinks were being spoken of in the same breath as the Beatles, the Rolling Stones, Manfred Mann and the Animals, all of whom had picked up the music of black America and begun to make of it a sound, and a style, that spoke to the unique circumstances of growing up working class in 1960s Britain.

The genesis of 'You Really Got Me' has been anatomized, mythologized and argued about so extensively that there's no point in rehearsing the story here. For the record, it seems most likely that it was Dave's idea (not Ray's) to slice the speaker cones of the little green amp with a razor blade (not his mother's knitting needle, as Ray has claimed) to see if he could get his guitar to play the same angry, distorted sound that he had so often heard from the blown speaker on the family radiogram. Dave was by all accounts an extremely angry teenager, and that rage was the crucial ingredient that gave 'You Really Got Me', and the Kinks, their unique sound. But in most other respects it was Ray's song, and it reflected the deep well of American influences from which he had been drinking for years.

It is ironic that one of rock's great storytellers should have had his first hit with a song of such minimal verbal dexterity. In just over two minutes Ray repeats the song's title no fewer than nineteen times, and the rest of the lyric amounts to minor variations on the same theme of primitive, slightly obsessive lust. But as with most teenage music then and since, the words aren't really the point. 'You Really Got Me' is a frenzied hormonal dance song designed to express and arouse teenage passion; the words are just there to accentuate the primal emotional state of the music. 'I always liked the idea of making a record which was repetitive,' Ray explained in *X-Ray*, 'like an African tribal chant. That's the secret of all great dance music: it's tribal. People fall into it naturally because they knew the dance before they were born.'[47] In this sense, while it bears little sonic resemblance to the acoustic blues of Big Bill Broonzy, it is perfectly accurate to call it, as Ray did in a 2010 documentary, a sort of 'north London blues'.[48] It is what Broonzy might have sung to his mysterious lady admirer in that smoky Belgian pub if he had been born in 1940s London instead of 1890s Arkansas – and if he had been able to squeeze a rowdy backing band of likeminded ne'er-do-wells onto the stage behind him.

But 'You Really Got Me' is much more than just 'Big Bill Broonzy with drums'. In fact, it reflects nearly the whole range of Ray's musical tastes as a teenager, from his early fascination with Duane Eddy's guitar instrumentals to more recent enthusiasms like the jazz saxophone of Gerry Mulligan. Ray was a music-first, words-second kind of teenage music fan, more interested in the ways musical instruments could express mood and feeling than in the stories that a song might tell. His earliest solo performances were of guitar instrumentals by the likes of Tal Farlow, Charlie Christian, Chet Atkins and Arthur 'Guitar Boogie' Smith.[49] One of his earliest compositions was an Atkins-style instrumental called 'Rocky Mountain' that, he says, was inspired by 'the rocky skies of Arizona',[50] which of course was a part of the world that he had never seen (although Duane Eddy was from there, and the 1955 movie *Oklahoma!* was filmed there). When he bothered to pay attention to vocals, it was usually their sound – such as what he has called the 'crying quality' of Hank Williams's songs – that captivated him, not the meaning of the words.[51] Indeed, whatever their early interest in the vocal ballads of Perry Como and *Oklahoma!*, by 1964 both Davies brothers were into much more abstract and artful music than their parents and sisters had been. Shortly before 'You Really Got Me' was born, they had been particularly captivated by the documentary *Jazz on a Summer's Day* (1960), which featured performances by Mahalia Jackson, Gerry Mulligan, Thelonious Monk, Jimmy Giuffre and a show-stopping Chuck Berry at the Newport Jazz Festival in 1958.[52] Like many of those performances – recorded in the very same year that Ray and Dave first saw Big Bill Broonzy on television – the Kinks' earliest songs were more abstract expressionism than representational art, aiming for a fundamental intensity of emotion that would only be diluted and confused by too much verbal sophistication. The vocal ballads of their childhood would eventually find their way into the Kinks' sound, but for now it was mood, not words, that mattered.

You can hear most of these early influences on 'You Really Got Me'. Like Ray's earliest compositions, the song began life as an Atkins-style instrumental, which he combined with a Mose Allison-inspired jazz-blues piano piece to create the distinctive, chugging riff.[53] The panting vocals – listen to Ray's gasps between the lines of the chorus – might be his version of the 'crying' sound he heard in Hank Williams's voice, as expressive as any of the words that he's saying. And the trance-like quality of the song, with its insistent riff and repetitive lyrics, has something of the hypnotic, bouncing quality that Jimmy Giuffre brought to his Newport Jazz Festival performance. And the girl? 'I was playing a gig at a club in Piccadilly', Ray once recalled, 'and there was a young girl in the audience who I really liked. She had beautiful lips. Thin, but not skinny. A bit similar to Françoise Hardy. Not long hair, but down to about there. Long enough to put your hands through . . . long enough to hold. I wrote "You Really Got Me" for her, even though I never met her.'[54] This was teenage longing in its purest form.

Yet in its soul 'You Really Got Me' remains a blues song, a howl of discontent from a particular time and a particular place that expressed the frustrations and passions of its performers just as surely as the folk-blues of the Mississippi Delta had done in their time and place. 'It's a love song for street kids,' as Dave once said.[55] Its very inarticulacy tells us more about what it felt like to be a teenager in post-war, post-rationing, post-National Service north London than a hundred well-crafted words could do. But what the song does not do, not really, is tell us exactly what there was to be so upset about. A few years earlier, after watching John Osborne's incendiary play *Look Back in Anger* for the first time, Noël Coward had confided to his diary, 'I wish I knew why the hero is so dreadfully cross and what about. I . . . cannot understand why the younger generation, instead of knocking at the door, should bash the fuck out of it.'[56] A year after the release of 'You Really Got Me', Ray Davies would seemingly come to a similar conclusion about his own songs.

The songs that he wrote next would be much more articulate – much more akin to Coward's own arch-sophisticated cabaret, in fact – than the teenage blues of 'You Really Got Me'. And in place of Dave's rage would be Ray's distinctive, though somehow just as angry, mix of sensitive observation and scathing satire.

The Kinks on TV: *Ready, Steady, Go!* (1965).

2

The Kinks vs Swinging London

When Dave Davies first heard 'You Really Got Me' on a friend's car radio, he knew that they had made the big time. 'It sounded and felt so real, so positive, so powerful, seductive and hypnotic. As if its earthiness could cut through walls,' he recalled.[1] The fierce, distorted sound that they had hit upon in the front room of 6 Denmark Terrace would propel the Kinks into the front rank of British beat bands. Scruffier than the Beatles, angrier than the Stones, hornier than the besuited celibates grinning out from countless record jackets up and down the country, the early Kinks made virtually no concessions to respectable taste. Their name was a deliberate provocation. Their behaviour on stage and screen – Dave playing a gig with his balls hanging out, Ray and Mick dancing cheek to cheek on American television, Mick nearly decapitating Dave with a cymbal during an onstage row in Cardiff – was similarly provocative, if somewhat less calculated. Their records were gritty and a little sloppy, full of power chords, distortion and occasional feedback. Their LPs were padded with R&B and rock 'n' roll covers that often featured Dave singing in a sort of whining sneer. In their songs, both originals and covers, they were either lusting after girls, complaining about girls or celebrating their love of girls – no other topic seemed to interest them. The songs were great for dancing, though, and at their concerts the crowds went crazy, jumping and screaming and, several times

– usually in Scandinavia, for some reason – starting full-blown riots. From mid-1964 to mid-1965 the Kinks seemed to embody all the traits that the conservative scolds detested about this new wave of teenage musical hooliganism. And then, in the autumn of 1965, the Kinks abruptly switched course.

It is easy to pinpoint the moment of the Kinks' transformation from north London troglodytes into swinging sophisticates, less easy to pinpoint the reasons. The moment was September 1965, when they released Ray Davies's new composition, 'A Well Respected Man', on the aptly titled *Kwyet Kinks* EP. The song was not the lead track – that was Dave's countrified 'Wait Till the Summer Comes Along' – but it was the standout track among a batch of four songs that were a sonic, if not altogether thematic, departure for the band. Gone were the crunchy riffs and heavy beats of the early hits. Here were the Kinks in a more thoughtful mood, singing about the joys of marital fidelity and the sadness of a loveless winter, but mostly still singing about love. 'A Well Respected Man' was not a love song, however. Its gently strummed opening chord was as gutsy in its way as the blown-speaker distortion with which the Kinks had proclaimed their impure intentions to the world a year earlier, but the truly remarkable thing about it was that it was *about somebody*. It was not about the singer, or the singer's girl, or the singer's romantic rival. It was not about a generic nowhere man who couldn't find meaning in life, or war profiteers, or out-of-touch parents, or archetypes of any sort. It was about a young bachelor who commutes to the City, longs to inherit his father's money, enjoys working in the garden and lusts after the girl next door while recognizing that she's probably not marriage material (unless his mother says she is). It is also about the young man's father, who likes to have it off with the maid, and his mother, who likes to flirt with young men at society gatherings. It is simultaneously a satire of the hypocrisy of the upper classes in the tradition of what Davies has called the 'English twit' movies of Terry-Thomas and a character sketch

Ad for a Kinks double bill with the Animals in Croydon, suburban London. *New Musical Express*, 5 March 1965.

that is drawn so precisely that it invites speculation as to who its real-life referent might be.[2]

Thus began what I have come to think of as Ray Davies's Dickens phase, which ran from mid-1965 to mid-1967, with occasional recurrences thereafter. During this period, in a torrent of hit singles and two LPS – *Face to Face* (1966) and *Something Else* (1967) – Davies did for Swinging London what Charles Dickens had done for Victorian London, peering behind the facade of self-congratulatory comfort and prosperity to find the complex human dramas within. He was still writing love songs and songs of emotional release, but now he was also inventing characters and telling stories. His songs became more lyrically ambitious as he poked fun at the British class system, questioned the narrative of Sixties progress that was being peddled by the media and celebrated the small pleasures of small lives. At the same time, his musical arrangements became quirkier and more old-fashioned; more East End music hall than Chicago juke joint. He began, in short, to write about the world around him rather than (or in addition to) the world inside him.

In the early days the Kinks had actually flirted with Dickensian imagery in their performances, adopting stage names drawn from his novels (Dave, naturally, was the Artful Dodger) and dressing up in Victorian costumes, but it was during the 1965–7 period that Ray's writing was most like that of Dickens. The two men were quite similar, in fact. They were both insomniacs prone to overwork and anxiety, conditions made worse by an early rush to fame that created intense pressure to keep coming up with hits. Both men were

The *Kwyet Kinks* EP, released in September 1965, marked a departure from the rowdy sound of the band's early hits and signalled a new direction for Ray Davies's songwriting.

also magnetic performers capable of impersonating a wide range of characters, and they both seemed to revel in live performance as a way to escape their own skins. More to the point, both were also insatiable observers of London life, which provided much of the raw material for their art. Dickens was famous for taking long strolls through the streets of London in search of characters and stories, sometimes walking 20 miles a day. At the beginning of his novel *The Old Curiosity Shop* (1841), the narrator (a stand-in for Dickens) explains that he has recently fallen into the habit of taking long nocturnal walks around London and 'speculating on the characters and occupations of those who fill the streets'. Driven by a 'never-ending restlessness', he says, he goes forth at night to observe the people and places of London, 'the crowds forever passing and repassing on the bridges', the scent of flowers at sunrise in Covent Garden, the 'old clerks' who hurry past on their way to work.[3] 'My walking is of two kinds,' Dickens wrote in a later essay titled 'Shy Neighbourhoods',

> one, straight on end to a definite goal at a round pace; one, objectless, loitering, and purely vagabond. In the latter state, no gipsy on earth is a greater vagabond than myself; it is so natural to me, and strong with me, that I think I must be the descendant, at no great distance, of some irreclaimable tramp.[4]

Ray Davies was a similarly restless tramp in London. Many years after the fact he would vividly recall taking a long bus ride at the age of fifteen from north London to Leicester Square, and then getting out to walk around Soho. 'This was my first solo venture . . . into the dark, seedy world of sleaze.' Soho was 'a new world, a dark world of neon lights and nightclubs, cafés, street-walkers, small-time underworld crime characters. I spoke to no one, I just walked and observed.'[5] Over the years he continued these long walks around London, taking note of the characters he passed and imagining his way into people's lives. Fortis Green, the King's Road, Regent Street, Waterloo Bridge: there were stories everywhere. He has often said that people carry with them a sort of musical aura that only he can hear. 'I usually write a theme song in my head for nearly every person I encounter in the real world,' he wrote in his second autobiography, *Americana*. 'They exist as part of my musical memory so that afterward I cast them in my own musical version of life, which is often more truthful than reality.'[6]

A 'more truthful' version of reality was of course exactly what Dickens, with his keen eye for detecting and then exaggerating people's mannerisms and foibles, was attempting in his fiction. Dickens was a skilled ventriloquist, alert to the ways that quirks of inflection and repetition in his characters' speech could provide windows into their souls. Every time Harold Skimpole in *Bleak House* insists that he is a 'mere child' he becomes a bit more contemptibly irresponsible; every time Fagin in *Oliver Twist* calls someone 'my dear' he becomes a bit more sinister. The hobby-horses upon which Dickens set his characters, as the critic John Killham once observed, 'are more compelling than other men's horses'.[7] Davies's technique was similar. His characters came from across the social spectrum – during this period they included a modish fashionista, a session musician, a Muswell Hill gardener, a clutch of conformist commuters and several indolent aristocrats – and in order to convey their unique personalities and social statuses he often exaggerated certain characteristics, showing a great fondness, for example, for extravagant accents (toff, Cockney, BBC English and so on) that could serve as a sort of Dickensian shorthand for a character's identity. This shorthand was even more essential to Davies, who had to work within the constraints of three-minute pop songs, than it was to Dickens, who could let his characters' eccentricities spill across hundreds of pages of prose, but the effect was similar. Both writers' characters are larger than life, often more caricatures than real people, but this just makes their stories all the more vivid.

Another thing Davies and Dickens have in common is their keen appreciation of the intricacies of the British class system. Each Dickens novel is a cavalcade of the social classes, running from absent-minded aristocrats and heartless capitalists all the way down to penniless orphans. For most of Dickens's characters, class determines consciousness, sets the bounds of the possible and shapes their moral outlook: the poor-but-honest tradesman, the rich-but-frivolous aristocrat, the spiritually dead businessman. The same is true of Davies's characters. The essential thing about the Well Respected Man and his family, for example, is their membership of the upper-middle classes: this makes their behaviour hypocritical in a way that similar behaviour by a working-class family never would be. The situation in which the hero of 'Tin Soldier Man' finds himself – setting off on a daily commute that resembles an absurd military route march – is unquestionably middle-class suburban; indeed, it is possible to position him just a notch or two down the social scale from the Well Respected Man, whose life is similarly ruled by timetables but who will one day escape the tedium of commuting when he inherits his father's money. The smug but cuckolded hero of 'Mr Pleasant', meanwhile, has clearly worked his way into middle-class comfort from a lower social station, while Suzy and Johnny in 'Situation Vacant' are happy enough with their modest circumstances until Suzy's social-climbing mother encourages them to strive for more, with disastrous results. Working-class people are less prominent in Davies's songs of this period than they will be later, but certainly the couple in 'Dead End Street' would qualify as working-class (if not lumpenproletarian), as would the people who smoke 'harry rags' – cigarettes (fags) in Cockney rhyming slang – in the song of that title. Not all of Davies's characters occupy a clear place on the class spectrum – Terry and Julie of 'Waterloo Sunset' could as easily be aristocrats as factory workers – but enough of them do to make the songs and, especially, the albums of this period into a panoramic snapshot of British society in the 1960s, much like Dickens's novels of the mid-Victorian years. Much had changed since Dickens's time, but the British class system, these songs remind us, has endured.

So how do we explain Ray Davies's shift to this more Dickensian style of songwriting at this time? Partly it was a consequence of new domestic arrangements. In December 1964 Davies married Rasa Emilija Halina Didzpetris, a young woman from Bradford whose parents were Lithuanian refugees. According to Dave, Rasa and her family were people with 'high moral values, polite, nice people with

87 Fortis Green, where Ray and Rasa Davies moved shortly after their marriage, was built in 1805 and boasted a spiral staircase and nine rooms. Though just a two-minute walk from his childhood home, it was a significant step up the social ladder for the twenty-year-old pop star.

impeccable manners who were somewhat austere', qualities that Dave found a bit off-putting (he ended up making an obscene speech at their wedding) but which probably appealed to Ray's desire to distance himself from his own less-than-impeccable roots.[8] In June 1965 the couple purchased a pricey, Regency era semi-detached house at 87 Fortis Green, a modest but elegant structure on the same street as Davies's childhood home. Like the marriage, the house was an act of social climbing on Davies's part, but the fact that it was just a two-minute walk away from his parents' home says a lot about what it meant to 'make it' by the standards of the London working class. This was a world in which you were expected not to get too far above yourself, not to 'put on airs', even if you were a world-famous rock star, and Davies was certainly conforming with that expectation in choosing to live in a house that he had walked past countless times as a child. But this was also a world in which success meant having something to show off to the neighbours; there was no point in 'making it' if you couldn't rub it in people's faces a bit. The new house fit the bill precisely, an extravagance by neighbourhood standards that nevertheless advertised Davies's continued allegiance to the community that had made him.

The Fortis Green house did several things for Davies. It provided a refuge from the pressures of the pop business, which included not just the touring and recording but the decadent lifestyle that was supposed to go with it. While his brother was throwing himself into the rock star lifestyle with self-annihilating abandon, Ray was hunkered down in his suburban semi with his wife and, soon, his infant daughter Louisa, churning out songs by the dozen. Most of them never made it onto record, but many of those that did bore the distinctive marks of the neighbourhood in which they were born. This is because another thing that the Fortis Green house did for Davies was to keep him surrounded by the very same people among whom he had always lived, including his large and tight-knit family. According to Rasa, the Davies clan 'were very interfering' in the couple's life. 'It was too incestuous, too close. They were quite powerful and controlling in their way. I just felt out on a limb because there was just me and all of the Davieses.'[9] Dave also continued to live nearby, first with Mick Avory in Connaught Gardens (around the corner from Mike and Peggy's flat in Onslow Gardens), then for a short time back in Denmark Terrace, and then in Cockfosters, a ten-minute drive from Ray.[10]

This was all a very working-class way to behave. Even at the height of Swinging London, working-class kids far more smitten with the celebrity lifestyle than Ray Davies rarely strayed too far from their families. 'All the East End boys loved their families in the way I never saw middle-class people love their families,' recalled one scenester of the era.[11] Even Terence Stamp, the cinematic idol of Swinging London, famously forsook his fashionable West End flat every Sunday to go and have dinner with his mum in the East End. With little precedent for how to behave after becoming rich and famous, working-class kids like Stamp and the Davies brothers did what people in their world had always done: they stayed within shouting distance of their parents. What made Ray Davies different from most of the others was that his artistic imagination stayed rooted in the old neighbourhood along with the rest of him.

The second factor that pushed Davies's songwriting in new directions was the blacklisting of the Kinks by the American Federation of Musicians (AFM) after a disastrous three-week tour of America in the summer of 1965. This was the group's first visit to America, and whatever romantic notions they had harboured about the land of Big Bill Broonzy, *Oklahoma!* and Elvis Presley were quickly dispelled. 'I had started playing music because it was the only way I could express myself as an individual,' Davies recalled, 'and yet America, the country that had always inspired that sense of freedom inside me, was somehow one of the most repressed, backward-thinking places I had ever been to.'[12] If America wasn't quite ready for the Kinks, it was even more the case that the Kinks weren't ready for

America. 'We were on our own planet,' says Davies. 'Planet Kink. And if they weren't on our planet it was difficult for them to get along with us. So it was a collision of cultures.'[13] While the Beatles and Rolling Stones benefited from savvy management and carefully devised (if, in the latter's case, calculatedly outrageous) public personas, the Kinks were simply themselves: foul-mouthed, long-haired north Londoners with a reputation for onstage violence and offstage surliness. It did not go down well.

To this day, Ray claims not to know precisely what caused the AFM to blacklist the Kinks. It may have been the contract proffered by a union official that Dave refused to sign, or it may have been the scuffle that Ray subsequently got into with the same official. It may have had something to do with the radio station in Denver whose programme director complained of 'vulgar, rude, [and] disgusting' behaviour by the group during a record store autograph party, an episode that led the station to ban their records.[14] Most likely it was due to complaints to the AFM by the promoter Betty Kaye, who quarrelled repeatedly with the group and its management during concerts in Reno, Sacramento and San Francisco. The dispute seems to have revolved around Kaye's refusal to pay the group's fees in advance, which led the Kinks to fill half of their 45-minute slot in Reno with an extended version of 'You Really Got Me' and to refuse to play the San Francisco gig altogether.[15] Whatever the precise reason, it was the culmination of a tour that was marred, in Ray's words, by 'complete differences of opinion, divergent attitudes to culture, a lack of business compatibility, and total misunderstanding on all sides'.[16]

It would be four years before the Kinks were able to return to America. Any hope of maintaining their strong American following began to fade as other British groups, most notably the Who, swept in behind the Beatles and Stones to become transatlantic superstars. Davies never lost his fascination with the sounds and culture of America, but for a time he was relieved of the necessity of writing songs that Americans might buy, since no British band (other than the Beatles) was going to sell many records in such a competitive market without heavy touring. The ban was of course a huge commercial setback, but it also had unexpected artistic benefits. 'The American ban had a profound effect on me,' Davies told Andy Miller, 'driving me to write something particularly English in a way which made me look at my own roots rather than my American inspirations. I realised that I had a voice of my own that needed to be explored and drawn out.'[17] Less time touring also meant more time for writing songs and honing sounds; he now felt he could write songs that were 'deliberately chancy', secure in the knowledge that he could always write another hit if necessary, even if it only ended up in the UK charts.[18]

Of course, just because the Kinks couldn't tour America anymore didn't mean that Davies had to start writing about England, any more than living on his childhood street with his wife and child meant that he had to start writing about suburbia. He could have played it safe and continued to write lusty love songs of the old north London blues variety for the rest of his life. That he didn't do so is due, I think, to a third factor beyond these personal and professional ones. Pop music was becoming much more self-consciously artistic around 1965, at least in certain quarters, as both audiences and performers began looking for something more than mere love songs. They still wanted these, of course, but increasingly they also wanted songs that said something meaningful about what it was like to be a person, especially a young person, living through this decade. Before the mid-1960s, music that had 'something to say' was generally confined to the folk scene, but this had limited appeal to teenagers or to the radio stations and record labels that served them. Deliberately artistic music, meanwhile, was largely the province of either classical composers or avant-garde jazz musicians, most of whom sold even fewer records than the folkies. What changed around 1965 was that artistic, socially aware music began to be made and consumed on a much larger, more commercial scale, and suddenly it made sense for groups whose chief merit was their ability to make pubescent girls scream to start pushing for something more.

The reasons for this larger shift in the pop music landscape lie well beyond my scope here – they have been lucidly analysed by Simon Frith, among others[19] – but two factors of particular relevance to the Kinks deserve a brief mention. The first was Bob Dylan, whom Ray Davies once described as one of the great 'piss artists' of the twentieth century (along with Picasso) and whose distinctive blend of sarcasm, sociological curiosity, poetic lyrics and self-concealing personas resembled Davies's own emerging style.[20] Not only was 1965 the year of Dylan's genre-defying albums *Bringing It All Back Home* and *Highway 61 Revisited*, it was also the year when Dylan 'went electric' at the Newport Folk Festival, symbolically welding together folk and rock 'n' roll to create a new kind of popular music that was starting to be called simply 'rock'. The second factor was Phil Spector, whose innovations in the recording studio were changing the sound of popular music and challenging musicians to think beyond the standard formulas. In December 1965 Davies credited the Righteous Brothers' Spector-produced hit 'You've Lost That Lovin' Feeling" with pushing him to pursue a new sonic palette in his music. 'That was the end,' he told Keith Altham, 'That was the perfect pop disc – as far as anyone could go.'[21]

The Kinks were not the only British group who were moving away from blues-based love songs towards a new rock aesthetic in 1965. That year the Rolling Stones released their generational anthem 'Satisfaction' as well as the B-side oddity 'The Under Assistant West Coast Promotion Man', a song that was quirkily Kinksian in both tone and title. The Who's 'My Generation' and the Animals' 'We Gotta Get Out of This Place' moved beyond simple teenage lust to embrace a wider vision of teenage rebellion, and the Beatles – under the watchful eye of another innovative producer, George Martin – took their first tentative steps towards artful vignettes and surrealism with 'Nowhere Man' and 'Norwegian Wood'. By the following year the tide had definitely turned. The Beatles quit touring and released their sitar-flecked, horn-drenched, drug-induced, goofy and observational masterpiece *Revolver* in August 1966. The Stones took on topics like suburban drug abuse and urban alienation in singles like 'Mother's Little Helper' and 'Paint It Black'. The Who invented outcast characters and gave them theme songs with 'Happy Jack' and 'I'm a Boy'. The Yardbirds went psychedelic with the trippily nostalgic 'Happenings Ten Years Time Ago', the new blues-jazz-psych outfit Cream released their debut album, a band called The Pink Floyd began performing far-out gigs at London's UFO club (which opened in December 1966) and Manfred Mann had a hit with a song called 'Semi-detached Suburban Mister James' that owed a distinct (if unacknowledged) debt to the style and preoccupations of Ray Davies. It was all a bit of a free-for-all, this first great flowering of British rock, a technicolour scramble of sounds and ideas shooting free from the earthbound blues that had nurtured them.

And where did the Kinks figure in the scrum? Along with the Beatles, the Stones, the Who and the rest, Ray Davies now felt free, thanks to the path forged by the likes of Dylan and Spector, to pursue his own artistic vision – indeed, he was significantly freer than those other British groups, who still had to worry about selling records and concert tickets in America. As Dylan had done at a slightly earlier period in his own artistic development, Davies decided to take a good look around the place where he lived, its rulers and its ruled, its pretensions and its authenticities, and he decided that he was up to the challenge of capturing its essence in song. And as Davies gazed out of his modest suburban semi upon the lights of Swinging London – feeling a bit experimental now that he needn't bother with America; feeling a bit detached, in his settled domestic life, from the hedonism of his fellow musicians; thoughtful and gloomy by nature, but with a growing sense of his own creative powers – as he looked around London he saw the one thing that nobody else seemed to have noticed: the whole thing, the whole Sixties myth of progress and joy and endless sunshine, was a colossal fraud. And so he decided to write songs about that.

'The Sixties was a lie,' Ray Davies once said, 'a total lie.'[22] The image of the decade as a time of unprecedented liberation, he felt, was 'like a carrot held up to youth to distract us so that we would not rebel against the ruling classes and all the backhanders and corruption that were actually present in politics'.[23] Davies's scorn for the very culture that made his career possible has the air of a one-time innocent who has been seduced, ravaged and subsequently betrayed. Like many working-class teenagers, he had believed the post-war you've-never-had-it-so-good rhetoric of the press and politicians. Expanded economic and educational opportunities, greater material comfort and a more permissive moral environment were supposed to be creating a new era of classlessness, an end to hidebound prejudices, perhaps the eventual toppling of the Establishment itself. That was the promise; as Davies was coming to sense by the middle of the decade, the reality was quite different.

The usual line on Sixties London was that, as *Time* magazine put it in a famous April 1966 cover story, a new 'colorful and ebullient pop culture' was causing the city to 'shed much of its smugness, much of the arrogance that often went with the stamp of privilege, much of the false pride – the kind that long kept it shabby and shopworn in physical fact and spirit'. Now, the magazine declared,

> Britain is in the midst of a bloodless revolution. This time, those who are giving way are the old Tory-Liberal Establishment that ruled the Empire from the clubs along Pall Mall and St James's, the still-powerful financial City of London, the church and Oxbridge. In their stead is rising a new and

surprising leadership community; economists, professors, actors, photographers, singers, admen, TV executives and writers – a swinging meritocracy.[24]

As they buzzed around town in their minicars, haystack hairdos flying in the summer sun, the youth of London were supposedly crashing through ancient class barriers and overturning age-old prejudices. Harold Wilson, 48 years old at the time of his elevation to prime minister in 1964, was heralded as the benevolent lord of this cult of youth, and the fact that he was a Labour PM underscored the fact that Swinging London (as it was coming to be known in the press) was largely a working-class accomplishment, the product of working-class teenagers' new-found affluence, taste and self-confidence. For the first time in British history, it was fashionable to be working class.

For much of 1964 and '65, it would not have been unreasonable to see the Kinks as standard bearers in this 'bloodless revolution', harbingers of the rough-edged but liberated culture of the future. Yet within a year of the group's initial success, Davies was beginning to sense that things were not going according to plan. The more he saw of British society, the more he felt that it was just as class-ridden as ever, and that the garish and disposable culture of Swinging London was not so much evidence of the working class's liberation as evidence of its gullibility. That the Kinks themselves were among those who had been duped only made him all the more bitter and withdrawn. But Davies's instinct as a songwriter was never to let that bitterness overpower his music. Instead of writing angry tirades about the hypocrisy of British society, he transmuted his anger into satire, balancing his vitriol with a large dose of humour and wry insouciance.[25] 'Dedicated Follower of Fashion', released in February 1966, is a good example of this. The song is a jaunty send-up of the trendy young men flitting around the boutiques of Carnaby Street and Leicester Square in a whirl of frivolity and self-regard. Its false-front opening, a few distorted strums on an electric guitar, soon gives way to Ray's acoustic guitar, strummed (he says) to sound like a ukulele, the signature instrument of George Formby, whose trebly pre-war character sketches the song resembles in many respects.[26] The lyric is gently mocking but never vicious, its protagonist described as a member of a narcissistic Carnabetian Army whose regiments march in lockstep according to the capricious commands of the fashion police. Is it polka dots this week, or stripes? The harshest words that he has for the character is to accuse him of a fondness for flattery and of being (here he sings in a put-on posh voice) 'as fickle as can be'. You would never know that the immediate inspiration for the song was a punch-up that Davies had had during a party in his Fortis Green house with a fashion designer who'd had the temerity to accuse him of wearing flared trousers. 'I kicked him,' Davies recalled. 'I kicked his girlfriend up the arse. It was awful, there was blood. I was grovelling in the gutter with him – it was sad. The next day I said to myself, "Fuck all this. This has got to stop. Take it out on your work," and I wrote that song, typed it up straight off.'[27]

'Dedicated Follower' may have been a poisoned dart aimed at one of Davies's enemies, but when the full band played it onstage it also became an exercise in self-mockery – 'Have your cake and throw it away,' as Davies once said[28] – a sort of verbal counterpart to Pete Townshend's guitar-smashing 'auto-destruction' during the Who's live sets. Ray might not have cared much about fashion, but the other Kinks certainly did, so the song effectively functions as an artful piss-take of the other members of the band. Dave, who was never particularly adept at detecting irony, enjoyed promoting the song because it gave him the chance to 'camp it up in public, especially at photo shoots, or on TV'. He recalls one particular floppy hat with purple and pink stripes that he had bought on Carnaby Street simply because 'it was by far the silliest item in the store'. He wore it everywhere, even to bed. 'I wasn't happy until somebody made some comment or the other about it, whether complimentary or not. It didn't matter as long as it was "noticed".[29] Pete was probably the most 'dedicated' fashionista of the four, a Vespa-riding, parka-wearing Mod who used to have lunch with future *Ready Steady Go!* star Cathy McGowan when she was still a secretary.[30] After the single's release, Ray told the *New Musical Express* that the frilly underpants mentioned in the song were, in fact, Pete's. 'Pete's underpants are the big thing in Europe now . . . He wears the nylon variety that I sing about in "Dedicated" and when he sent his to the hotel laundry they became the talking point of the place.'[31] Mick Avory, meanwhile, briefly became a model for the fashion designer John Stephen, appearing in photo spreads in *Vanity Fair*, *Disc and Music Echo* and *Men Only*.[32] 'I don't think Mick actually lived anywhere in 1966,' Ray later joked. 'He stayed in the clubs.'[33]

'Dandy', which appeared on *Face to Face* in October 1966, is a sort of sequel to 'Dedicated Follower', recounting the sexual exploits of a fashion-conscious lothario who has multiple girls stashed here and there but who one day must face a reckoning. Its immediate inspirations were the 1966 film *Alfie*, in which a chatty and devious Michael Caine philanders his way across Swinging London, and Alan Sillitoe's 1958 novel *Saturday Night and Sunday Morning*, in which the young factory worker Arthur Seaton philanders his way across less-than-swinging Nottingham.[34] Yet the song was also a fairly accurate summary of Dave's hedonistic lifestyle, which, the singer predicts (with what might be a touch of brotherly concern), will eventually catch up with him. In fact, much of Ray's disillusionment with Swinging London was a form of envy of his brother's exciting and carefree life. The song 'Two Sisters', which appeared on *Something Else* in September 1967, was an oblique acknowledgement of this. It told of a housewife's jealousy of her free-spirited sister who spends her time partying with dandies like Dave and his crowd. '"Two Sisters" is about Dave and me in a way,' Ray once recalled. 'I was the dowdy one.'[35] While it ultimately comes down in favour of the domestic life, 'Two Sisters' is somewhat more sympathetic towards London's swinging scenesters than 'Dedicated' and 'Dandy' are. The 'dowdy' sister can see the appeal of her sister's wayward life, though by the song's end she has come to affirm the superiority of her own lifestyle: an early instance of the ambiguities (or indecisions) that would structure many of Davies's later songs.

Davies was not alone in his scorn for the bright young things of the period. No sooner had *Time*'s 'swinging city' cover story appeared than cultural commentators from across the political spectrum began dumping cold water on the idea of Swinging London. In a *New York Times* article titled 'Britain Seems Willing to Sink Giggling into the Sea', the English social critic Henry Fairlie declared, 'If I were given to conspiracy theories, I would believe that there is a plot to denigrate Britain by praising everything in it which is mindless and nasty, which is senseless and corrupting, which is meaningless and deadly.' Denouncing the whole Swinging London phenomenon as decadent and self-obsessed humbug, he quoted John Ruskin on the 'final ruin' of Renaissance Venice, which he felt had an uncanny parallel in modern Britain: 'By the inner burning of her own passions, as fatal as the fiery rain of Gomorrah, she was consumed from her place among the nations; and her ashes are choking the channels of the dead, salt sea.'[36] Fairlie's diatribe was one of several emanating from middle-class and traditionalist quarters in Britain, which resented the liberated London scene on aesthetic as much as moral grounds, but there were other lines of attack coming from elsewhere. Serious political and economic observers worried about Britain's decaying industrial base and contracting empire, insisting that, whatever its surface-level prosperity, the nation was living on borrowed time. In these analyses, Britain's giddy youth culture was at best an irrelevant distraction and at worst actively undermining the country's long-term viability.[37] A third line of attack came from the scenesters themselves, among whom it soon became fashionable to pooh-pooh the very idea of Swinging London. Dismayed that their little world of hip had been sussed by the masses (especially American tourists), they chose to close ranks and become even more exclusive, ruthlessly discarding last year's clubs and boutiques as irretrievably outré and moving on to something else. Swinging London, according to the 'in' set, was an American fabrication devised to sell magazines and holiday packages, not a reflection of the real culture of the city.[38]

Davies's critique combined elements of all of these positions. He distrusted the superficiality of the dandies and the fashionistas, and at times he could sound like a middle-aged, Fairlie-style traditionalist (without, however, evincing the middle-class disdain for working-class vulgarity that coloured Fairlie's critique). In the coming years he would also criticize the postcardification of the English landscape for the consumption of American tourists, thereby aligning himself somewhat with the scenesters. But, as someone who had lived in London his whole life and was interested in how ordinary people lived, one of his strongest impulses was to question the economic and political premises upon which the myth of Swinging London rested. Had Britain really entered a new era of prosperity and classlessness? He doubted it. How much was changing in Britain, really? Too much in some directions, his songs suggested, and not enough in others. In many of his songs, Davies was responding to what he saw as a youth culture that was gleefully complicit in its own exploitation. The dandies swanning around the boutiques of Chelsea and Carnaby Street, the hip trendsetters losing themselves in nightly debauches at the Ad Lib and the Scotch of St James, the young girls screaming their way through each and every one of the Kinks' gigs around Britain – in his eyes, they were all doing the Establishment's bidding for them, propping up a facade of liberation and equality in a society that was anything but.

He came at this problem from a number of different directions. Some of his songs, such as 'Dandy' and 'Dedicated Follower', directly satirized the kinds of people who adorned the covers of the glossy magazines. Others, such as 'Dead End Street' – a deceptively jaunty tune about the persistence of inner-city poverty amid the heedless prosperity of Swinging London – attempted a sort of sociological analysis of the state of the nation, albeit with a wry (and somewhat self-defeating) grin. To me, some of Davies's most interesting critiques of Swinging London are those that focus on the experiences of women. These are interesting partly because it was rare to hear male rock musicians of the 1960s writing about women in this way, and partly because these songs tap into one of the primal themes of English art and literature: the innocent country girl who goes to London and is seduced, and ultimately ill-used, by the shady characters of the metropolis. The first of these songs was 'Big Black Smoke', which appeared as the B-side to 'Dead End Street' in 1966 and provided (in Dave's words) 'a perfect complement in atmosphere and sound and feeling' to the A-side's Dickensian tale of urban poverty.[39] The other two songs were slightly later: 'Polly', B-side to the April 1968 single 'Wonderboy', and 'Starstruck', an album track on *The Kinks Are the Village Green Preservation Society*, released in November 1968. In all three songs a young girl abandons her dull rural life for the excitement of London's clubs and streets, where she generally finds more than she was bargaining for and worries the daylights out of her parents in the process. The narrative of 'Big Black Smoke' is the most fully developed of the three, its young ingénue becoming addicted to purple hearts (the Mods' amphetamine of choice), sleeping in cafés and bowling alleys and ultimately getting robbed by a guy named Joe with whom she's taken up. By the end of the song it is clear that the girl has been ruined both financially and morally, and it is an open question whether her mother will ever recover her pure, frail, formerly innocent girl. The heroine of 'Polly' has a similar adventure but avoids ultimate ruin when she confesses her sins to her parents and returns home to understanding and forgiveness. The eventual ruin of the unnamed protagonist of 'Starstruck', meanwhile, is hinted at but not quite certain: repeatedly warned that her addiction to drinking and partying will 'ruin' her, she remains suspended in a precariously 'starstruck' condition by the song's end.

All three songs depict Swinging London as a den of turpitude capable of destroying the morals, health and possibly lives of the women who are seduced by it. They are part of a long tradition of depicting London as a 'city of dreadful delight', a place that entices women with promises of liberation but which ultimately works their ruin.[40] Ever since the Restoration, English writers had been warning of the dangerous temptations that the city held for young women, although, particularly during the Restoration, this was not always presented as a bad thing. In William Wycherley's play *The Country Wife* (1675), for instance, a young married woman named Margery Pinchwife finds a life of licentiousness in London to be far preferable to the constraints of married respectability in the countryside. 'I have got the London disease they call love,' she swoons in the midst of her affair with a charming London rake named Harry Horner, whose attentions she finds much more exciting than those of her 'musty Husband', to whom she must ultimately return.[41] Most writers were much less sanguine about the moral perils of the city, however. A woman who has gone 'upon the town', as Laura Rosenthal writes, 'was generally represented as the bottom of a slippery slope that began with seduction, moved to a "keeping", slid to a series of temporary situations with different men, and finally ended with indiscriminate availability as a streetwalker, the most dangerous form of prostitution'.[42] In the depths of their despair, such women often ended their lives by throwing themselves into the Thames.

In 1732 William Hogarth published a series of prints entitled *A Harlot's Progress* that graphically depicted this descent from country virtue to urban vice. The first print shows the heroine, Moll Hackabout, arriving in town along with a wagonload of fellow rustics. She stands outside a tavern, pure and well dressed, while a crone named Mother Needham strokes her lily-white chin as if appraising a horse. The subsequent prints show Moll's descent: first

In the first scene of *A Harlot's Progress* by William Hogarth (1732),
the young and innocent Moll Hackabout arrives with a group of rustic
girls at a Cheapside brothel, where she is appraised by the proprietress.

she is living as a kept woman with a wealthy man, then she sits in her
lodgings while bailiffs come in to arrest her, then she is incarcerated
and beating hemp in Bridewell Prison, and then she is shown per-
ishing in an untidy room amid quarrelsome doctors. The final panel
shows the mourners at Moll's funeral, some in mock grief, some
enjoying a light drink and others locked in an intense flirtation. As
a cautionary tale about the dreadful delights of the city, *A Harlot's
Progress* makes for an oddly appropriate visual accompaniment to
'Big Black Smoke', from the antiquated church bells that open the
song to the shouting town crier and bells (again) that end it. Davies
has acknowledged that Hogarth was indeed an influence on him:
'I liked the way Hogarth really tells things the way they are in his
pictures,' he told Jon Savage, pointing out that he knew a girl, the
president of the Kinks' first fan club, who followed a similar path

from country innocence to prostitution and a drug-related death.[43] Whatever its superficial charms, Davies's songs seem to warn us, Swinging London is still the same perilous place for young women that it has always been.

There is something oddly parental about Davies's perspective here, the songs nudging us towards sympathy with the worried mothers and fathers rather than the thrill-seeking girls. His perspective aligns fairly closely with what was in fact something of a moral panic that broke out in the mid-1950s, as the promise of lucrative employment began drawing hordes of provincial young women to the booming capital. In 1956 the BBC broadcast a television programme called 'A Girl Comes to London', part of its *Special Enquiry* series, in order to find out just what was happening to the five hundred girls who (it said) were arriving in London every week. 'How do they live?' asks the presenter, Robert Reid. 'What sort of digs do they find? And what sort of people are they meeting and palling up with?' Most of the girls interviewed for the programme were doing just fine, it turned out, working in shops and factories during the week and having a grand time in the West End at the weekend, but the producers also found lurid tales of 'good-time girls' coming to London with no real purpose other than to partake of its carnal delights. One employer reckoned that 25 to 30 per cent of the girls his firm brought over from Ireland went missing within the first month. 'There's no doubt at all', says Reid, 'that some girls who come to London just for a good time end up by earning their living on the streets.' The camera shows us a room at Scotland Yard where special cabinets contain files on young women who have come to the notice of the police or who have been reported missing. We also visit a grim shelter operated by the London County Council for women who have run out of money and are often in desperate circumstances. Reid is careful to insist that for every 'good-time girl who drifts into sordid ways of life in the lower depths of the big city', there are many more good girls who do quite well for themselves.

Nevertheless, the idea that the city contains hidden dangers amid its many delights was clearly every bit as potent during the post-war boom as it had been in Hogarth's day.[44]

In a way, the moral danger confronted by the women in 'Big Black Smoke', 'Polly' and 'Starstruck' is the flip side of the philandering of the male characters in 'Dandy', 'A Well Respected Man' and so on. Neither men nor women come off particularly well in these songs, but the social opprobrium, where there is any, falls largely on the women rather than the men, and this fact elicits the singer's sympathy. Polly and her female colleagues may be silly and gullible, and they may be susceptible to a kind of moral corruption that doesn't apply to the men, but in Davies's hands it is generally the male characters who are shown to be hypocritical, cruel, pompous or ridiculous. At a time when other male songwriters were still depicting women primarily as objects of love or lust, and in a rock world in which misogyny was still the default setting for many groups (the Rolling Stones released both 'Under My Thumb' and 'Stupid Girl' just six months before 'Big Black Smoke'), Davies's sympathy with his female characters, and his contempt for many of his male ones, is striking. Perhaps he identified with these characters' experiences of seduction and betrayal, for this was also how he was coming to feel about his own time in the pop music business. Regardless, virtually alone among his male peers (with the possible exception of David Bowie in his 1967 song 'Maid of Bond Street'), Davies showed an interest in exploring what it was like to be a woman in Swinging London, making so bold as to suggest that the scene's famous 'dolly birds', with their geometrical haircuts and Mary Quant handbags, might have feelings, too.

This attitude was evident not only in his songs of female endangerment, but in songs such as 'Two Sisters', which, fraternal allegories notwithstanding, also explores the divergent lifestyle choices that were available to women at the time, and 'Little Miss Queen of Darkness', which tells of a girl who tries to mask her loneliness by flirting with boys at discotheques. Even Dave's songs from this period, notably 'Funny Face' and 'Susannah's Still Alive', began to take an interest in women as subjects rather than mere objects. In June 1967 the Beatles would reach a much broader audience than the Kinks ever could with *Sgt Pepper*'s girl-gone-to-the-city narrative 'She's Leaving Home', but in this case, at least, the Kinks had got there first.

One of the most pervasive myths of Swinging London – indeed, of the entire post-war period up to that point – was the myth of classlessness, or the idea that working-class affluence and the democratization of culture was starting to erode Britain's notorious class divisions. The earliest discussions of this phenomenon had occurred in the mid-1950s, when working-class playwrights such as John Osborne and Arnold Wesker had stormed the battlements of respectable culture with jarring theatrical depictions of an insurgent plebeian culture. When these 'Angry Young Men' were embraced by the very establishment they were kicking – when, in Osborne's case, *Look Back in Anger* became a hit in the West End and Sir Laurence Olivier agreed to play the lead role in his next play – it began to seem to many (middle-class) commentators that class divisions were starting to crumble. These young men may be angry, went the thinking, but the future clearly belonged to them.

The rise of Swinging London a few years later appeared to confirm this. Working-class youths, now more giddy than angry, gave the scene some of its most iconic figures: photographers (David Bailey, Terence Donovan, Brian Duffy), actors (Terence Stamp, Michael Caine), models (Twiggy, Jean Shrimpton), fashion designers (Mary Quant, John Stephen) and of course musicians (not just the Kinks, but also the Beatles, the Stones, the Who, the Dave Clark Five, Small Faces, the Pretty Things, the Animals, Helen Shapiro, Adam Faith, Sandie Shaw and dozens more) all found their way up from the lower depths into the limelight. Together with the more switched-on portion of the upper classes, they formed a new hipoisie, a media-friendly cultural elite who worked, played, partied and slept with one other with a promiscuity that was mostly (if not entirely) heedless of class distinctions. David Bailey, who rose from East End obscurity to become the most celebrated fashion photographer of the 1960s, felt that, however talented he might be, he would not have been able to achieve such fame prior to this decade of liberation. 'Until the sixties,' he once said, 'the class structure here was almost like the caste system in India. If things had gone on as they were, I would have ended up an untouchable. But that all broke down.'[45] His fellow East Ender Terence Stamp was more blunt. 'Had the sixties not happened,' he said, 'I would never have been able to spend the night with a young countess because I would never have met her.'[46]

The problem with the classlessness myth was that, real though the phenomenon might have been on the bohemian or artistic fringes, it did not really describe the lives of ordinary people. As historian Arthur Marwick has noted, the working classes may have 'attained unprecedented *visibility*' in the post-war era, but the class structure itself proved remarkably resilient.[47] Throughout the 1960s middle-class people continued, on the whole, to live in middle-class neighbourhoods, go to middle-class schools and pursue middle-class careers, even if their children did occasionally listen to working-class pop music. The upper classes were even more insular, as they had always been, despite the odd renegade countess. And, while it is true that the working classes were experiencing more drastic changes than the others, the ways they experienced those changes were still conditioned by their social status. Working-class people still faced disadvantages in the realms of education and housing, for example, and by some measures the gap between the rich (or the merely comfortable) and the poor was actually growing. When asked about these matters by sociological researchers, nearly everybody was able to place themselves somewhere in the class hierarchy; even though they were not always clear on precisely where the dividing lines lay, they knew to which class they (and their neighbours) belonged.[48]

Of course, Britain had changed a lot since 1845, when Benjamin Disraeli famously described the country as consisting of 'two nations; between whom there is no intercourse and no sympathy; who are as ignorant of each other's habits, thoughts, and feelings, as if they were dwellers in different zones, or inhabitants of different planets'.[49] Now the classes were much more familiar with one another, and the boundaries between them were far blurrier. Whole new occupational groups had arisen that were not part of any historically recognized class (where did 'fashion photographer' fit on the traditional manual/non-manual worker axis, for example?), and people of all classes tended to read more of the same books and watch more of the same films than ever before. There was, on the whole, a certain 'levelling up' of society (as the *Daily Telegraph* put it in 1959) as living standards for working-class people began to improve. Nevertheless, to claim, as Harold Macmillan did (also in 1959), that the class war was 'obsolete' was a bit premature.[50] As long as people in different occupational and income groups continued to socialize in different ways, go to different schools, speak with different accents, vote for different political parties and identify with different cultural traditions, the 'two nations' still remained, no matter how many countesses Terence Stamp slept with. This was the key point, and the one that Davies explored in his songs: whatever the outward changes to British life since the war, people's consciousness of class – their intuitive sense of where they and others fit in the system – remained as sharp as ever.

The Kinks' own experiences in the music business bore this out. Upper-class enthusiasm for working-class culture had got the Kinks their first managers, the well-respected City men Grenville Collins and Robert Wace, who initially hired them as a backing band so that Wace (who was not musically gifted) could sing at parties for his well-bred friends. Many of these privileged kids found the whiff of the slums that these scruffy musicians carried with them quite thrilling, regarding them with the same mixture of fascination and condescension that genteel philanthropists had shown during the 'slumming' fad of the Victorian period. Wace and Collins – an advertising executive and a stockbroker, respectively – took up managing the Kinks much as their forebears might have taken up fox hunting, as an amusing but probably not especially profitable hobby on which to spend their free time. For their part, the band were always acutely aware of the gulf separating them from their managers, nick-naming Wace 'Bob the Snob' and mining their accents for creative effect (it is Collins's plummy voice that we hear answering the phone at the beginning of 'Party Line'). Although the relationship between the band and their managers was usually friendly, it was never free from class resentments and misunderstandings. 'The fact that they managed us must have made them radical and anti-establishment in their own circles,' Davies once conceded; but their circles were not the Kinks' circles, and this was what mattered: even in the supercharged world of popular music, management and labour still inhabited two very different nations.[51]

Nevertheless, by becoming pop stars the Kinks had also become slightly unmoored from their own working-class roots. Even if some of them still lived within walking distance of their childhood haunts, they were now moving in vastly different orbits than the people among whom they had grown up. They had wealth, fame and mobility. They had travelled the world, appeared on television and hobnobbed with the great and the good. Yet, despite all their achievements, they were never going to be accepted as true members of the upper classes. Their manners, accents, lifestyles and interests were too indestructibly 'common' for that. Like other working-class musicians, the Kinks were in an odd position: having achieved more success than anyone from their world was ever supposed to, they would never obtain full entry into the next world up.

The anxiety that this produced – a mixture of pride in his working-class background, resentment-cum-jealousy of the Establishment and uncertainty about where he fit into the class system now that he had 'made it' – could be heard in the many class-conscious songs Davies was writing at this time. It is most apparent in his songs about homeownership, a topic about which Davies wrote with surprising frequency. Famously reluctant to part with any amount of money, however trifling, Davies's decision to purchase the house in Fortis Green had been of monumental importance to him. On the one hand, it required him to spend more money than he would have liked (£9,000, quite a large sum for the time); on the other hand, he couldn't shake the feeling that, as a world-famous musician, he really ought to have an even larger home somewhere outside the city – a feeling that two of his older sisters, who had known the deprivation of the war years, encouraged him in. Davies would eventually purchase a grand suburban home in the summer of 1968, but in the meantime you could hear him testing out the implications of such a move, and what it would mean for his class standing, on songs such as 'House in the Country', 'Most Exclusive Residence for Sale' and 'Sunny Afternoon'. All three recall Noël Coward's song 'The Stately Homes of England' (1938), which had likewise used real estate as a sort of barometer for measuring the strength of the British class system. But whereas Coward had treated the nation's crumbling mansions as symbols of a declining aristocracy, Davies uses his grand homes as symbols of social aspiration, and his characters' struggles to obtain or retain such homes as confirmation that the class system, though strained, is still quite strong.

All three songs appeared on the 1966 album *Face to Face*, which was the Kinks' first serious attempt to break from the singles format and create an LP that could stand on its own as a coherent artistic statement. 'House in the Country' is the most venomous of the three, an angry rant about a haughty sociopath who is a brute at work and detested at home. He doesn't care what people think about him, though, because he has a fine country house for weekends and a fancy car to get him there. When the singer pledges to knock him off of his throne, it comes across as the petulant envy of a social inferior who simply can't stand the idea of someone who is so unflappably self-satisfied. Knowing that Davies will soon buy a country house of his own, it is hard not to hear the song as either an act of pre-emptive self-laceration or an attempt to inoculate himself against future criticism – as if, having committed his feelings about people who own country houses to record, he can retain some sort of working-class credibility should he eventually buy a country house himself. Whatever its intent, it is a fine example of pop music as class warfare.

'Most Exclusive Residence for Sale' strikes a softer, somewhat more sympathetic tone. It tells of a social-climbing profligate who, having made a pile of money, splashes it about on girls, jewellery and a great big house. But then hard times hit (possibly because of some financial improprieties on his part) and he has to sell his home and let the servants go. He takes to drinking and descends into a pit of despair, and there he remains at the song's end, while the Kinks sing some sympathetic 'la la la las' just before the fade. It's not satire, exactly, but rather a cautionary tale about the dangers of rapid wealth acquisition and the speed with which wealth quickly acquired can just as quickly disappear. It is almost certainly an expression of Davies's own anxieties about the transitory nature of wealth and fame. 'I was always frightened by having the house and the garage and all the things that go with it,' he told an interviewer in 2013. 'At the same time, I don't want to be homeless. That's a big fear.'[52] At the time he wrote the song, in 1966, there were still very few people who had managed to build a lasting career as a pop musician. Pop was a highly competitive world still largely at the mercy of the singles charts: just one or two dud singles could sink your career or relegate you to a lower division without a hope of climbing back up. The frenetic pace of recording and touring set by the record companies – an album a year, at least, plus endless live performances and interviews – was partly responsible for the extraordinary outpouring of pop music during the 1960s, but it was hard to see how it could be sustained for more than a few years. Davies was constantly under pressure to keep churning out hits, and he naturally worried about what would happen to his home and his family when his creative powers gave out. Would he have to sell his own semi-exclusive residence and tumble back into working-class mediocrity? Was his Regency semi-detached maybe a bit of an extravagance after all? At the same time that he was writing songs for *Face to Face* he also wrote the little-known song 'This Is Where I Belong' (later to be the B-side to the Dutch release of 'Mr Pleasant'), in which the singer promises his beloved that he won't look for a house upon a hill because he's happy right where he is. That song amounted to a pledge to be content with what he had; 'Most Exclusive Residence for Sale' was a warning about what could happen if he started putting on airs.

The third posh-chaps-and-their-houses song constructs a similar scenario to the other two, but its message and mood could not be more different. Where 'House in the Country' was all angry satire and 'Most Exclusive Residence for Sale' was all dour pessimism, 'Sunny Afternoon' was a celebration of delusional sangfroid in the midst of financial ruin. It is the only one of the three songs to be sung in the first person, a technique that leads us to empathize with the central character much more than we are able to do with the (objectively quite similar) protagonists of the other two songs. The narrative is simple: a wealthy cad has been hit with a crippling tax bill, and, having sold off his possessions and lost his girl, whom he has been drunkenly abusing, he has decided that there's nothing for it but to lie around in the sunshine sipping cold beer. The upper-class inflection of Davies's voice, the unexpectedly upbeat chorus and Nicky Hopkins's chirpy piano all tell us that, whatever the narrator's complaints, his situation is more comical than dire.

He has lost his yacht, his car and his girl, but he's not exactly eating bread and honey for Sunday dinner; the predicament from which he repeatedly requests salvation – big house, sunshine, beer and plenty of time on his hands – is of course no kind of predicament at all. He is a bit like one of Evelyn Waugh's spoiled aristocrats, bored and tipsy in a steaming bath, regretting the rising price of petrol while the Nazis invade Poland. You can tell that he's a spoiled and selfish scoundrel, but you can't help identifying with him. As the American critic Paul Williams once said of the song, 'Goods and bads don't enter into the picture.'[53]

Despite its jolly mood, however, 'Sunny Afternoon' is deeply rooted in Davies's own class anxieties. In Jon Savage's words, it demonstrates his 'fear that the classlessness of the 1960s has made him rootless . . . he has cast himself adrift – he is neither fish nor fowl'.[54] But this time there is political confusion to go along with the class confusion. The Labour government's taxes on high earners (including many rock stars) were astronomical at this time, sometimes reaching as high as 90 per cent, and 'Sunny Afternoon' is Davies's half-hearted and self-effacing letter of complaint. 'I was brought up believing that all Conservatives were cruel slave-drivers,' he reflected in *X-Ray*, 'who took advantage of the poor and cared little for the unfortunates on whom their whole financial empire had been built. Here was I, newly rich (on paper), singing songs about the woes of having money taken away from me by a Labour Government.'[55] The remarkable thing about 'Sunny Afternoon', however, was that its half-Tory outlook did not stop it from becoming a massive hit with the record-buying masses. Released in early June 1966, it became the unofficial anthem of what turned out to be an unusually warm summer, hitting #1 in the charts (where it displaced the Beatles' 'Paperback Writer') and serving as a theme song for the victory celebrations after England won the World Cup in July.[56] This was also the summer when Swinging London was at its peak, when working-class kids were adorning the covers of glossy magazines and talk of a new era of classlessness was everywhere. Despite Davies's own pessimism about this new golden age, he had somehow persuaded millions of people to identify, however briefly, with a debauched aristocrat whose very existence suggested that the class system was as robust as ever. Partly this was because it was such a catchy song – Davies says he wrote it to be the sort of thing that people could sing in pubs – but it also seems to have touched a collective nerve. 'Sunny Afternoon' offered ordinary people, people who were not David Bailey or Twiggy or Terence Stamp, the opportunity to enact the myth of classlessness for themselves, to pretend that all they had to worry about was the loss of their yachts and their cars while they lounged about in their massive homes sipping beer. Or perhaps it gave them an opportunity to cry crocodile tears for the poor, harassed aristocrats who were finally being taxed out of existence.[57] Whatever the case, as with the myth of classlessness itself, it was pleasant to pretend that the story told by 'Sunny Afternoon' was true, even if people's everyday experiences told a very different story.

Say what you will about the characters of Ray Davies's Dickens period, they are rarely boring, rarely neutral. They inhabit the extremes of poverty and wealth, exhibit hypocrisy and frivolity and evoke our pity, envy and rage. They are, like Dickens's characters, often larger than life, their flaws and virtues magnified for our amusement and, occasionally, our moral judgement. But this is to be expected, not just because there is only so much complex characterization that you can achieve in a short pop song, but because exaggeration is the very currency of satire. If Davies wanted to poke fun at the hype surrounding Swinging London, or to highlight the dangers of the city for innocent women, or to anatomize the nation's social hierarchy, he had to create characters who were exaggerated embodiments of the phenomena he was examining. Characteristics that would, in real life, be found scattered among a large group of people were, in songs like 'A Well Respected Man' and 'Sunny Afternoon', concentrated into one, somewhat grotesque, individual.

This pattern of songwriting began to change in the later 1960s. It was not so much that Davies's songs became less satirical, but that his satirical songs became softer and more ambiguous. It became less clear just who or what he was satirizing, or if he was satirizing anything at all. At the same time, his songs started to become more nostalgic (or were they just satirizing nostalgia?) as he began exploring a more durable sort of Englishness than that being proffered by the trendsetters of Swinging London. His characters, too, became less grotesque and more ordinary – not boring, exactly, but smaller and more relatable. They became, to use the epithet of the time, squares: the sorts of people who lived in semi-detached houses, drank tea by the gallon, holidayed in Blackpool (and enjoyed it!) and had about as much in common with the beautiful people of Swinging London as with the Man in the Moon. They may not have fit the world's idea of what London or England should be, but they fit Davies's experience of what the people around him were actually like. England was changing, sure, but not in the way that *Time* magazine said it was; what was happening went much deeper, and was much more troubling, than that. In the next phase of his career Davies would try to get at the essence of those changes, not by confronting them directly, but by retreating into a fantasy world of his own devising.

3

Ready, Steady, Stop!
(or, Rock Music as Historic
Preservation)

In late July 1968 Ray Davies and family – which now included a fox terrier named Alfie, in addition to Rasa and three-year-old Louisa – moved out of their modest semi-detached house in Fortis Green and into a suburban mock Tudor mansion at Borehamwood, Hertfordshire. This was the sort of thing you were supposed to do when you made it big in England. Whether you were an industrialist, a banker or, in the upside-down world of the 1960s, a rock star, the time-honoured way to demonstrate (and maybe even enjoy) your success was to abandon the hurly-burly of city life for a big house in the country. The Beatles had done it, the Stones had done it and now Ray Davies was doing it, albeit at the urging of two of his sisters and with the support of a wife who was desperate to put some distance between herself and her overbearing in-laws.[1] The new house, hidden in a quiet suburb 10 miles northwest of Muswell Hill, was hardly a secluded country retreat on the scale of, say, Keith Richards's Elizabethan cottage in Chichester, but to a homebody like Davies, Borehamwood seemed like a different world. Just before the big move he invited his family to the old house to hear him play his soon-to-be-released single 'Days', a song of wistful gratitude for a time that is irretrievably lost. 'I finished the song and there was silence in the room,' Davies recalled. 'It was obvious I was saying goodbye, not just to a house but to a way of life, a time, an inspiration.'[2]

The goodbyes turned out to be premature. Within fifteen months Davies was back in the house at Fortis Green (which he hadn't bothered to sell), along with a new addition, baby Victoria. The new house just hadn't suited. It was too big, too remote from family and bandmates, too stockbrokerish. Davies felt depressed living there, like he was 'betraying my class', as he once said.[3] Back in Fortis Green he was again surrounded by familiar streets and familiar people, and there he would stay until 1973, when his marriage fell apart and he moved away for good.

Although brief, Davies's detour through Borehamwood was nevertheless significant, as much for what it symbolized as for what it did for his music. It was not true, as Davies and others have sometimes suggested, that most of the songs on the Kinks' landmark album *The Kinks Are the Village Green Preservation Society*, released in November 1968, were written at Borehamwood – they were mostly written earlier[4] – but the pastoral tone of that album, its suspicion of city life and its longing for a true and essential (but endangered) Englishness were all very much in line with Davies's decision to move out of Muswell Hill for the first time in his life. Like the character in 'Days', time was dragging him forwards, but his face was still turned towards the past, as if he wasn't quite convinced that the future was somewhere he wanted to be.

If the period from mid-1965 to mid-1967 saw Davies anatomizing, and often scorning, the varieties of modern English life that he saw from his north London window, the succeeding period, which lasted until about 1971, saw him thinking in a more focused way about the English past, the attractions and perils of nostalgia, and the allure of the countryside as a refuge from the modern city. If the earlier period was Davies's Dickens phase, then perhaps this was his Romantic phase, a period when he sought refuge from the juggernaut of the modern world in the vanishing remnants of a simpler time.[5] His sojourn in outer suburbia was an expression of these concerns, but it did not cause them. As we will see, he had been flirting with nostalgia for several years before the move to Borehamwood, and he would continue to explore its implications for many years after he moved away. But 1967–71 were the years when he came closest to embracing a full-blown anti-modernism, an attitude that in some ways resembled the 'getting it together in the country' ethos of the hippies and the folk revivalists of the same era. Yet unlike those groups, Davies never quite took it all the way. As Nik Cohn once observed, 'he's an open romantic but there's always a slyness in it, some self-mockery.'[6] The past might be a nice place to visit, his songs often suggest, but it is not a place you can stay if you want to keep your sanity or your soul. So perhaps it is more accurate to call this Davies's semi-Romantic period, the period when he could never quite commit to living completely in the past. This ambivalence was most clearly evident in the songs that appeared on *Village Green*, which will be the focus of this chapter, but it would resurface in many other songs of the period, as we will see in the coming chapters.

'The major trend' of post-war British life, in the words of historian Edward Royle, 'has been an accelerating discontinuity with the past'.[7] For many people, of course, the changes could not come quickly enough, but there were also those who worried that in the rush to embrace the new, something valuable of the old was being lost. For most of his semi-Romantic period, Ray Davies counted himself among the worriers. Even Dave, who was much more eager to avail himself of the new freedoms than his brother, was coming to sense that newness was not a virtue in itself. As he recalled in his autobiography,

> While other songwriters were metaphorically tearing up the 'old' in favour of the 'new', the Kinks were trying to point a way to a future where the good from the past could be interwoven with the new and radical. The revolution, we felt, if

indeed there was to be one, could not happen purely by freeing ourselves completely from the ties to our past, our culture.[8]

The Davies brothers, as we know, had maintained strong ties with their own 'past' and 'culture' even during their early rush to fame. Now that things had slowed down and they had time to ponder it, they began to sense that some things were changing in the wrong sorts of ways. The working classes were richer and more mobile than ever before, but the very affluence that had made a band like the Kinks possible also seemed to be eroding the tight-knit urban communities in which the Davies brothers had their roots. Many of Ray Davies's songs of this period were a way of articulating, sometimes consciously and sometimes almost accidentally, this core idea: working-class life was indeed changing, but what was being gained did not always compensate for the loss of an old working-class world that had once been much more cohesive, proud and self-contained. Partly this was nostalgia for his own idealized childhood, but partly it was also nostalgia for an imagined world that had existed before he was even born.

We have already seen how post-war affluence and greater consumer choice were reshaping working-class youth culture in Britain, but what was it doing to working-class communities generally? As early as 1957, sociologists Peter Willmott and Michael Young were noting how the growing abundance of consumer goods and the rise of the mass media were transforming the structure of working-class Bethnal Green:

Fewer children, longer lives, more space in the home, less arduous work – these are some of the changes which have profoundly influenced the local community. It has been penetrated at a hundred points by the great society. Ideas, as well as people, now move more freely. The popular press, the cinema, the radio and now the television have put new models, drawn from other classes and other parts of the world, before the local people, creating new aspirations and new ideals.[9]

These 'new models' had of course provided the Davies brothers with their first musical inspirations, but their impact went well beyond that. A few years after Willmott and Young conducted their research, the sociologist Ferdynand Zweig found that televisions, along with more affordable motor cars, were profoundly altering the working classes' family and social lives.[10] Fathers, formerly stern and distant, were becoming more family-centred as they chose to stay home in the evenings to watch television and, at weekends, to take the family out for drives. 'Both innovations', Zweig wrote, 'strengthen the family circle, while actually weakening the ties with mates.'[11] Zweig saw working-class families becoming more harmonious and self-contained – more middle class, in fact – as a result of these innovations, but it is easy to imagine that many families might actually have got along better when dad was out of the house. In any event, there was no doubt that working-class lives were becoming more centred around the home thanks to televisions, cars and other forms of family entertainment, and this was having important knock-on effects across society.

One effect was that, by providing a greater range of entertainment possibilities that catered to more individual tastes, television and its confreres (record players, transistor radios and so on) were displacing the common culture that had previously bound the working classes together. The old variety theatres, which brought together a wide array of entertainment genres into one family-friendly package, were either closing or being converted into concert halls or cinemas – indeed, cinemas themselves were in decline (from 4,700 across Britain in 1946 to just 1,600 in 1971) as people chose to stay in and watch television instead.[12] The same was true of other mass leisure activities. Racetrack attendance was down (although betting shops and bingo halls were booming), working men's clubs were becoming less crowded and pubs were beginning to lose business to the greater comforts of the domestic hearth. Working-class teenagers were less likely than ever to listen to their parents' records or radio programmes, and even within teenage culture, fractures were emerging as kids gravitated towards different musical subcultures.[13] Young and old still socialized together more than they did in America – the American producer Joe Boyd recalls being surprised to find 'earringed boys with long hair . . . drinking a Sunday pint next to their dads in cloth caps'[14] when he moved to London in the mid-1960s – but that too was starting to change as cultural offerings became ever more narrowly targeted to specific age groups.

Another factor that was helping to fragment the working classes was accelerating migration into the suburbs. This had really begun between the wars, but it picked up dramatically after the Second World War, thanks in part to growing car ownership. By 1966 half of all British households owned at least one car, a trend that contributed not only to the rise of the suburbs but to the death of the corner shop, the rise of the supermarket and the massive expansion of the motorways.[15] As with television, the movement of people into the suburbs tended to strengthen the family at the expense of the broader community. In 1964 the sociologist J. H. Westergaard observed,

The closed, homogeneous, one-industry, one-class, one-occupation community, familiar from earlier industrialism, is no longer typical. Suburbs and new towns are taking the place of the old mining villages, textile districts, and dockside areas. And, through these and other changes, the street, the pub, the working-men's club are losing their importance as centres of local social contact, in a world where working-class families lead increasingly 'home-centred' lives.[16]

What was happening when factory workers, miners and railwaymen migrated from the inner cities to the suburbs was that they were abandoning (often quite willingly) a tight-knit world that was shaped by a broadly communal outlook. Lives that had previously been lived in the streets, the pubs and the music halls – or, for women, in cramped and dingy houses where the doors were always open and neighbours were always 'dropping in' – were now more private, more inward-looking. Childhoods that had been enmeshed in a comfortable, knowable web of extended families and close (sometimes too close) neighbours and parents' workmates became more circumscribed. The old neighbourhoods were places where children ran riot through the streets and mothers gossiped at doorsteps, where everyone expected to have the same sorts of jobs as their neighbours and the same sorts of lives as their parents, where everyone was equally deprived and therefore equally 'up against it' in their dealings with the rest of society. The new, suburban way of life was much more anonymous and self-contained, if also more comfortable. What historian Jerry White calls the 'mutual consolations' of the poor were no longer necessary now that people were not quite so poor and had new (often televised) means of consolation.[17] For many people the move to the suburbs was undoubtedly a step up, but something vital was also lost along the way.

The old neighbourhoods were not exactly hollowing out, however, for as the old working classes moved out, new people were moving in. Non-white immigrants from the Commonwealth, estimated by the Home Office to account for about 2 per cent of the population in 1968, not only moved into the inner-city neighbourhoods that had formerly been regarded as the heartland of the white working class, but they also tended to occupy the bottom of the labour market, which brought them into direct contact (and sometimes conflict) with the white residents who remained.[18] Many working-class whites, especially the younger and more culturally adventurous among them, enjoyed mingling with these newcomers, but many others blamed the immigrants for the break-up of the old neighbourhoods and the loss of the old culture. In such circumstances, the anti-immigrant scapegoating of Enoch Powell and the far right found many receptive working-class ears. As more immigrants continued to arrive, many whites who had not yet fled the inner cities began to do so, and the old communities eroded even further.

It didn't happen all at once or in the same way everywhere, and in several important ways the English working classes still retained a large degree of distinctiveness from the middle classes, but by the late 1960s the old inner-city neighbourhoods were visibly changing. By the time the Kinks released *Village Green* in 1968, the place you were most likely to encounter the pre-war culture of the working classes was not out in the streets but on the millions of televisions that tuned in twice weekly to watch *Coronation Street*, a soap opera that, since its debut in December 1960, had become a staple of British life. In tower blocks high above the sparkling cities, in suburban front rooms strewn along the commuter belt and in council flats built where the slums used to be, the atomized working classes of Britain would settle onto their sofas for what was, in a sense, a half-hour of collective mourning. Here on the screen was a small, cobblestoned street of cosy shops, brass bands and friendly neighbours tucked away somewhere in darkest Salford, a place where children played ball games in the street, old and young understood one another, outsiders were few and there was always someone ready to strike up the pub piano for a boozy sing-song. It was the kind of place that was rapidly disappearing out in the real world, a community that, in the words of its creator, Tony Warren, comprised 'a fascinating freemasonry, a volume of unwritten rules' into which the viewer was offered privileged access.[19] Roughly a third of the British population watched *Coronation Street* during the 1960s, a testament not only to the quality of the show's writing and acting (both unusually strong for the time) but to the deep emotional need people felt to hold on to the world that was slipping away.[20] In a sense, what *Coronation Street* was doing on television was what Ray Davies would begin doing in his songs: preserving the last traces of a pre-war culture before it finally disappeared, and mourning those elements that were already lost forever.

Although it took him several years to devote much concentrated attention to the topic, Davies's initial turn towards the past occurred surprisingly early in the Kinks' career – as early as November 1965, in fact, when the Kinks released 'Where Have All the Good Times Gone' as the B-side to 'Till the End of the Day'. The A-side is a fairly uncomplicated celebration of the liberating powers of true love, but 'Where Have All the Good Times Gone' is, as its title suggests, suffused with an uneasy nostalgia for a better world. The singer is fretful, depressed about the state of his life and longing for things to be like they were when he was young, when he was happy and the world wasn't so complicated. He also seems to long for a time before his own birth, back when 'ma and pa' had been poor and honest and didn't go looking for more than they had. These are remarkably rueful sentiments for a group of young men supposedly leading a youth insurgency (Ray was 21, Dave was 18), but, like Davies's later songs in this vein, it is never entirely clear if the Kinks are surrendering to nostalgia or simply making fun of those who do. The line in the middle of the song that describes how the singer's parents 'always told the truth', which Davies delivers with just the ghost of a smirk, sounds an awful lot like satire to me. It calls to mind the 1997 general election manifesto of the Monster Raving Loony Party, which promised to create a 'Ministry of Nostalgia' to restore 'a wonderful bygone age when everyone was paid in golden sovereigns, no one was ill or died, the weather was perfect, and you could get 200 pints of bitter for a quid'.[21] This sort of absurd romanticizing of the past is precisely what Davies seems to warn against when, towards the song's end, he tells his interlocutor to come down to earth and stop longing for a vanished yesterday. But the rest of the song certainly sounds earnest enough, with those crashing chords and the insistent repetition of the titular question. It is, in short, an early effort to resolve the dilemma that will be repeated in many Kinks songs to come: shall we surrender to the comforting embrace of nostalgia, or shall we acknowledge that the past is gone and accept the world as it is?

The other great pre-1968 song that foreshadows Davies's later concerns is 'Autumn Almanac', which was released as a single in October 1967. This song is less concerned with nostalgia as such than with describing (and thereby preserving) the more mundane aspects of working-class life that were somehow managing to survive the Swinging Sixties. The song's title recalls Louis MacNeice's poem cycle *Autumn Journal* (1939), a depiction of England on the eve of the Second World War that, like 'Autumn Almanac', acts as a kind of anticipatory requiem for a way of life that seems doomed to extinction. As the threat of bombing and invasion hang over England, some people prepare for the worst (the government, MacNeice observes, is cutting down the trees on Primrose Hill for anti-aircraft guns) while others seek comfort or distraction in the familiar rhythms of ordinary life.

> The workman gathers his tools
> For the eight-hour day but after that the solace
> Of films or football pools
> Or of the gossip or cuddle, the moments of self-glory
> Or self-indulgence, blinkers on the eyes of doubt,
> The blue smoke rising and the brown lace sinking
> In the empty glass of stout.[22]

Davies has said that 'Autumn Almanac' was 'inspired by Charlie, my dad's old drinking mate, who cleaned up my garden for me, sweeping up the leaves', but it could just as easily be about one of MacNeice's fatalistic workmen sipping stout after a day's labour.[23] It is a song about the small (if blinkered) pleasures that the character finds when he is at work – the musty colour of the leaves, a caterpillar creeping through the dew – and when he is at rest – holidays in Blackpool, Saturday football, Sunday joints. It is also about the contentment he finds on his street, which he vows never to leave, even if he lives to be 99. He celebrates Friday evening get-togethers, regrets the disappearing summer and complains about his rheumatism. There's also a portion of the song that Davies sings in a Northern accent that is either gently mocking or clumsily affectionate. 'I got some gyp from fans up North who didn't like it,' he recalled, 'thinking I was satirising them. I said, "I'm not satirising you, I'm celebrating you."'[24] As ever with Davies, the line between satire and celebration is wafer thin.

In 1958 the BBC aired a documentary about life in Bethnal Green that nicely encapsulated the outlook of people like the protagonist of 'Autumn Almanac'. The programme, presented by the inescapable Robert Reid, follows the Gladden family through their weekly routine, examining their work, pastimes, family relations and general ideas about the world. Asked at one point about his 'idea of life', Johnny, a middle-aged jack-of-all-trades, replies, 'I like to build my life around me pleasures. I go to work, I don't think about work, I just do me work. But I'm thinking of me pleasures all the time. Me dart match. What I'm gonna do at the weekend. Me little bit of golfing or football. I like to build me life around that.' When Reid asks him if he ever worries about the future, Johnny replies, 'No, no. I just worry about today. Let tomorrow come. Just go to work, do me work, and enjoy meself for that day.' This delight in small and momentary pleasures is precisely the outlook that Davies captures in 'Autumn Almanac'. But there is a twist to the Gladdens' story. The programme ends by noting that the family are about to be rehoused in a new council flat. 'They don't expect to alter their way of life,' says Reid. 'They feel freer than most people. That's how they like it. That's how they want it – from now 'til kingdom come.'[25]

Postcard from Blackpool, Lancashire, c. 1967. Since the 19th century Blackpool had been a popular seaside resort for the working classes of the industrial north.

The Gladdens might be optimistic about the change, but we know that the slum clearance and rehousing that they are about to undergo is going to transform Bethnal Green utterly – and, in all likelihood, to change the Gladdens' way of life as well. By 1967, when Davies wrote 'Autumn Almanac', the way of life depicted here would have seemed like a transmission from a lost world. A few decades on, and 'Autumn Almanac' would start to have a similar feel.

In fact, as several scholars and Davies himself have acknowledged, this side of Davies has quite a bit in common with another chronicler of disappearing Englishness, the painter L. S. Lowry. Like Davies, Lowry's paintings of the 1940s and '50s showed great interest in the quotidian pursuits of ordinary people: trooping off to work, gathering at train stations, flocking to football matches, amusing themselves at fairs and festivals.[26] 'My characters?' Lowry once said, in words that anticipate Davies's own explanations of his writing process, 'They are all people you might see in a park. They are real people, sad people; something's gone wrong in their lives. I'm attracted to sadness, and there are some very sad things you see.'[27]

Scenes of working-class life. The Gladden family of Bethnal Green
in *The More We Are Together* (1958).

As Elizabeth Field has pointed out, Lowry's paintings share with
Davies a 'refusal to glamorize the underclass'.[28] Instead, both artists
recognize the limitations with which their characters must con-
tend, their drab and uniform surroundings, the inescapable
tyranny of the factory clock and the limited and somewhat shabby

pleasures to be had at the weekend. These are not bucolic images of a bygone Englishness, but there is nevertheless something nostalgic in them, a fondness for the pieces of the past that have somehow survived into the present.

Lowry's painting *The Old House, Grove Street, Salford* (1948) is a good example of this. The pure white sky and street, neither blue nor grey, the three figures in old-fashioned clothes strolling heavily towards a gate that appears to open on to a cemetery – this all gives a mournful quality to the mustard-and-slate semi-detached house with the misaligned windows that dominates the scene. A dozen years after Lowry painted this scene, a similar Salford street would become the setting of *Coronation Street*, a place where (in Dominic Sandbrook's words) 'change came only slowly and gently, if at all'.[29] Like the disappearing world that *Coronation Street* hymned and preserved, Lowry's street – with its gas lamp, iron gate and apparent lack of motor cars and television aerials – seems to have changed little since the Victorian era. And like 'Autumn Almanac' and many

L. S. Lowry, *The Old House, Grove Street, Salford*, 1948, oil on canvas.

of Davies's other semi-Romantic songs, it focuses on the sturdy continuities that connect the working classes' past to their present. It is somewhat nostalgic but not fully, recognizing working-class life for what it often is: a bit drab, perhaps, but also somehow dignified, and definitely rooted in its own history.

As with much else that Davies was writing at the time, 'Autumn Almanac' seems totally oblivious to the fact that there was supposed to be a generational war going on. Not only does Davies sing like an old man, rheumatic back and all, but, with its pub piano and music-hall brass (actually a Mellotron), the song brazenly appropriates the sounds of the music hall in a manner calculated both to appeal to the

George Formby entertains British troops in Normandy, 1944.

older generation and to preserve that generation's vanishing world.[30] Earlier singles like 'Mr Pleasant' and 'A Well Respected Man' had also adopted the chirpy melodies and ramshackle instrumentation of the music hall, so much so that by March 1966 people were starting to refer jokingly to the Kinks as 'The George Formby Quartet', after the ukulele-playing Lancashire man so beloved of Davies's parents' generation.[31] Yet the affinities between the Kinks and Formby lay not just in their musical style, but in their subject-matter as well. Like the Kinks, George Formby sang songs about Blackpool holidays ('With My Little Stick of Blackpool Rock'), eccentric local characters ('Gallant Dick Turpentine') and the quotidian pleasures of working-class life ('Sitting on the Ice in the Ice Rink'). His 'Biceps, Muscle and Brawn', about an unathletic weakling who wishes he were more attractive to girls, anticipates the Kinks' similarly self-deprecating 'David Watts'. His 'In a Little Wigan Garden', in which a lover tries to woo his darling while soot tumbles down from the chimneys and bees buzz dangerously around him, anticipates not only 'Autumn Almanac' but the later Kinks song 'Holiday' in its wry celebration of the glories, and limitations, of working-class leisure. There is satire in Formby's songs, but it is a kind of self-satire, sung for the amusement of a working-class audience who, in time-honoured fashion, preferred to laugh at their troubles so as not to be overwhelmed by them. As Richard Hoggart pointed out in *The Uses of Literacy*, 'The cheeky, finger-to-the-nose and ain't-life-jolly song is the song of the working-classes when they are refusing to be downhearted simply because they are working-class, when they are raucously confident.'[32] There are traces of this attitude in 'Autumn Almanac', particularly in the middle portion about Blackpool holidays, but it would be even more evident in the songs that Davies wrote next.

The Kinks Are the Village Green Preservation Society was the clearest sign yet that Ray Davies had become a man out of time – or at least that he would very much like to have been. It combined the ambivalent nostalgia of 'Where Have All the Good Times Gone' with the time-capsule sensibility of 'Autumn Almanac' to remarkable effect, becoming what many regard as the Kinks' masterpiece. Famously overlooked upon its release, it received glowing reviews in the music press but got little commercial traction and was virtually forgotten for decades. The album's obscurity was partly due to disputes between Davies and the group's record label, Pye, about how to package and promote it, but it was also the victim of bad timing. Not only did it appear within weeks of Jimi Hendrix's *Electric Ladyland* and the Rolling Stones' *Beggars Banquet*, but it appeared on the very same day as the Beatles' *White Album*. These three powerhouse albums easily drowned out the Kinks' much quieter 'song picture of the gentler aspects of British life', as the critic Judith Simons called it at the time.[33] Davies frequently insists that he prefers the demo versions of his songs to their final, packaged versions, and with *Village Green* he achieved a sound that, he says, resembled the liner instructions that used to accompany folk anthologies: 'to be played intimately, as if among friends'.[34] For its admirers, the album continues to have the quality of a shared secret, acting as a sort of litmus test of whether someone truly 'gets' the Kinks – their Englishness, their wistfulness, their humour – or whether they are simply drawn to the flashier pleasures of the singles.[35] 'Maybe', Davies reflected while discussing the album with *Rolling Stone* in 1970, 'people should have a winding down session before listening to our songs. Maybe they should be briefed. Or debriefed. I think they should be debriefed.'[36]

Davies's original plan for *Village Green* had been to create a piece of musical theatre or pantomime. He was inspired by Dylan Thomas's radio play *Under Milk Wood* (1954), an ensemble piece that portrays in intimate detail the dreams, longings, jealousies and shameful secrets of an imaginary Welsh coastal village called Llareggub ('bugger all' backwards). Thomas's village is an impossibly self-contained world that exists somewhere between Britain circa 1926 and Never Never Land, full of cartoonish eccentrics such as Willy Nilly, the unscrupulous postman who tells everyone what's in everyone else's mail; pretty Polly Garter, who has borne children by nearly every married man in the village (and whom Davies had earlier referenced on the song 'Polly'); and blind old Captain Cat, who dreams of the ghosts of his drowned comrades and invites us to listen with him to the hubbub of the town: the women gossiping at the pump, Cherry Owen stumbling home from the Sailors Arms, Utah Watkins cursing his cows. 'Only you', a soft voice intones at the play's opening, 'can hear and see, behind the eyes of the sleepers, the movements and countries and mazes and colours and dismays and rainbows and tunes and wishes and flight and fall and despairs and big seas of their dreams.'[37] As a picture of village life, *Under Milk Wood* is pure fantasy, an escapist journey into a rural Britain that never did or could exist. Yet there is something in its essence – something in the ways people act towards and think about each other, in the things they eat and the decor of their homes – that is purely British, purely Welsh. If you could strip away all the unnecessary ugliness and hassle of modern Britain, all the pylons and bus fumes and television licences, all the queues and tabloids and pesticides, then you just might find a sweet centre that smells strongly of liquorice and herring, soapflakes and Guinness, and this sweet centre would be something like Dylan Thomas's Llareggub. It would also be something like the Kinks' village green.

It took a couple of years for Davies to realize his idea for the album – the oldest song, 'Village Green', was written two years before the album's release – and lack of support from Pye ensured that it didn't become the soundtrack to a piece of musical theatre as Davies had hoped, but much of *Village Green* still has the flavour of *Under Milk Wood* in its composite portrait of village life, its gentle rhythms and its quiet intimacy. Both *Village Green* and *Under Milk Wood* fit into the long-standing British literary tradition of imagining the countryside as the only place where one could still find what Raymond Williams calls 'knowable communities'. Unlike the city, with its 'increasing division and complexity of labour' and its 'altered and critical relations between and within social classes', the countryside had long figured in British literature as the 'epitome of direct relationships: of face-to-face contacts within which we can find and value the real substance of personal relationships'.[38] *Village Green* was partly, I think, an effort by Davies to restore the 'face-to-face contacts' that had once characterized working-class life but which were now being eroded by modernity. As he once told Jon Savage, it was an effort to create an 'ideal place, a protected place. A fantasy world that I can retreat to.'[39] It was also (and not for the last time) an attempt to reconstruct the family life Ray and Dave had known as children, back before people began emigrating, dying or becoming famous rock stars. It wasn't so much a retreat into the countryside as a retreat into the leafy inner suburb of their youth. 'If Hollywood had designed Muswell Hill and written it in a film script,' Ray said many years later, 'it would have looked like the Village Green.'[40] But there was also something very post-war, even post-modern, about the album. Its uneasiness with nostalgia, its refusal to commit to any fixed attitude about the past and its omnivorous appropriation of the sounds and images of global pop culture all mark it as something that was more attuned to its time than either its creators or its fans often recognize. Savage has called the album 'appallingly out of sync with the time', and many other critics agree, but, as I will explain below, it is actually one of the most avant-garde things the Kinks ever did.[41]

The opening song is a sort of White Paper for the preservation project that Davies is proposing. It lists the kinds of things the Village Green Preservation Society would like to see preserved, an inventory of a certain kind of Englishness rooted in comic books, Victorian morality and cosy pleasures. It is an arresting blend of the playful and the earnest, the satiric and the sincere. On the one hand we have the increasingly absurd names that the Society adopts as the song progresses (the Custard Pie Appreciation Consortium, the Skyscraper Condemnation Affiliate), the triviality of some of the things they want to preserve (strawberry jam, Fu Manchu) and the recurring falsetto 'ooh-ooh-ooohs' that sound just a touch insincere. On the other hand, many of the 'old ways' that the Society lists do seem to be worth preserving, for they were under genuine threat. Corner shops were collapsing under the onslaught of supermarkets and shopping centres, draught beer was being standardized and pasteurized by the big breweries, genteel china cups were giving way to disposable plastic and the variety theatres were practically extinct. As will be the case throughout the album, Davies is trying to have it both ways. Nostalgia certainly is fun, he seems to say, but isn't it also just a little bit silly?

The other songs on the album offer a variety of different answers to this question. Some completely surrender to an uncomplicated nostalgia rooted in the countryside. 'Village Green', the most antique-sounding song on the album, is the story of a boy who leaves his bucolic village and the lovely Daisy for the big city. He returns to find Daisy married and the village overrun with camera-clicking American tourists. He can't ever go back to the old ways, but he can, by the end, envision sipping tea with Daisy and reminiscing about the village green. 'Sitting by the Riverside' is a celebration of lazing around outside and doing nothing much at all, with a music-box melody (occasionally broken by a few bars of wordless, carnivalesque fantasia) and a simple lyric inspired by fishing trips that the Davies brothers took as children. Another straightforwardly nostalgic song is 'Animal Farm', which, despite its Orwellian title, is about an actual, joyous, unmetaphorical farm where the protagonist used to live and to which he pledges to take his 'little girl' someday. Like 'Village Green' and 'Sitting by the Riverside', it proposes the quietness and simplicity of the country as an antidote to the crushing pace of city life. It also offers an insight into the optimism with which Davies regarded his impending move to the outer suburbs, a touching promise from a father to his young daughter to take her to a farm where she can play with pigs and goats in the sunshine and be happy.

The songs on *Village Green* that most closely resemble *Under Milk Wood* are the ones about identifiable characters, of which there are at least six. 'Johnny Thunder' is about a rebel without a cause who drives the highway and subsists on a strict diet of water and lightning. 'Starstruck' is one of Davies's 'going upon the town' narratives about a young girl who leaves her life of rural simplicity for the moral dangers of the city, a sort of 'Animal Farm' in reverse. 'Phenomenal Cat' is about a literal cat who has travelled the world in search of enlightenment, a state that he seems to have attained by eating great quantities of food (hark ye, Johnny Thunder). 'Wicked Annabella' is the neighbourhood witch who lives in a scary old house and haunts the children's dreams. 'Monica', one of several Kinks songs to experiment with calypso rhythms, is about the village beauty (and possible prostitute) whom all of the lads lust after but none can have, at least not in body *and* soul. She is a bit like the beautiful schoolteacher Gossamer Beynon in *Under Milk Wood*, whom the men of Llareggub mentally undress as she walks primly past the pub, or Polly Garter, who happily carries on with the married men of the village right under the noses of their wives. The hero of the music-hall ditty 'All of My Friends Were There' isn't named, but he is clearly another inhabitant of the village green. His story of onstage calamity was inspired by a disastrous Kinks gig at Blackheath in July 1967, when a drunk and feverish Ray performed terribly while his friends watched from the front row. None of these characters directly interact with one another, but it is easy to imagine them all coming together under the benevolent (but non-interventionist) 'Big Sky', who watches over them like Captain Cat watches over the inhabitants of Llareggub, gossiping in Johnny Thunder's garage, drinking draught beer at the village pub, decorating the church hall at Christmas: a sort of Llareggub crossed with *Coronation Street*.

These character songs make up almost half of *Village Green*'s fifteen tracks – more, if we include the song 'Do You Remember Walter?', which is obviously about a character named Walter but which, I think, belongs in a separate category that also includes the songs 'Picture Book', 'People Take Pictures of Each Other' and 'Last of the Steam-powered Trains'. These are all songs about the instability of memory, a concept that is far more complex than simple nostalgia and which is, I think, the underlying theme of the album as a whole. In 'Walter' the singer fondly remembers a childhood friend and the fun they used to have: the rainy games of cricket, the illicit cigarettes, the grand dreams. But now things are changed, life has become complicated and the two have lost touch, never to connect as they used to do. As if to stave off the decline that 'Walter' laments, the characters in 'Picture Book' and 'People Take Pictures of Each Other' try to freeze time and, in so doing, to overcome the deficiencies of memory. 'Picture Book' follows directly after 'Walter' and acts as a kind of coda to it, instructing the listener to imagine getting old and looking through a family photo album at images of happier times. It offers several jolly images – baby pictures, holiday snaps, pictures of parents frolicking with their friends – but it also suggests there's something kind of pathetic in taking so many pictures, as if we think we can photograph, and thereby preserve, love itself. 'People Take Pictures of Each Other' elaborates upon this idea, describing people taking snapshots in order to prove their love of one another – indeed, to affirm their very existence – but, the song suggests, it's impossible to prevent the passage of time in this way. What's gone is gone, and it's pointless to try to preserve it. This idea is reinforced in 'Last of the Steam-powered Trains', a dirty blues song with a harmonica riff lifted from the Howlin' Wolf song 'Smokestack Lightning' (1956). It expresses Davies's sense that he belongs to an earlier time, still chugging over the same old tracks while all his friends have gone electric. British Rail's last steam-powered passenger train had just made its final run two months before the song was recorded, so in addition to Davies's own feeling of back-datedness there is a certain end-of-empire melancholy, a recognition that Britain's glory days as an industrial power are now behind it and whatever relics remain are just dusty museum pieces. This was a notion that Davies would return to on *Arthur* the following year.

The standard critical interpretation of *Village Green* is that, for all of its apparent ambivalence about the past, it is essentially a conservative and nostalgic album – as Michael Mooradian Lupro puts it, 'The village green is a nostalgic stand-in for all that is good and worth preserving and protecting.'[42] But this, I think, is to impute to the album too much of a social or cultural agenda, to see it as proffering answers instead of simply raising questions. *Village Green* does create a cosy, self-contained community into which the listener (and the performers) can escape from the modern world, but it is not exactly directing us to do anything out in the real world once the record stops spinning. It alternates between basking in and withdrawing from the comforts of nostalgia, telling stories, sketching characters and having quite a bit of fun along the way. It is constantly undercutting itself, surrendering to romantic notions of the past only to whip around and declare that such a surrender is pointless and self-deluding. It celebrates the simple life of the countryside but can't resist the lure of the city. It is both quintessentially English and unabashedly cosmopolitan, the soundtrack to a morris dance one minute and to a Belgian blues bar the next. All of this makes it entirely too slippery and evanescent to be any one thing for very long, and this of course is its strength. Many years later, when asked by Daniel Rachel if he liked 'revisiting the past', Davies replied, 'It's hell. The past is something you can't take back. It's wonderful.'[43] That answer is *Village Green* in a nutshell.[44]

However, if we must categorize *Village Green* as one type of thing, then I would argue that it is an unusually well-camouflaged piece of Pop art.[45] The key to this interpretation lies with a certain cartoon duck who appears on the opening track of the album.

Before I began writing this book, one thing that had long confused me about 'The Village Green Preservation Society' – and which no critic or commentator had ever satisfactorily explained – is the prominence of Donald Duck among the inventory of items that the Society wants to preserve. True, Donald Duck occupies the same realm of childhood nostalgia as the comic book hero Desperate Dan and the literary-stroke-movie villains Fu Manchu, Count Dracula and Professor Moriarty, but Desperate Dan was a purely British phenomenon (even if most of his adventures were in the American Wild West), and the stomping grounds of the other three were almost exclusively British. Donald Duck is not British, nor, to my knowledge, has he ever visited Britain, yet he gets four separate mentions in the song, the most of any item in the inventory other than 'vaudeville and variety' (which are the American and British terms, respectively, for what became of nineteenth-century music hall). Why?

Former scenester George Melly tells us that in the late 1940s and early 1950s there was a sort of fad among British intellectuals for American cartoons. But not just any cartoons: 'Disney was rejected as dated in technique and sentimental in content', and people also objected to 'the extreme modernity of the UPA cartoons'. Warner Bros. cartoons, on the other hand, were unanimously regarded by the with-it crowd as 'everything an animated cartoon should be': sophisticated but not arch, revealing the elevated tastes of the animators but without being too obvious about it.[46] As a Disney character, Donald Duck would have been rejected as irretrievably square among the British hipoisie of the 1950s, and you might assume that he therefore deserves a place among the antique tables and china cups of the Kinks' village green. But then, in 1961, Donald Duck played a starring role in the birth of Pop art when the American painter Roy Lichtenstein depicted him in his groundbreaking work *Look Mickey*. The painting is almost a direct copy of a scene from a Disney comic book, showing Donald accidentally hooking himself in the tail feathers while trying to cast his fishing line into the water.

Mickey Mouse stands nearby covering his mouth while Donald yells, 'Look Mickey, I've Hooked A Big One!!' The painting was a sensation. The object of furious denunciations from the art establishment, it marked the arrival of a new artistic movement that refused to recognize distinctions between high and low culture, finding inspiration in the emblems of mass culture just as readily as from more approved sources.

Lichtenstein's bold appropriation of comic-book art launched a thousand imitators, and Donald Duck became, quite unexpectedly, the herald of a new world of collapsing cultural hierarchies. I doubt Ray Davies had this painting in mind when he wrote 'The Village Green Preservation Society', but the fact that Davies and Lichtenstein should both hit upon Donald Duck is more than mere coincidence. As an emblem of childhood in the middle of the twentieth century, you could hardly ask for a better figure than the spluttering and irascible Donald, who may have been American by birth but had long since flown the coop to become a citizen of the world.[47] Like Lichtenstein, Davies (who confessed in a 1966 interview to watching Disney cartoons 'twice a week on the box'[48]) was reaching for something that was innocent, universal, unpretentious and perhaps a wee bit incongruous. Donald Duck has no more business waddling around an English village green than he does hanging on the wall of an art gallery, but there he is in both places, attesting to the inescapable reach of American mass culture into even the stodgiest or cosiest of institutions. He's the stereotypical crass American, flapping about and causing a ruckus wherever he goes, complaining about the food, trampling the delicately sodded lawn, demanding to be treated like the centre of the universe. He's utterly incapable of blending in, more prone to make an ass of himself (in the manner of 'All of My Friends Were There') than to appreciate the local colour (in the manner of 'Village Green'), and for that we both love and loathe him. He's an embarrassment, but he's also kind of funny. He is the essence of Pop art.

Roy Lichtenstein, *Look Mickey*, 1961, oil on canvas.

'Acceptance of the mass media entails a shift in our notion of what culture is,' the English critic and Pop art evangelist Lawrence Alloway wrote in 1959:

> Instead of reserving the word for the highest artifacts and the noblest thoughts of history's top ten, it needs to be used more widely as the description of 'what a society does.' Then, unique oil paintings and highly personal poems as well as mass-distributed films and group-aimed magazines can be placed within a continuum rather than frozen in layers in a pyramid.[49]

Pop artists embraced, in Robert Hewison's words, 'a splendid pluralism of forms', recognizing 'no hierarchy of value' and 'no hierarchy of subject-matter'.[50] But unlike the vernacular cultures from which they drew, Pop artists were always at least one step removed, lifting mass-produced fragments of popular culture out of their contexts and dropping them into new ones – a comic strip painted on canvas, a soup can in a museum. 'It was an ambivalent thing,' writes Melly, 'part tongue in cheek, part sincere, but never unconscious.'[51] Ray Davies, inveterately ambivalent and tongue-in-cheek himself, had been at art school at the very time that the work of the great Pop artists was filtering into the curriculum. Despite later dismissing Pop art as 'pretty pretty and petty', it was inevitable that he should have absorbed something of its ethos, if only partially and by degrees.[52] The atmosphere in these schools was, as Brian Harrison says, 'experimental, international, and creative', and the Pop art that Davies and other musicians of his generation (Townshend, Richards, Clapton et al.) encountered there 'was youthfully populist in tone, subversively witty, hedonistic in its unashamed alignment with Americanized consumerism, unsnobbishly adventurous in its working materials, and seeking immediate impact rather than a timeless and universal permanence'.[53]

Every one of those traits (with the possible exception of the last) characterizes not just the opening track on *Village Green*, but the entire album. The juxtaposition of Donald Duck with Desperate Dan, Mrs Mopp (a character in the 1940s radio comedy *It's That Man Again*), Old Mother Riley (a music-hall and film character played by Arthur Lucan), the George Cross and assorted fictional villains is pure Pop art, a humorous, incongruous aural collage akin to Peter Blake's pop-culture fever dream on the cover of *Sgt Pepper's Lonely Hearts Club Band*.[54] The musical styles across *Village Green* are similarly eclectic and cosmopolitan, drawing from English folk-pastoral traditions, music hall, psychedelia, calypso, blues and even (on 'Wicked Annabella') horror movie soundtracks. It is, as Simon Frith and Howard Horne have said of 'Pop art pop' generally, full of 'music as bricolage, quoting from other work, incorporating "real" sounds, recontextualizing familiar sonic symbols'.[55] Like the Pop artists and magazine editors of Swinging London, the album is also obsessed with photography: if Davies doubts the value of photography as a true record of the past, he also offers us many examples of the kinds of things that people take pictures of, which together add up to another kind of Blakean collage. Furthermore, the inhabitants of the village green, far from being the musty, old-fashioned sorts traditionally associated with rural England (sturdy yeomen, blacksmiths, pretty milkmaids and so forth), are, in fact, a very modern hotchpotch derived from the mass culture of the 1960s: a motorcycle freak, a couple of dolly birds, a fairy-tale witch and a world-travelling, enlightenment-seeking feline. With its whimsy, ambiguity and giddy appropriation of the symbols of mass culture, *Village Green* is, to my ears, much more of a Pop art object than an exercise in backward-looking conservatism. As ever when listening to the Kinks of the 1960s, we must remember that this is the work of a group of young, working-class musicians who had come of age in affluent post-war England, American pop-culture obsessives who had risen to fame in the same hothouse pop industry that had created many of their idols. Their yearnings may have been old-fashioned, but the eclectic vocabulary in which they expressed those yearnings was utterly contemporary – even, or especially, when they were mimicking the tones and inflections of their elders.

This point becomes clearer if we compare the Kinks' ambivalent, pop-culture-infused nostalgia with the kind of nostalgia that was being embraced by middle-class intellectuals at the time. Probably the most famous intellectual anti-modernist of the 1960s was John Betjeman, the kindly, tubby, permanently dishevelled poet and architecture critic who spent most of the post-war period (and a good portion of the pre-war period) complaining about the ravages of development in his innumerable poems, lectures, radio talks and documentaries. For decades, Betjeman was a more or less permanent fixture on the BBC, forever peering into ancient churches or riding around on little-used branch lines while a camera crew captured his pensive gaze and a voiceover (contributed by himself) read off a bit of his poetry. Jocelyn Brooke once described him as 'a writer who uses the medium of light verse for a serious purpose: not merely as a vehicle for satire or social commentary, but as a means of expressing a peculiar and specialized form of aesthetic emotion, in which nostalgia and humour are about equally blended'.[56] This makes him sound very much like Ray Davies, as do poems like the highly facetious 'Inexpensive Progress' (1966), with its foreboding opening lines: 'Encase your legs in nylons, / Bestride your hills with pylons / O age without a soul'.[57] Like Davies, Betjeman was troubled by any so-called progress that cut him off from memories of his own idealized childhood. He distrusted and satirized executives, speculators, planners, vulgar suburbanites, neon signs, motorways, clean straight lines and young people who seemed to be having too good a time with their modern gadgets. In a memorable poem of the 1950s called 'The Town Clerk's Views' he roasted planning officials who envisioned turning open fields into fluorescent-lit playing fields, but who, in the manner of the tourist-trap village green of Davies's imagination, had deigned to 'keep one ancient village just to show / What England once was when the times were slow'.[58] In place of such fakery, Betjeman treasured church bells, rusty iron gates, birdsong, buttercups, elm trees, winter jasmine, the Cornwall coast, inglenooks, tennis lawns and sugar cubes soaked in port. He could be savage, but he could also be quite funny, capable of mixing (again in Brooke's words) 'fun and nostalgia . . . irony and romantic feeling' in order to sweeten the sting of his fury.[59] Given these traits, it is little wonder that Betjeman was briefly mooted as a collaborator for Davies on his 1969 *Arthur* project.[60]

In addition to his poems and broadcasts, Betjeman was also something of a one-man preservation society, working through community action to protect the nation's natural and architectural heritage. 'All people who spoil decent country should go to prison or be heavily fined,' he said in one especially pungent anti-speculator broadcast in 1937.[61] Among his many projects was the Victorian Society, which he helped to found in 1958, a body whose aim, in

John Betjeman statue in London's St Pancras Station, one
of many Victorian structures he helped to save from the
wrecking ball. Sculptor: Martin Jennings.

historian Christopher Inwood's words, was 'to defend what was left
of old London from the hitherto triumphant march of functional-
ism, modernism and big business'.[62] As if to pave the way for the
Kinks' revival of the sounds of the music hall, Betjeman also worked
with the British Music Hall Society to save London's oldest music
hall, Wilton's, in 1964. He also had an affection for steam-powered
trains and the stations that housed them: it was thanks to Betjeman
(and a sympathetic British Rail worker who leaked the demolition
plan to him) that London's magnificent St Pancras station escaped
demolition in 1967.

There were plenty of other intellectuals at this time who worried about the costs of progress in a Kinksian sort of way. In 1972, for example, Philip Larkin published a deeply pessimistic poem called 'Going, Going' that blended the concerns of the emerging environmental movement with Betjeman-style preservationism to worrying effect. Renouncing his earlier attitude that there would always be more fields and trees beyond the built-up areas, more unpolluted oceans than mankind can possibly destroy, the poet now frets about 'bleak high-risers' crowding out the old and pleasant streets and new factories spoiling 'the unspoilt dales'. He has now come to fear that England itself will disappear before he dies, that it will all be 'bricked in / Except for the tourist parts', its shadows and meadows vanished, its guildhalls and 'carved choirs' destroyed. A few vestiges might survive in old books and galleries, 'but all that remains / For us will be concrete and tyres.'[63] This sort of modern nightmare was precisely what led Ray Davies to see the 1960s as a period of greed and deceit. 'The countryside was being eroded and trees pulled up in order to build motorways,' he wrote in *X-Ray*, 'I was writing songs and the country was gradually being sold out. Cheated.'[64]

Yet despite the apparent similarities, the outlook of middle-class intellectuals like Betjeman and Larkin was not entirely congruent with Davies's working-class view of the world. There was little room in their conceptions of the English good life, for example, for comic books or bad horror films; indeed, such products of the American mass media were precisely what they set themselves against. Here is Betjeman in a 1943 talk for the BBC Home Service laying out his personal war aims:

For me, at any rate, England stands for the Church of England, eccentric incumbents, oil-lit churches, Women's Institutes, modest village inns, arguments about cow parsley on the altar, the noise of mowing machines on Saturday afternoons, local newspapers, local auctions, the poetry of Tennyson, Crabbe,

Hardy and Matthew Arnold, local talent, local concerts, a visit to the cinema, branch-line trains, light railways, leaning on gates and looking across fields.[65]

Few of these items, with the possible exception of local concerts, railways and trips to the cinema, would have found a place on the Village Green Preservation Society's list of protected properties. Nor, in all likelihood, would Larkin's books, galleries and carved choirs make the cut. Davies's outlook was much more proletarian, much more Saturday football, Sunday joints and American pop culture than that. In 1959 Betjeman had greeted the creation of the Noise Abatement Society with the decidedly un-rock-and-roll aphorism, 'God is worshipped in silence but the devil is worshipped with noise.'[66] One can hardly imagine Ray Davies (let alone the other Kinks) endorsing such a view of the world.

Seen from this perspective, the concept behind *Village Green* begins to look positively subversive, for essentially what Davies was doing on this album was translating the nostalgic longings and fears of the modernity-shunning elite into the vocabulary of post-war working-class youth. Indeed, there was something subtly subversive in the very idea of a working class rock band fronting a preservation society, however tongue-in-cheek the concept might have been. Prior to the 1960s, almost without exception, preservationist organizations had been the province of the upper crust. According to historian Paul Readman, the membership lists of organizations like the Commons Preservation Society (founded 1865), the Society for Checking the Abuses of Public Advertising (founded 1893) and the National Trust (founded 1895) 'resembled extracts from a Who's Who of the British Establishment', encompassing aristocrats, bishops, dons, prime ministers and the like.[67] In many ways the elite nature of these organizations was a good thing: it is thanks to the power and influence of their members that Epping Forest, Hampstead Heath, Wimbledon Common, the Malvern Hills and Ashdown Forest are not currently car parks or housing estates. Yet these bodies could also be quite conservative, if not downright reactionary, for often what they were trying to do was to check the spread of the unwashed masses into the unspoiled regions of the country. The Council for the Preservation of Rural England (CPRE), for instance, was founded in 1926 to halt the expansion of suburban housing developments, motorways and petrol stations – the habitat of the upwardly mobile working classes – around major cities and towns.[68] One of the CPRE's most prominent supporters was the philosopher C.E.M. Joad, who in a 1931 pamphlet theorized that the constant interaction of workers with factory machines had made them incapable of appreciating nature: 'it is not to be expected that a population so trained and so employed can do other than spoil the country, when it depends upon it,' he mused.[69]

None of this meant that the lower classes were indifferent to the cause of preservation, simply that their perspective was not often considered, except in a negative way, by the elite groups who led the preservationist charge. In reality, as Readman has shown, during the Victorian and Edwardian periods the working classes were increasingly drawn to the countryside by cheap rail fares, more abundant leisure time and the proliferation of rambling and cycling clubs. As a result, many working-class people came to believe that certain parts of the English landscape ought to be the common property of all, not the private property of speculators and developers. 'If anything,' Readman writes, '[preservationism] challenged the property rights of elite groups; the capitalist railway speculator and the commons-enclosing or footpath-stopping landlord were its enemies.'[70] In other words, preservationism had the potential to become an act of anti-establishment resistance, a people-powered rebellion against the unholy alliance of speculative capital and corrupt or cavalier governments. It need not simply be about preserving old or beautiful places: it could also be about protecting portions of the country as the common birthright of all.

The common people's efforts to combat property speculation and ruthless development actually went back much further than the Victorian era. From the fifteenth to the nineteenth centuries, the rural poor had mounted their own sort of preservation campaigns by resisting the enclosure of common lands by profit-driven landlords. These struggles were about much more than preserving the beauty of the countryside: they were about preserving people's ability to scratch out a living from the woods, fields and other common spaces in the manner of their ancestors. Sometimes they resisted through violence and sometimes through legal channels. Their resistance ultimately failed to prevent the seizure of most of the nation's open countryside by the wealthy, but they did often manage to prevent the enclosure of village greens, thereby ensuring that communities continued to have places to come together to gossip, trade and celebrate. In fact, if by 1968 England had any village greens left at all, this was due less to the petitions of elite preservation societies than to the refusal of ordinary people to allow the local squire to steal their common spaces. It wasn't God who saved the village green, in other words, but the people of England themselves.[71]

Some of this tradition of resistance can be seen in the poems of John Clare, the untutored 'peasant poet' of Northamptonshire who gained some fame in the 1820s and '30s for his Romantic poems of rural life. Clare's anti-enclosure laments and poems of childhood innocence trampled by greedy progress have a strongly Kinksian ring to them, and they make an interesting contrast with the refined nostalgia of Betjeman and his middle-class colleagues. Clare's poem 'Remembrances', for example, dwells upon joyous seasons spent amid the wild countryside, 'where bramble bushes grew and the daisy gemmed in dew', before the landlords came along to enclose the land:

Inclosure like a Buonaparte let not a thing remain
It levelled every bush and tree and levelled every hill

And hung the moles for traitors – though the brook is
    running still
It runs a naked brook cold and chill[72]

Clare's love of the countryside – his pleasure in its rhythms and
seasons, his countryman's intimacy with the songs of the birds and
the subtly different greens of the grasses – was a love derived not
from aesthetic contemplation but from constant, daily interaction
with the land as a source of sustenance and survival. Like the upper-
class Victorians who would later create the Society for Checking the
Abuses of Public Advertising, Clare also had an abhorrence of signs,
but not because they blocked his view of the countryside. He hated
them because they literally made it harder for him and people like
him to survive.

There once were lanes in nature's freedom dropt,
There once were paths that every valley wound –
Inclosure came, and every path was stopt;
Each tyrant fix'd his sign where paths were found,
To hint a trespass now who cross'd the ground
Justice is made to speak as they command;
The high road now must be each stinted bound:
– Inclosure, thou'rt a curse upon the land,
And tasteless was the wretch who thy existence plann'd . . .[73]

This was preservationism like a strong snapping of the jaws. It dif-
fered from the genteel preservationism of Betjeman and company
like draught beer from fine wine: both tended towards the same
outcome, but one had a decidedly earthier tang.

Where elite preservationists tended to blame the vulgar masses
for the denuding of the countryside and the destroying of the
nation's heritage, writers like John Clare and Ray Davies, whose
origins and sympathies lay with those same vulgar masses, tended

to blame the rich and the profit-hungry for what was happening. In Clare's day, wealthy speculators had been abetted in their enclosure schemes by thousands of 'Inclosure Acts' passed by their allies in Parliament. In the 1960s, this collusion between capital and the state continued in the form of redevelopment schemes hatched by urban property developers in alliance with local councils. But, as in Clare's day, the vulgar masses were starting to fight back. In 1959–60 a private plan to redevelop Piccadilly Circus into a massive office complex was halted after a furious public outcry that included all classes of Londoners. A similar thing happened to the planned redevelopment of Covent Garden in 1971, which would have destroyed about two-thirds of the existing (largely working-class) area and replaced it with roadways, office blocks, a sports ground and other large-scale amenities. This preservation effort spawned the Covent Garden Community Association, an alliance of local residents and market sellers whose success inspired similar community organizations around the country.[74] These grass-roots campaigns were not particularly reactionary, conservative or anti-modern; mostly they reflected a growing determination by ordinary people to preserve the freedom that came with the unplanned diversity of the city and the undeveloped simplicity of the countryside (as well as the affordable rents and prices that would be threatened by gentrification). As one Covent Garden campaigner put it, they saw themselves as engaging in 'a freedom struggle against oppression, exploitation, and, subsequently, colonisation' by the forces of property speculation and global capitalism.[75] Celebrities like John Betjeman often joined these campaigns and brought them greater publicity, but the heavy lifting was done, as often as not, by the common people themselves.

This kind of historic preservation – this demotic and antiauthoritarian preservationism of the little man – was the preservationism with which the Kinks were in tune. Dave Davies once said that the tightly woven opening harmonies on 'The Village Green Preservation Society' symbolized a certain 'bonding' and 'strength' among the singers. 'It was like, "We're impenetrable. We might not have a lot, but you can't kill us. You're going to have to *shoot* us."'[76] This was not the signboard-smashing, America-despising, modernity-shunning, port-sipping preservationism of the intellectual anti-modernists, despite certain strong resemblances. I said above that *Village Green* is too ambiguous and indecisive a record to be heard as promoting a positive agenda out in the real world; it is an escapist record, not an activist record. But you can still tell where its sympathies lie. Its uncertainty about the merits of nostalgia, its inclusion of such vulgar items as Southend holidays and cartoon characters among its inventories of Englishness, its openness not just to the music of America but to that of the world at large – all of these characteristics set it apart from the intellectual anti-modernists and fox-hunting conservationists who had so far dominated the preservationist landscape. *The Kinks Are the Village Green Preservation Society* was Ray Davies's attempt to create a Pop art fantasyland into which none of the bulldozing speculators, capitalists or bureaucrats of the modern age would be allowed. Beyond that, though, it was open to all sorts of influences, especially American ones, just as the English working classes had always been. It is an open-armed, big-hearted, ambivalent and forgiving kind of record, a far cry from the snobbishness and certainty that infused much of the elite-driven nostalgia of the past century, to say nothing of the small-minded English nationalism that Enoch Powell and his latter-day descendants would so cynically exploit in the years to come. Almost despite itself, it offers a vision not so much of an idealized English past, but of a possible future in which Donald Duck and calypso music could become as English as afternoon tea.

4

The Glory of Being Boring

One day perhaps a Dickens of the suburbs will arise,
to immortalize the life and language of suburbia.

J. M. Richards,
The Castles on the Ground: The Anatomy of Suburbia (1946)

To get to Borehamwood by train from central London you pass through several miles of open countryside. This gives you the mistaken impression that you are headed for a quaint rural hamlet, but the place you encounter when you exit the station is not all that different from any modern English suburb or small town. The high street is strewn with the usual array of estate agents, charity shops and piri-piri takeaways, and behind the busy main strip is a new shopping complex enclosing a wide asphalt sea full of cars and shopping trolleys. Today Borehamwood and its conjoined twin, Elstree, market themselves as a destination for movie tourists. Parts of the *Star Wars*, *Superman*, *Indiana Jones* and *Harry Potter* franchises were filmed here, and *EastEnders* and other BBC television series continue to be shot at the local studios. The two towns even have their own version of the Hollywood Walk of Fame, with plaques placed here and there along the high street honouring some of the celluloid heroes who have come to the area to make movies. Ray Davies does not have a plaque here, but if you visit the Elstree & Borehamwood Museum on the top floor of the public library, the friendly volunteers will be able tell you exactly how to get to the site of The Gables, the large mock Tudor manor that he bought from *The King and I* actor Martin Benson in 1968. The manor no longer exists, but the gatehouse that Davies and the band used for rehearsals is still there, hidden behind a tall white fence. It is just steps away from the big shopping centre, but neither the shopping centre nor the surrounding scatter of brown-shingled semis were there when Davies lived here. Back then, it was mostly countryside.

Borehamwood today is not an especially quiet place, but in 1968 Davies found the quiet of outer suburbia unsettling to the point of distraction. 'I miss things like having people bang on the walls when I play music too loudly,' he told a journalist shortly before he gave up on Borehamwood and moved back to Fortis Green. 'I just want to be surrounded by people again.'[1] Not only was the place too quiet, it was too far away from the people who had been most important to him for most of his life – his parents, his siblings and of course his bandmates. In order to learn the new songs Davies was writing, the other Kinks had to take the tube all the way up to High Barnet, where they would be fetched by a car and brought round to the echoing manor to await Davies's pleasure.[2] This arrangement was quite irritating – Pete Quaife, who would leave the band in early 1969, complained of feeling more sidelined than ever – and it clearly troubled Davies as well. What was there to write about in such a place? Where was the street life? Where were the stories? The locals remember Davies drinking at the Wellington pub, which still stands a few steps away from where The Gables used to be, but it seems he found little in the way of inspiration there. Borehamwood was a sleepy kind of place then, filled with a class of people to whom he found it difficult to relate, but whom he feared he might one day become. Now *he* was the well-respected man with a most exclusive house in the country, and if he wasn't exactly a member of the tin-soldier army that marched off to the train station every morning, his neighbours certainly were. Was it for this that he had abandoned the comfortable world of his childhood?

Suburbia can be a lonely place. During the great suburban boom of the interwar years, some people – usually people who didn't live in the suburbs – spoke of something called 'suburban neurosis',

The Gatehouse, Borehamwood: all that remains
of Ray Davies's 'house in the country'.

which supposedly afflicted housewives who stayed at home all day while their husbands went off to work. 'The causes of this malady', writes historian Alan A. Jackson, 'were said to be threefold: lack of social contacts, leading to boredom; worries about money and the home; and a false set of values derived from novels and films which implanted expectations of thrills and excitements not likely to be found in the suburban environment.'[3] Whether this condition was as widespread as people believed is open to question, but it seems like some such malady afflicted Ray Davies during his fifteen-month sojourn in outer suburbia. The strongest evidence for this is the album he produced there, the only Kinks album wholly written at the Borehamwood house: *Arthur (or, The Decline and Fall of the British Empire)*. Although it returned to many of the themes Davies had explored on *Village Green* – childhood, nostalgia, the pleasures of the countryside – *Arthur* was in many ways a record of suburban loneliness, charting the journey of one small man from the Victorian slums of inner London to suburban isolation in the affluent 1960s. *Arthur*'s story was a microcosm of recent working-class history in England: like *Village Green*, it was a response to the changes that the working classes were undergoing, but it was a response in a somewhat different register. If *Village Green* had seen Davies retreating from the slow death of working-class London by creating his own version of Llareggub, *Arthur* was a more realistic picture of what was actually happening to working-class people who made the great migration from inner-city terraces to privatized suburbia. It was not, on the whole, a happy tale.

Yet *Arthur* is more than just a document of suburban loneliness. In fact, as I will argue here, it is not even particularly hostile to suburbia, or in anyway to the people who lived there. Rather, by exploring the history of Britain's twentieth century through the eyes of one small man, it makes the case that each suburban semi-detached house contains entire worlds – of experience, of longings, of memories – that are much larger and grander than the four walls that confine its inhabitants. The heyday of the Victorian empire, the catastrophes of the world wars, the trials of the Depression and the disorienting changes of the post-war era all haunt the rooms of the anonymous suburban home in which the story's protagonist, Arthur Morgan, lives out his final days. Continuing in the cut-and-paste Pop art style he had developed on *Village Green* – a style hinted at by the Pythonesque cartoons on *Arthur*'s cover – the songs are a mixed-media collage of old song lyrics, advertising slogans, political speeches and sound effects. It is a little like a 1969 version of the 1951 Festival of Britain, which Simon Rycroft has described as 'Pop Art on a grand scale, a disassembled, cut-up and reassembled collage of the nation's past'.[4] Viewed from without, which is where most writers would have stayed, Arthur Morgan is a sad and boring little man. But viewed from within, which is where Davies takes us, he contains multitudes.

Like *Village Green*, *Arthur* was originally conceived as the soundtrack to a piece of musical theatre. In January 1969 Davies, who had begun writing songs for television and was looking for ways to blend rock music with film and performance, finalized arrangements with Granada TV to write a 'pop opera' about the decline of the British Empire. The list of potential collaborators included John Betjeman and the satirist Alan Bennett, both of whom had a sharp wit and a sardonic sensibility that nicely matched Davies's own. Betjeman, as we have seen, shared Davies's suspicion of modern life and affection for the gentler ways of the past, even though his particular brand of nostalgia was mustier and more patrician. Bennett had been at the forefront of the 'satire boom' of the early 1960s, one of the four principals (alongside Dudley Moore, Peter Cook and Jonathan Miller) in the *Beyond the Fringe* comedy revue that had laid the groundwork for much of the anti-Establishment British humour of the decade. It is interesting to speculate about just how different *Arthur* would have been if either Bennett or Betjeman had ended up working on it – with Bennett it would almost certainly have been funnier; with

Betjeman there would almost certainly have been more trains – but in the end the job went to the playwright and novelist Julian Mitchell, a less well known but equally sympathetic partner.

In 1964 Mitchell had written a novel, *The White Father*, about a colonial officer named Hugh Shrieve who returns to Britain just as the empire is crumbling to advocate for the protection of the Ngulu, a small African tribe of whom he has oversight. This 'white father', as he is known to his subjects, is alarmed and confused by the changes sweeping through England, particularly the hedonistic new youth culture that seems to have sprung up overnight. Shrieve forges a relationship with an aspiring musician who resembles an earlier version of Davies and his bandmates, and much of the story is about the gulf that has emerged between the old, morally certain world of the empire and this new world in which all values seem to be up for grabs. 'Do you ever see young people at all?' Shrieve asks at one point. 'They have a sort of cult of detachment – moral detachment, moral neutrality – they don't seem to want to get involved in anything. They don't criticize much, they just don't seem to believe in anything.'[5] The novel is essentially about the consternation that people feel when their solid, taken-for-granted values dissolve into something new and unfamiliar, and it made Mitchell peculiarly well suited to working on *Arthur*, which Davies had conceived as only partly a tale about the fall of the empire as such. The empire bit had been Granada's idea: Davies's instinct was to make it about an old man's disillusionment with the course of his life and the things in which he has been brought up to believe, a crisis of confidence that mirrors what journalist Anthony Sampson called, in 1962, 'the decay of the sense of overriding purpose' in the country at large.[6] The actual fall of the empire happens mostly offstage, framing the story and establishing an elegiac tone but not really central to the action. The real 'decline and fall' is that which occurs to Arthur himself.

The action of *Arthur*, such as it is, is largely confined to a modest home somewhere in the wastelands of suburbia. The central character, Arthur Morgan, is a retired carpet layer living in what he once fancied a sort of suburban paradise, his shiny car parked in the driveway and his warm slippers awaiting him after a long day at work. But Britain isn't what it used to be, and Arthur isn't doing so well himself. After losing a brother in the First World War, suffering and struggling through the Depression and losing a son in the Korean War, he finds himself lonely and disillusioned in the brave new world of the late 1960s. Tomorrow his surviving son is leaving with his young family for Australia, and most of the story concerns the events prior to this leave-taking. There's a family dinner, an evening at the pub, a sullen trip the following morning to the Australia-bound boat – and there are Arthur's memories, mostly fond but also painful, of a life spent pursuing a dream that never quite materialized. Davies based the character on his brother-in-law Arthur Anning, who had married his sister Rose. As I noted in Chapter One, when he was a teenager Davies had lived for a time with Arthur, Rose and their son Terry in their house on Yeatman Road, and he got to know them quite well. The real Arthur was a welder in a plastics factory who had lost his brother Stuart in the Second World War. He was a strict disciplinarian and a rather unhappy man. As Davies remembered, 'The world Stuart had died to protect had turned its back on Arthur, making him a tormented, empty person.'[7] Davies had been crushed when Arthur, Rose and Terry emigrated to Australia in the early 1960s, but he understood the impulse. 'A lot of people in the family thought that he was a bitter man, but he was just frustrated. People gave up their lives and their youth for the war. They had been promised a new world, and what did they get? Motorways and concrete.'[8] It was this sense of disappointment, of 'being left behind in an old world that was in decline', that Davies and Mitchell sought to capture in their television play.[9]

It is difficult to say if this downbeat premise would have worked on-screen, however, because the programme was never made.

A director was chosen and actors were cast, but the funding dried up and Granada pulled the plug at the last minute (what we know about the story comes mostly from Mitchell's liner notes). To add insult to injury, by the time the album was finally released, on 10 October 1969, the Who had released a 'rock opera' of their own called *Tommy*, thereby taking the credit for producing the first such concoction in history (although both albums were preceded by two near-rock operas the previous year: Small Faces' *Ogdens' Nut Gone Flake* and the Pretty Things' *S. F. Sorrow*). Like *Village Green*, *Arthur* received strongly positive reviews but failed to make much of a showing in the charts, particularly in Britain. In the U.S., where a tour was finally being planned thanks to some belated fence-mending with the American Federation of Musicians, Reprise launched an advertising blitz that lifted the album (and a single, 'Victoria', backed with 'Brainwashed') into the nether reaches of the charts. The American critics were gushing in their praise: Greil Marcus called it 'by all odds the best British album of 1969', and *Rolling Stone*'s Mike Daly called it 'a masterpiece on every level: Ray Davies' finest hour, the Kinks' supreme achievement'.[10] This critical response set the stage for the Kinks' triumphant return to the States a week after the album's release, where they found a small but loyal fanbase awaiting them. Nevertheless, the experience of making *Arthur* was quite dispiriting for Davies and Mitchell, who had spent a year on the project only to see half of it disintegrate before their eyes.

Had it aired, there is a strong possibility that the characters in *Arthur* would have borne a strong resemblance to another televised suburban household that was appearing on British screens at the time. The BBC series *Till Death Us Do Part*, which ran from 1965 to 1975, centres on the snivelling, reactionary cockney blowhard Alf Garnett, who loyally keeps a portrait of Churchill on the wall, complains about the swarms of immigrants who are ruining the country (and the Jews who are running it) and is the only one in the cinema who still stands when they play 'God Save the Queen'.

An inspiration for the character of Archie Bunker in the 1970s American programme *All in the Family*, Alf Garnett might almost be Arthur Morgan's obnoxiously racist doppelgänger. In fact, Davies wrote the title song for a 1969 film version of *Till Death Us Do Part*, so the comparison is not entirely fanciful. But Arthur turns out to be a much sadder and more introspective character than Alf, one who feels duped after years of living his life according to the official line that patriotism, sacrifice and hard work will bring him material comfort and spiritual contentment. Davies avoids the trap of making Arthur an Alf-like buffoon who exists simply for our satirical amusement. Instead, he invites us to consider the whole of Arthur's past and present – his sorrows and joys, his longings and regrets – in such a way that if, by the end, we end up feeling sorry for Arthur, it is because we sympathize with him, not because we feel superior to him.[11]

The opening track, 'Victoria', takes us back to the themes of *Village Green*, introducing us to the childhood nostalgia that afflicts Arthur in his old age. Back in Victoria's time, Davies tells us in an affected old-man voice (undoubtedly Arthur's), the world was purer, people didn't talk about distasteful things like sex (echoes here of the 'virginity' that the Preservation Society wanted to preserve) and everyone knew their place. There were village greens, croquet lawns, rich people living in large houses and poor people who, though deprived, were nevertheless loyal to a monarch who cared equally for rich and poor alike. These sentiments are riveted into place with patriotic slogans and the band's enthusiastic and frequent repetition of Victoria's name, which also happened to be the name of Davies's second daughter, who had been born in Borehamwood just before he wrote the song. About halfway through, a triumphant brass band comes in to complement the standard rock instrumentation, emphasizing the pride with which Arthur contemplates the geographic scope of Victoria's domain (Canada, India, Singapore, even Cornwall!), and by the end the band are really going for it, singing Victoria's praises to the heavens amid the trilling brass and the guitars chiming out like church bells. Things won't get this exuberant again until Side B, when Arthur gets a chance to sing about his house.

'Victoria' establishes the young Arthur Morgan as a member of the patriotic, naturally conservative working classes whom Benjamin Disraeli had identified as a potential source of Tory votes back in the 1870s. 'I mean that the people of England,' he told a crowd at the Crystal Palace in June 1872,

> and especially the working classes of England, are proud of belonging to a great country, and wish to maintain its greatness – that they are proud of belonging to an Imperial country and are resolved to maintain, if they can, their empire – that they believe on the whole that the greatness and the empire of England are to be attributed to the ancient institutions of the land.[12]

This is a fair summary of Arthur's outlook at the beginning of his story, but soon the disillusion starts to set in. In his Victorian childhood, Arthur had promised to fight for the land that he loves; the next two songs reveal the consequences of that promise. 'Yes Sir, No Sir' is a send-up of the class-riven British army and the unthinking obedience with which working-class recruits were expected to behave. Pushed around by superiors who see him as little more than cannon fodder, Arthur and his comrades find the army to be a kind of conspiracy to keep the lower classes in their place, even when their place is within the sights of a German machine gun. They're subjected to ludicrous levels of bodily discipline – they can't even breathe without asking permission – and all they get in return is a pack of cigarettes and insincere assurances that their sacrifice is essential to victory. As in 'Victoria', 'Yes Sir, No Sir' is full of sonic gestures to the era it depicts, with parade-ground snare drums and a quotation from the chins-up trench song 'Pack Up Your Troubles in Your Old Kit-bag'. The message here is clear: whatever youthful idealism Arthur may once have had is being sorely tested by this rich man's army and its meaningless war.

Towards the end of 'Yes Sir, No Sir', Davies imitates an officer who, in a contemptuous upper-class sneer, promises to do the minimally decent thing of sending a medal to a dead soldier's wife. In the next song, 'Some Mother's Son', we get to hear what it feels like to be on the receiving end of such a gesture. The song is a lament for a dead son (Arthur's brother in the narrative, who dies in the Battle of the Somme), the mother's grief acting as a sombre rejoinder to the triumphant patriotism of 'Victoria'. Look, the song seems to say – look at what is happening to Victoria's children in this enlightened twentieth century of ours. Look where the paths of glory have led. Just before the soldier dies he is described as lying in a trench and looking back on games he played as a child, but there can be no escape into the safety of the past here: the reverie ends, and in the next second he is killed. Back home, his mother puts his photograph on the wall and places a flower in the frame, but, as we know from *Village Green*, photographs only encourage nostalgia. They can never bring back what is lost.

It will take more than one disastrous war to snuff out Arthur's patriotism, however, as the song 'Mr Churchill Says' makes clear several tracks later. On the surface this is a straightforward celebration of the 'Blitz spirit' of stiff upper lips and calm-keeping carrying-on. Here we find Davies in high Pop art collagist mode, appropriating snippets of Churchill's speeches verbatim ('We will fight them on the beaches . . .') and crowding the canvas with real historical characters. Lord Beaverbrook, wartime Cabinet member and press baron, calls upon Britons to recycle their metal goods into war supplies. National sweetheart Vera Lynn sings the morale-boosting ballad 'We'll Meet Again'. General Bernard Montgomery and Lord Mountbatten exhort the people to courage and sacrifice.

There's even an air-raid siren followed by a fearsome guitar solo that evokes the desperation of a city under attack. As ever, it is difficult to tell if Davies is being earnest or satirical here. Like 'Victoria', 'Mr Churchill Says' draws from a rich fund of patriotic platitudes – and Davies has often said that he admires what his parents' generation went through during the war – but coming after the anti-war, anti-authoritarian sentiments of the two First World War songs, these phrases ring rather hollow. Davies's pompous recitation of Churchill's words makes the song sound more irreverent than patriotic, as does the chipper singalong towards the song's end, suggesting that the consoling myths of the Second World War are perhaps not so much evidence of collective heroism as of a well-intentioned but gullible British public doing the bidding of the greedy and powerful.

It is not all war and class resentment on *Arthur*, however. There are also several penetrating portraits of working-class life between the wars. 'Drivin'', which appears directly after 'Some Mother's Son', lifts us out of the mud and death of the Western Front and deposits us in the Morgan family's motor car on a Sunday drive. A petrol-powered tune of rural escape along the lines of 'Sitting by the Riverside' and 'Animal Farm', 'Drivin'' takes place during the 1930s, when Arthur is making a bit of money as a carpet layer and starting his own small family. As a hymn to long-ago, carefree days, it neatly complements track ten on the album, the somewhat maudlin 'Young and Innocent Days', in which an aged Arthur looks back wistfully on the 'soft white dreams' of his youth. This nostalgic component is not accidental. According to Dave Davies, 'Drivin'' was inspired by Sunday outings that he and Ray took as kids in their dad's black Vauxhall 12, which only their Uncle Arthur (as the lone one in the family with a driver's licence) was permitted to drive.[13] For working-class men like Fred Davies and Arthur Morgan, cars were an important marker of status, a reward for hard work and a sign of being able to provide for one's family. 'The car gives him self-confidence, self-assurance,' wrote Ferdynand Zweig in 1961. 'He is no more at the bottom of the social ladder. He takes pride in having such a glittering smooth-looking and smooth-moving thing which gives him a sense of achievement.'[14] The drive is just part of the pleasure; the other part is the pride of car ownership itself.

In what has by now become a familiar Kinksian attitude, there is a certain whistling-past-the-graveyard quality to 'Drivin'', a sense that if the characters stopped laughing they would start to cry. Back in the city the landlords and debt collectors are knocking at the door, and beyond England's shores the world is going to hell in a handbasket (particularly, as the song notes, in Russia, Spain and China – this is 1937, or thereabouts), but motoring through the countryside allows Arthur and company to momentarily forget their cares. Another song in this vein is 'She's Bought a Hat Like Princess Marina', which sounds like Bob Dylan's 'Leopard-Skin Pill-Box Hat' as rewritten by Noël Coward for kazoo orchestra. The title refers to Princess Marina of Greece and Denmark, who had married Prince George, Duke of Kent, in 1934. At the time she was the height of ladies' fashion in Britain, and it appears that Rose Morgan, Arthur's wife, has gone and bought a hat that resembles the princess's even though she can barely afford to feed her own children. This is the Depression, after all, as Davies reminds us when the song abruptly lurches into a jumped-up, kazoo-led adaptation of the 1930s American song 'Brother, Can You Spare a Dime?' Arthur has had his little indulgence as well, buying a homburg hat of the sort Anthony Eden, Conservative Foreign Secretary for much of the 1930s, made fashionable. Both Arthur and Rose are clearly aping their superiors in a somewhat ridiculous manner, splashing out on frivolities when they can hardly afford the necessities, but they've decided that they won't let mere material deprivation prevent them from having a bit of fun. It's the old *carpe diem*, 'finger-to-the-nose and ain't-life-jolly' attitude of the working classes that we've seen in other Kinks songs, the feeling that life is short and times are hard so you might as well grab your pleasures now and let tomorrow worry about itself.[15]

It would be a mistake to dismiss these hats merely as vain indulgences, however, for they also serve the very serious purpose of enabling Arthur and Rose to maintain their respectability among their neighbours. The suburbanite's obsession with 'keeping up appearances' is easily mocked (most famously in the 1990s sitcom of that name), but it is not as trivial as it seems, particularly for newly suburbanized members of the working class. In the old inner-city neighbourhoods of open doors and shared walls you got to know your neighbours intimately, but in the inward-facing streets of suburbia you needed other ways to show you belonged. Arthur and Rose are living in a time when people could still judge a person's social status by the clothing they wore, and when to wear the wrong clothes in the wrong environment could be acutely embarrassing. In the nineteenth century, the poor had often stayed away from church on Sundays because they couldn't afford nice clothes. Now, in the 1930s, similar considerations applied. In 1939 a sociological survey of the Watling Estate in Burnt Oak, northwest London, reported that 'clothes lend social status, assurance and even personality to the wearers, whose standards of judgement upon frocks and suits are determined by films and magazines depicting the rich and leisured. Many Watling residents . . . are deterred from mixing with others because of the embarrassing consciousness that their outfits are shabby.'[16] Status anxiety was a real problem for people like Arthur and Rose, who have clearly calculated that what their fine hats will buy them in respectability is worth whatever they might cost them in caloric intake. For all that the song's lyrics poke fun at their frivolity, the boisterous, kazoo-driven singalong at the end seems also to celebrate it. The dilemma of the working-class suburbanite has been resolved, at least momentarily: as in 'Drivin'', they have refused to surrender to the despair that their objective circumstances would seem to require. And for that they deserve at least a thimbleful of respect.

Not all of the songs on *Arthur* are about the past, however. Several take place in the present (that is, the late 1960s), when Arthur is an old man preparing to watch his son depart for Australia. These songs allow us to see into the minds of some of the other characters in Arthur's story, specifically his son Derek and grandson Ronnie. The latter, clearly a member of the Kinks' own idol-smashing generation, gets to voice his disdain for Arthur's nostalgia through the angry and self-righteous 'Brainwashed'. He accuses Arthur of spending his life kowtowing to his social betters – literally on his knees, a function of his profession as a carpet layer – and receiving nothing in return but contempt from the upper classes who want to keep him in his place. It's a fierce denunciation of the Disraelian 'poor but loyal' mentality that has shaped Arthur since childhood, the cry of an all-knowing younger generation convinced of its own ability to see things as they really are. But coming just after 'Drivin'', with its joyous celebration of motoring freedom, it seems Ronnie is misinformed about the nature of Arthur's predicament. Arthur might be caught within a class system that will let him rise only so high, but within the limits of his confinement Arthur has actually managed to find quite a bit of contentment, even joy. To an outsider like Ronnie he might seem brainwashed, but we, who have seen inside his memory, know better.

Derek's two songs are more measured. The first, 'Australia', is written like a pamphlet from the Australian tourist board, extolling the cleanliness, fun and employment available for the enterprising Englishman willing to emigrate to the other side of the world (such immigrants were known as Ten Pound Poms, a reference to the price they paid for a one-way ticket). In Australia, we are told, Christmases are sunny, there's no class system, nobody's on drugs and the people are always smiling. It is clear from the ad-copy hype that Derek is being sold a bill of goods here: he will undoubtedly have his share of struggle and hardship in his new home, for such is always the fate of the immigrant, and he may find it no better abroad than it was in England (this had been the real Arthur's experience after he and Rose emigrated). Derek's second song, 'Nothing to Say', enacts a failed attempt to make conversation with his father just before he sails away. Recalling his fond memories of walks with his dad and Sunday dinners at home, he ruefully concludes, as other characters had done on *Village Green*, that the joys of yesterday cannot ever be retrieved, seemingly resigning himself to the fact that he and his dad are destined to live distant lives. He tries several conversational gambits – asking about Arthur's health, enquiring after Auntie Mabel, commiserating over Arthur's noisy neighbours – but the two men have nothing to say to each other, and (one suspects) after the move to Australia they never will.

Sequenced just after the similarly regretful 'Young and Innocent Days', Derek's failure to connect with his father threatens to end the story on a note of frustration and despair, but just at the last moment the closing track, called simply 'Arthur', arrives to save the day. It summarizes the tale of Arthur's life: his youthful ambition, the disappointments thrown in his way, the constraints of his social class, his sadness and sense of betrayal as he watches his country decay and his only living son sail across the ocean. But all is not lost, for an unnamed 'we' (presumably the Kinks themselves) are there to tell Arthur that they love and care for him, a fact that they insist upon over and over as the song and album fade away. This, the final song says, has been the portrait of a man who did everything that he thought he was supposed to do and ended up disappointed with his life; what he deserves is our love and help, not our pity, and certainly not our derision.

This attitude is the key, I think, to understanding the strongest song on the album – indeed, one of the strongest Davies ever wrote: 'Shangri-La'. I have left this song for last, even though it is the first track on Side B, because a full appreciation of it requires a bit of an excursion. This is rock's greatest song about suburbia, a topic that has fascinated British writers and artists long enough to have acquired its own sort of artistic canon. 'Shangri-La' deserves a place in that canon, I think, largely because it is one of the few works on the suburbs to successfully combine the two competing strands of English suburb-writing, which we can broadly if crudely classify as pro-suburban and anti-suburban. Part of what makes 'Shangri-La' such a great song, apart from the simple, visceral pleasures to be had from listening to it, is the seamless way that Davies moves between those traditions while never fully committing to either one. The song is a perfect example of his ability to unite contradictory ideas within a single, coherent piece of art, the arguments for and against the suburban lifestyle pulling the listener in opposite directions in a way that ultimately generates a far richer experience than if it were to come down on one side or the other. To grasp the nature of that artistic achievement – and of *Arthur* generally – we need to know something about the traditions from which it draws.

The modern English suburbs date from about the 1820s.[17] They were designed to provide homes (but little else) for commuters who worked and socialized in the city but longed for the tranquillity of the countryside. The first suburbanites tended to be well-off professionals who could afford the expensive and time-consuming daily commute, but, as new forms of transportation came along, new kinds of suburbanites emerged. In the 1860s and '70s new tramlines and the London Underground brought the suburbs within the reach of lower-middle-class clerks, and in the succeeding decades a few skilled workers began to afford the move as well, although the working classes would form but a small fraction of suburbia before the First World War. The Davies family's own neighbourhood of Fortis Green was an early example of a former village that had been absorbed into the sprawling octopus of London thanks to the expansion of the railways in the 1870s. A mix of terraced and semi-detached houses, it was rather more densely settled than later suburbs – more *urb* than *sub* – but still leafy and quiet, definitely not part of the urban core: just the sort of place that appealed to clerks and other members of the Victorian petite bourgeoisie.

For most of the late Victorian and Edwardian periods, fictional suburbia – particularly that portion of it closest to the city – tended to be depicted as a faceless brick-and-concrete desert inhabited by petty conformists. George and Weedon Grossmith set the standard for clerk-kicking fun with their novel *Diary of a Nobody* (serialized in *Punch* in 1888–9 and published as a single volume in 1892). A resident of then-suburban Holloway (where the Davies family had its roots), the book's hero, Charles Pooter, was the archetype of the 'boring, respectable [suburbanite], full of inflated self-importance and a social climber obsessed with outward show'.[18] His house, pompously named The Laurels despite its distance from anything resembling bucolic countryside, is his primary obsession. He is complacent but also wracked with class anxiety, resenting the smallest slights from people he deems his inferiors and compulsively monitoring the propriety of his and everyone else's clothing and behaviour. He commutes by horse-drawn omnibus into the City, quarrels with butchers over mutton chops and frets about the future prospects of his callow son, Lupin. Pooter is snobbish but also ridiculous in his snobbery, a little man incapable of grasping his own littleness, and much of the humour of the novel comes from the distance between his sense of his own importance and his actual importance in the grand scheme of Victorian society.[19]

The characters of *Diary of a Nobody* quickly entered the popular lexicon of late Victorian England. To accuse somebody of Pooterism was to dismiss them as essentially trivial and insular, more concerned with the state of their wardrobe than with the state of the world. Where Pooter had been a figure of gentle condescension, however, subsequent writers often adopted a more pitying tone. In his social survey *The Condition of England* (1909), C.F.G. Masterman found the suburbs to be home to 'a life which, with all its energies and satisfactions, has somehow lost from it that zest and sparkle and inner glow of accepted adventure which alone would seem to give human life significance'.[20] Writers like H. G. Wells, E. M. Forster, George Gissing and Edward Thomas similarly depicted the suburbs as bleak, stultifying and often reactionary places where beauty and optimism go to die.[21] Thomas, on setting out to 'the heart of England' (that is, the countryside) in 1906, saw the streets of suburban London as 'a great storehouse where yards of goods, all of one pattern, are exposed, all with that painful lack of character that makes us wish to rescue one and take it away and wear it, and soil it, and humanise it rapidly'.[22] There was for Thomas a kind of horror in the vast anonymity of the London suburbs. 'More than battlefield

Charles Pooter paints his servants' washstand in *The Diary of a Nobody* by George and Weedon Grossmith (1892).

or library,' he writes, 'they are dense with human life. They are as multitudinous and painful and unsatisfying as the stars.'[23]

The suburban male was a particular worry for these writers.[24] 'He is a hen-pecked, shrew-driven, neglected, heart-sick man,' wrote the journalist Thomas Crosland in a book-length attack on the suburbs in 1905.[25] Many writers saw suburbia as a space ruled by wives, a feminine space of softness and triviality that robbed men of their vigour and independence. This was a problem not just for the individual male but for the nation and empire as a whole: as Todd Kuchta has noted, 'the suburban male's degeneration from an imperial pioneer to a colonized slave' was a source of considerable anxiety for people (usually non-suburban males) who made it their business to monitor the health of what was then called the imperial race.[26] Scorn for the pettiness and self-indulgence of the male suburbanite was very much in line with fears, particularly strong in the Edwardian era, that the British Empire was headed for the same 'decline and fall' that the Roman Empire had undergone. 'They had become too effete and nerve-ridden to guide the destinies of the world,' wrote Elliott Evans Mills in his book *The Decline and Fall of the British Empire* (1905), a work of retrospective fiction that purported to be a school primer produced 'for use in the national schools of Japan' in the year 2005.[27] Mills identified the same corrosive decadence in the British Empire that the eighteenth-century historian Edward Gibbon had perceived in ancient Rome, including a 'Growth of Refinement and Luxury', a 'Decline of Literary and Dramatic Taste' and a 'Gradual Decline of the Physique and Health of the English People', all failings commonly associated with suburbanites in general, and male suburbanites in particular. In this way of viewing suburbia, the lifestyle of somebody like Charles Pooter – or, indeed, Arthur Morgan – was no mere private failing: it was weakening the entire British Empire by robbing it of the manly virtues necessary to keep it going.

The true heyday of anti-suburban literature was probably the period between the two world wars, which saw a massive expansion of suburban housing in so-called ribbon developments outside most British cities and towns. Stretching like red-scaled tentacles along arterial roads up and down the country, the characteristic home design in these developments was the three-bedroom semi-detached: 'bow window, front door, bow window, front door – for miles,' as John Betjeman described Swindon in 1937.[28] This ubiquitous British home design was the perfect symbol of suburbia. Neither a bastion of rural, free-standing solidity nor a link in an interlocking urban chain, the semi, like the suburbs, is neither self-sufficient nor joined in solidarity with others – it is mostly private, but not quite, capable of expressing the owner's personality, but only within the boundaries set by the surrounding homes. Semis spread during the interwar years thanks to a number of historical trends: rising middle-class affluence, especially in the south; more affordable motor cars; low interest rates and the rise of hire-purchase schemes; planning-oriented local councils undertaking slum-clearance programmes (often in order to provide ex-soldiers with the 'homes fit for heroes' that they had been promised during the First World War); and a general lack of zoning regulation that enabled private speculators to gobble up vast swathes of countryside unchecked. The resulting mass-suburbanization provoked angry protests from middle-class preservationists who, motivated both by a genuine desire to protect the countryside and by an instinctual distaste for suburban mass culture, began attacking the suburbs as a threat not so much to the health of the imperial race as to the very soul of England itself.

The language of these anti-suburbanites could at times be almost comically hostile. In his 1931 book in support of the Council for the Preservation of Rural England, luridly titled *The Horrors of the Countryside*, C.E.M. Joad described suburbia as a disgusting red rash of 'bungaloid growth' that was as tragic for the landscape as for the people living there. 'Cut off from the life of the spirit, outcasts from the great herds of their kind, without part in a community or roots in the soil', suburbanites, Joad noted sadly, were spreading 'like locusts over the land'.[29] In 1937, amid widespread fears about the prospect of German aerial bombardment, John Betjeman called upon the expected bombs to focus their attention on the town of Slough, on the far western reaches of Greater London, which he felt had become a sort of prefabricated no-place. 'Come, bombs,' he wrote, 'and blow to smithereens / Those air-conditioned, bright canteens, / Tinned fruit, tinned meat, tinned milk, tinned beans, / Tinned minds, tinned breath.'[30] In that same year, W. H. Auden, in his 'Letter to Lord Byron', drew a scathing picture of the suburban commuter that prefigured many of Davies's own dull, regimented commuters: 'There stands our hero in his threadbare seams; / The bowler hat who strap-hangs in the tube, / And kicks the tyrant only in his dreams'.[31] In 1939 George Orwell, in his novel *Coming Up for Air*, described the fictional suburb of West Bletchley as 'a prison with the cells all in a row. A line of semidetached torture-chambers where the poor little five-to-ten-pound-a-weekers quake and shiver, every one of them with the boss twisting his tail and his wife riding him like the nightmare and the kids sucking his blood like leeches.'[32] To escape this humdrum existence, Orwell's hero, George Bowling, sneaks off to visit the village of his birth, only to find it swamped with rehoused Lancastrian slum-dwellers who have turned his childhood idyll into a vulgar nightmare that is even worse than his own middle-class 'torture-chamber'.

As the suburbs started becoming more working class, the tone of the anti-suburb argument shifted slightly.[33] No longer was suburbia ridiculed simply as the land of the puffed-up clerk pretending to live like a country squire. Now it was also the home of a shabby sort of sameness and spiritual emptiness that its inhabitants were too blind – or, what came to the same thing, too unsophisticated – to see. One of the boldest attacks along these lines came after the Second World War, at a time when planner-designed New Towns and council estates were starting to replace the unregulated sprawl of the interwar years. In June 1955, in a special issue of the *Architectural Review* titled 'Outrage', the architecture critic Ian Nairn issued 'a prophecy of doom – the doom of an England reduced to universal Subtopia, a mean and middle state, neither town nor country . . . the world of universal low-density mess'. This was the first use of the term Subtopia – defined by Nairn as 'making an ideal of suburbia' – which soon became a sort of journalistic shorthand for the delusional mediocrity of the suburbs. For Nairn, Subtopia was as much a state of mind as a physical place, one that he feared was poised to 'drift like a gaseous pink marshmallow over the whole social scene, over the mind of man, over the land surface, over the philosophy, ideals and objectives of the human race'.[34] The problem with suburbia, he argued, was that it blurred the lines between what was man-made and what was nature-made, leaving people in a state of dull confusion about their place in the world.

> Insensible to the meaning of civilization on the one side and, on the other, ignorant of the well-spring of his own being, [twentieth-century man] is removing the sharp edge from his own life, exchanging individual feeling for mass experience in a voluntary enslavement far more restrictive and permanent than the feudal system.[35]

This was not just about beauty, in other words, it was about personal liberty. Could anybody living in such a grey world ever be truly free?

A decade later still, on 12 June 1964 (just two days before the Kinks entered the studio to record 'You Really Got Me'), the BBC aired a programme called *A City Crowned with Green* that was every bit as worried about the spiritual consequences of suburbia as was Nairn's 'Outrage'. Written and edited by Nairn's colleague at the *Architectural Review* Reyner Banham, the programme offered an indignant history of the territorial expansion of London in the twentieth century and a clear plan for remedying it. Banham's thesis was that Greater London had simply grown too big ('hopelessly, incomprehensibly too big'), that the roughly two million people who commuted to the city every day were missing something vital by living so far away from the urban core and that the solution was more high-density accommodation within the city. He advocated what was then a new idea, 'urban renewal', as a way to invigorate both the city itself and the lives of the people who lay scattered beyond it. Banham insisted that, whatever they told themselves, no one could be truly happy living in 'the great nowhere of fake half-timbering that rings London on all its most desirable sides'. Suburbanites were people who had somehow been brainwashed into the 'tragic illusion that this is any kind of a way to live in a great city, that to live like this is to be a Londoner in anything but the name'.[36] For their own good, people needed to be rescued from the suburbs and restored to the activity and excitement of city living.

By the time Ray Davies and Julian Mitchell set to work on *Arthur* in 1969, suburbia had become, among both the young and hip and the old and sophisticated, a byword for mediocrity, repression and conformity: a place that you first had to escape before you could live any kind of meaningful life. And, in one way of listening to it, 'Shangri-La' seems to fit right into this anti-suburban ethos. The 'little man who gets the train' can trace his origins back through the henpecked George Bowling, through Auden's purblind straphangers, to the self-important Charles Pooter himself. His materialism and pettiness are precisely the qualities that the Edwardians had predicted would bring about the fall of the British Empire – which, by 1969, was nearly complete. The characterless houses on Arthur's street are the same cookie-cutter dwellings that Edward Thomas had wanted to 'soil' and 'humanise' in 1906. The mortgage that oppresses Arthur and the radio and television set for which he pays seven shillings weekly are instances of the same 'voluntary enslavement' that Nairn had warned of. Indeed, Arthur's whole existence is the very essence of the 'tragic illusion' of Subtopia. He has spent his life pursuing creature comforts – the house, the car, the television, the radio, the rocking chair – but he has found that life in Shangri-La is not what he'd hoped. He's lonely, beset by nosy neighbours, stuck in his place like an infantryman in a trench and 'too scared to complain' because of how he's been conditioned (Ronnie would say brainwashed) into accepting his lot. This is no way to live in a great city.

But does Arthur really want to live a different sort of life, and does Ray Davies think that he should? Shortly after the album's release, Jonathan Cott of *Rolling Stone* interviewed Davies at Kenwood House, a seventeenth-century manor on Hampstead Heath that is the very opposite of suburban mediocrity. 'What do you think of the people you sing about in "Shangri-La"?' Cott asked. Davies's lengthy response, which I give here only in part, is a revealing glimpse into the contradictory (or confused) impulses that gave rise to the song:

I played 'Shangri-La' to somebody – an old friend of mine – and I knew half way through it that he was embarrassed by it because it was about him, and he realized it, and I didn't want him to realize it, and I can never sort of talk to him again. I wanted him to hear it, and then I realized: there he is.

I'm not laughing at those people in the song at all. They're brainwashed into that, they brainwash themselves. She says, 'That's it, I don't want a new dress,' not because she really doesn't want it, but because she can't afford it. Their minds are like that; they're happy, really. It becomes a religion to them. The glory of being boring. It's a glory. He shows you his stamp collection. It's a sense of greatness he's got around him that you can't penetrate because you feel you might upset him, he's got that aura of *stuff*.

The chorus of 'Shangri-La' is a bit of a chant – like 'See My Friends.' It's a religious thing. You accept it as your religion because you can't have anything else, and whatever you've got anyway is what you accept yourself. You let yourself believe it . . . No, perhaps not. If you lived there [Kenwood] and you accepted this, and this was as far as you could go, you'd be a lot happier. Well, no, perhaps not. See, I've tried living in a big house and I can't. I'm going back to a little house. I don't think people really want to live in a posh house, as much as a rich person doesn't want to live in a slum. I don't like to say what I've got and be happy with it. I'd wear hobnail boots by my fire rather than slippers. I can't stand slippers 'cause they symbolize giving up to me. But at the same time, I love the people who are like that. But I hate what's handed down when people get into the state where that's all they want.[37]

Somewhere in this tangle of digressions and contradictions is, I think, a fundamental point that can help us make sense of 'Shangri-La'. Superficially, it may be a straightforward satire of suburban life, but it also recognizes that there is a certain dignity to that life, a certain 'glory of being boring'. Davies had done unambiguous suburban satire before – as recently as the March 1969 single 'Plastic Man', in fact, which had imagined the suburbanite as literally made of plastic, every bit as lifeless and mass-produced as his environment – but 'Shangri-La' is not like this. The secret, as Davies recognized, is in that chant-like chorus. Despite a certain formal similarity with 'See My Friends' (or even 'You Really Got Me'), the chorus of 'Shangri-La' is quite unlike anything else the Kinks had done up to that time. It is grand and stirring, more 'Ode to Joy' than 'See My Friends', the harmonizing voices rising plaintively as the horns soar and the plunking bass struggles to keep up. The drums become more expressive with each repetition, climaxing in virtuosic rocket bursts that make you wonder if Keith Moon has somehow got hold of Mick Avory's kit. It is a long song, with at least three different movements, each one leading you down a barbed chain of images and emotions that don't really add up to a single idea. Is suburbia a prison? Is it nirvana? Davies has recently said that he feels uneasy about the song because it seems to satirize his own way of life at the time. 'It's thrown at myself,' he told Nick Hasted. 'I am that person. I have a kind of guilt feeling about it.'[38] Yet I think Davies is being too hard on himself. The verses of 'Shangri-La' might be satirical, but that chorus certainly is not – it is triumphant. Has anyone ever felt about their small patch of semi-detached Subtopia quite as fondly as Arthur Morgan feels about his?

In his memoir, Dave Davies complained that listeners 'got hold of the wrong end of the stick' with 'Shangri-La', which was released as a single several weeks before the full album appeared. People had missed the 'underlying sympathy' with which the song treated its subjects, he said, and this is why it never became a hit.[39] This may not be the only reason the single didn't chart, but it is easy to see how listeners could miss the song's multifaceted picture of suburbia. For not only is the song's 'sympathy' for suburbia definitely 'underlying', but it is also the kind of song whose meaning changes when you isolate it from the rest of the album on which it appears. Without the other songs to give it context – without the simple pleasures of 'Drivin'' and 'She's Bought a Hat Like Princess Marina', without the suffering and sacrifice of the war songs, without the songs of arrogant youth and melancholic nostalgia – the character at the centre of 'Shangri-La' can come across as simply pathetic, a conformist little Pooter who needs Ray Davies to point out to him the limitations of his own existence. But heard within the context of the album, and always bearing in mind that triumphant chorus, it is possible to see 'Shangri-La' as part of a minor, but still significant, tradition of English thought that is much more friendly towards suburbia than Nairn, Orwell and the Grossmiths. It is a tradition that doesn't ignore the shortcomings of suburbia, but it does manage to find the human dignity, humour and joy that exist there.

The novelist Arnold Bennett was an early example of someone who could look out upon limitless miles of suburban semis and see something more than just a sea of faceless Pooters. Like Davies, he got his story ideas from eavesdropping on the ordinary people around him: on the streets, in the cafés, wherever the unremarkable masses might be found. He offers a glimpse into his modus operandi in his first novel, *A Man from the North* (1898), in which an elderly writer living in Fulham, southwest London, rebukes his niece for an anti-suburbs outburst.

> 'Child,' he said . . . 'the suburbs, even Walham Green and Fulham, are full of interest, for those who can see it. Walk along this very street on such a Sunday afternoon as today. The roofs form two horrible, converging straight lines, I know, but beneath there is character, individuality, enough to make the greatest book ever written . . . How many houses are there in Carteret Street? Say eighty. Eighty theatres of love, hate, greed, tyranny, endeavour; eighty separate dramas always unfolding, intertwining, ending, beginning, – and every drama a tragedy . . . Why, child, there is more character within a hundred yards of this chair than a hundred Balzacs could analyse in a hundred years.'[40]

Even more than Davies, Bennett was able to suspend his own judgement about people's lives and to see things as they saw them. As Lynne Hapgood says, 'What makes Bennett's characters extraordinary is their own sense (not Bennett's) of the uniqueness of their experience and importance of their lives: they do not think that they are ordinary.'[41] William Pett Ridge showed a similar aptitude in his novel *Outside the Radius* (1899), which focuses on working-class suburbanites living on a street called The Crescent: 'I find that to declare life in The Crescent dull and monotonous is a mere pretence; outwardly that may be so; in point of fact there are romances in every house.'[42] Ford Madox Ford, in *The Soul of London* (1905), likewise asked that his readers 'not sniff at the suburbs as a place of small houses and dreary lives', for 'in each of these houses dwells a strongly individualised human being with romantic hopes, romantic fears, and at the end, an always tragic death.'[43] Many who wrote in this vein were of a lower social class than their suburb-scorning contemporaries – Pett Ridge, for example, was a former clerk whose father had been a railway porter – and this undoubt-edly contributed to their sympathetic outlook on suburbia, just as it did with Davies.

Other writers chose to depict suburbia as exactly what it says it is on the tin: an Arcadian refuge from the trials of city life. In 1861 Charles Dickens invented a castle, complete with a little moat and drawbridge, in suburban Walworth as the home of the clerk John Wemmick in *Great Expectations*. Dry and officious at work, Wemmick becomes warm and personable in his suburban retreat, observing that 'the office is one thing, and private life is another. When I go into the office, I leave the Castle behind me, and when I come into the Castle I leave the office behind me.'[44] Decades later, as Hapgood observes, novels like Arthur Conan Doyle's *Beyond the City* (1892) and Keble Howard's *The Smiths of Surbiton* (1906) portrayed the suburbs as 'purpose-built for the convenience and pleasure of ordinary men and women . . . promising a new civilisation of physical and economic liberation and of moral and physical health'.[45] These novels often come across as more artful versions of the speculative builder's brochure, a kind of escapist fiction written for already existing suburbanites who longed for an even more ideal version of suburbia than the one they had got. R. C. Sherriff's novel *Greengates* (1936), about a retired couple who find autumnal contentment in suburban Surrey, is typical of the genre:

He stepped over the tapes and stood upon the only piece of land in the world that could make him happy. The wiry grass

Subtopia on the Northern Line: London Underground poster advertising
Golders Green, 1908.

sent a thrill of understanding up his legs: he felt the iron-
rooted muscles of the giant that towered above them.

'This is our place', he said.[46]

This is 'Shangri-La' without the irony – and without the working
classes, either, for working-class people and the grimy environments they inhabited were precisely what the suburbs were meant
to rescue people from. These stories may be pro-suburb, but they
are not pro-suburb in quite the way that 'Shangri-La' is.

A few years after the publication of *Greengates*, another pro-
suburb voice began to be heard in a rather unexpected quarter. In
1940 John Betjeman, formerly the scourge of Slough, issued a public
apology for his previous attitude in a talk for the BBC Home Service.
Referring to his rubbishing of Swindon in a talk in 1937 (the same
year he published 'Slough'), he now said, 'I *like* suburbs; nothing is
ugly.' Determined to find beauty in such things as 'the sham Tudor
beams, the standard roses, the stained glass in the front doors, the
pram in the hall, the drainpipes running zigzag down the side door',
he concluded, a tad grudgingly, that the suburbs were now an inescapable part of England, so he might as well 'put up with them'.[47]
Years later he would offer a more full-throated celebration of suburbia in the television documentary *Metro-Land* (1973), although
in choosing to film among the older, upmarket suburbs along the
Metropolitan Line rather than the newer and more working-class
communities elsewhere, Betjeman made it clear that his tastes still
ran towards the refined and bourgeois, not the new and seemingly
antiseptic.

A somewhat less qualified defence of suburbia came in 1946
when J. M. Richards, the editor of the *Architectural Review* (future
home of the anti-Subtopia crusaders Nairn and Banham), published
a curious little book called *The Castles on the Ground*. Seeking to
explain 'the appeal [suburbia] holds for ninety out of a hundred
Englishmen', Richards urged architects and planners to stop scorning

the suburbs and start taking them more seriously.[48] 'If democracy means anything, it means deciding – for a change – to pay some attention to the expressed preference of the majority, to what people themselves want, not to what we think they ought to want.'[49] *Pace* Orwell, the suburbs were, in Richards's view, the very opposite of prisons: from furnishing the home to working in the garden to choosing a name for the house, many people found suburbia to be the only place where they could arrange their world in their own way, without anybody telling them what to do. The very predictability that Davies alludes to in 'Shangri-La' is for Richards one of the chief virtues of suburbia, whose architecture 'can be described as an attempt to create a kind of oasis in which every tree and every brick can be accounted for, to exclude the unpredictable as far as possible from everyday life'.[50] With the rest of the world so changeable and uncertain, people seemed to crave a bit of dull security in the places they called home.

The suburban dweller might be a slave, but, for sympathetic observers like Richards, 'he is a willing slave, enjoying the one benefit of slavery, that it spares its victims from being burdened by the uncertainties of other worlds besides the one they know.'[51] This was only part of the picture, however. As the growing post-war sociological literature about working-class suburbanization was starting to show, the suburbs also represented an escape from the previous worlds people *did* know. One new suburbanite who had been relocated from Bethnal Green to Woodford told Peter Willmott in 1963, 'The things that pleased us most when we first moved here was to have a house of our own, with electric light and a bathroom and a scullery with running water. We'd been in two rooms in Bethnal Green with a tap and wc three flights down and shared with two other families . . . I thought it was just like a palace.'[52] In 1961 Ferdynand Zweig argued that, from the perspective of the man of the house, suburban life was far preferable to that which had come before. 'As he sits by his fireside and watches TV he feels free and happy . . . The foul air, the vermin, the outside, smelling lavatory, the broken chairs have been removed as if by magic.'[53] This passage anticipates, almost verbatim, the lyrics of 'Shangri-La', whose protagonist sees the pleasures of indoor lavatories and relaxing by the fireside as fitting compensations for a life of deprivation and struggle. In this version of suburbia, the suburban male is not the harassed and emasculated clerk of the anti-suburban imagination, but a weary warrior enjoying a necessary respite from his battles with the world.

For all that they might miss their old neighbourhoods and the culture that went with them, working-class people often found suburban life to be a step up from where they had been. At the most basic levels of physical comfort, health and hygiene, the leap from urban to suburban life for the poor could not be otherwise than transformative. 'The fact was', says historian John Burnett, 'that, for all its limitations and failings, the suburb represented a kind of utopian ideal, an arena for a new and better life for family and children, based on a house with substantially improved space and amenity standards.'[54] Moreover, despite an initial feeling of loneliness, as Alan A. Jackson notes, most people adapted quite well to the idea of 'keep[ing] themselves to themselves . . . They chose instead to sink into the comfortable anonymity which still remains a strong feature of London suburban life, rarely extending their acquaintance beyond their immediate neighbours.'[55] In many cases family life was also improved. In his study of a slum district in pre-war Holloway, Jerry White found little to mourn in the passing of the family life of that era, which included 'interminable rows between husband and wife . . . the use of violence against children, frequently to excess; the exploitation of children by parents who might ignore their youngsters' needs; [and] the contradictory discipline which reinforced a child's alienation from its parents' mode of life'.[56] In the suburbs, cramped and quarrelsome families had a chance to start anew, and many found that with a little more space and a little less household drudgery, domestic peace was much easier to maintain.

There is even evidence that people liked being involuntarily rehoused into council flats as a result of slum clearance, at least at first. We will discuss the negative aspects of this phenomenon in the next chapter, but here it is worth pausing to appreciate that, for all the well-justified criticisms of London's tower blocks and modernist estates, there were many people who found them to be a great improvement over their old way of life. In a film produced in 1967 by the Greater London Council (GLC), an elderly woman who has been rehoused in a tower block declares, 'I'm really better off than I've ever been I think since I've been married.' Another woman, evidently the first woman's daughter, chimes in: 'Well of a night-time, it's just like, exactly like fairyland . . . We never get fed up here, because it's so lovely.' Another family reports that they love being able to have warm baths for a change. A younger woman says that she enjoys living close to shops, doctors' offices and so forth.[57] Some of this was undoubtedly pro-resettlement propaganda by the GLC, but, along with the copious sociological evidence of suburban contentment, and the simple fact that millions of people willingly chose (and continue to choose) to live in such places, these testimonies point to a fairly straightforward conclusion: most people who live in the suburbs like it there.

Taking all of this evidence together, it turns out that Davies was right: for many people there is, in fact, a certain glory in being boring. This is the overall impression one gets, if not from 'Shangri-La' alone, then from *Arthur* as a whole. Across the album's twelve tracks we find characters struggling with all sorts of things – poverty, class snobbery, warfare, grief, loneliness – but still managing to find enjoyment in small pleasures such as Sunday drives and fancy hats. In 'Shangri-La' these small pleasures include such activities as sitting in a rocking chair, polishing the car and using an indoor lavatory – activities that might seem utterly mundane to an outsider, but for the person performing them they are nothing short of glorious. Arthur's home is an escape both from the hurly-burly of city life and from the poverty into which he was born; the absence of worry and care is something that he has worked hard to achieve – and something that Arthur's creator found it difficult to attain in his own life. As much as Davies might pity Arthur for being 'brainwashed' into pursuing his Subtopian ideal, there was also, I think, a part of Davies that envied him. That's how I read the long excerpt from the Jonathan Cott interview I quoted above. The 'glory of being boring' was something that Davies had tried to achieve during his abortive experiment in suburban Borehamwood. He had failed, but he still saw something noble in the pursuit.

5

Muswell Hillbillies vs Big Brother

If there is hope [wrote Winston] it lies in the proles.

George Orwell, *Nineteen Eighty-four* (1949)

People do not always respond to oppression in the ways that we expect them to. Sometimes they resist, to be sure, but sometimes they find reasons to collaborate with their oppressors. In Arthur Morgan, Ray Davies created a character who swallowed the ruling ideology and, in exchange for a small measure of material comfort, allowed himself to become a cog in the very system that exploits him. A similar condition afflicts other Davies characters, such as the Dedicated Follower of Fashion and Mr Pleasant: they are victims of what a Marxist would call false consciousness, hoodwinked by a hegemonic Establishment into thinking that what really matters is not spiritual fulfilment or national decline but nylon underwear and petty respectability. But there are other Davies characters who strain against their chains, who refuse, often against long odds, to submit to the impoverished existences that their rulers would subject them to. Johnny Thunder, the Phenomenal Cat, Terry and Julie, the protagonist of 'I'm Not Like Everybody Else' – each find a measure of self-respect, even contentment, in ignoring the strictures of society and pursuing their own notions of the good life.

The two albums that the Kinks released at the start of the 1970s, *Lola Versus Powerman and the Moneygoround, Part One* (1970) and *Muswell Hillbillies* (1971), mostly tell the stories of such resistors and rebels. With a handful of exceptions, these are songs of defiance and alienation and biting, sometimes vicious humour. But there has been a change from the Kinks' earlier songs in this vein: now the odds against attaining self-respect or contentment seem longer somehow, the structures of oppression more formidable. As the candy-colour dreams of the Sixties sputtered into a dusty haze, the Kinks pivoted once again, away from the gentle rhythms of *Village Green* and the historical miniatures of *Arthur*, towards something much more bitter and disturbed. Though not entirely without hope, these two albums portended a more difficult decade ahead, not only for the Kinks but for Britain itself.

There is a little-remembered Ealing comedy from 1952 called *The Happy Family* that sheds a surprising amount of light on these two albums, particularly *Muswell Hillbillies*. The film stars Stanley Holloway and Kathleen Harrison as Henry and Lil Lord, owners of a small corner shop (cheekily named the House of Lords) on the south bank of the Thames, near what will become the site of the 1951 Festival of Britain. The neighbouring houses have been demolished to make way for the festival site, but the Lords are still there, carrying on their trade among the dwindling number of families who still call the area home. One day Aunt Ada, the eccentric spiritualist in the family, receives a visit from the ghost of William Shakespeare, who tells her, 'Ada, beware of the men in black, for they shall invade your precious plot, set in a silver sea.'[1] Soon a man from the government, wearing a black suit and (as one family member remarks) an Anthony Eden hat, comes to the shop to tell the Lords that their house must be destroyed to make way for an access road to the festival grounds. If they cooperate, they will be rehoused at government expense in a more comfortable home with all mod cons in South Harrow, in far northwest London. But the Lords, with typical cockney independence, insist that they won't move an inch. Lil explains to the government man that they had gone hungry in the 1930s and worked their fingers to the bone to purchase this little house and shop. They had lost a son in the war, made tremendous sacrifices for their country, and now they just want to be left alone. When the man in black insists, the Lords decide to fight back. At first they try to work through official channels, but after getting the run-around from politicians and bureaucrats they decide to take matters into their own hands. When the police finally arrive with a battering ram to force them out, the Lords, who had begun talking in terms of the French Revolution and the Suffragettes, pelt the coppers with tinned peas, eggs and other items from their shop, and in the end the government is forced to capitulate. The shop is allowed to stand on the festival grounds as a monument to English liberty and a testament to the eternal truth that an Englishman's home is his castle, and the family emerges from the ordeal stronger and happier than ever.

The Happy Family fits rather awkwardly with popular memories of the Festival of Britain and of the Labour government that organized it, which may be why it is so little remembered today. The official line on the festival, in the words of its director general, was that it was 'the people's show, not organized arbitrarily for them to enjoy but put on by them, by us all, as an expression of the way of life in which we believe'.[2] This aligned with the goals of the 1945 Labour government generally, which had swept into power promising a New Jerusalem of equality in matters of health, education, housing, employment and economic opportunity. The festival was meant to celebrate all that had been accomplished so far and to prepare the way for even better things tomorrow. But *The Happy Family*, which appeared several months after Labour lost the 1951 general election, suggested that the optimism of the post-war years was already starting to wear thin. The government men who try to force this honest cockney family from their home might have good intentions, but really they are just as pushy and paternalistic as the ruling classes have always been. The central conflict of the film – of well-meaning but arrogant officialdom against stubbornly individualistic common folk – was one of the central conflicts of post-war Britain. Far more than ever before, the state was accepting responsibility for the welfare of its citizens. Many people welcomed the change as long overdue, willingly granting the 'men in black' much greater control over their lives in exchange for better access to good-quality housing, healthcare, education and jobs. But as the idealism of 1945 began to fade, people's attitudes towards the state began to change. The bureaucrats and politicians who were planning out this New Jerusalem did not, it seemed, always have the people's best interests at heart. They might claim to be giving the little man what he wanted, but were they actually bothering to ask him what, precisely, that might be? The story of the Lord family was indicative of a dawning public suspicion, as early as 1952, that the deep inequalities of British society were not disappearing as quickly as many people had hoped.

Two decades later, when the Kinks recorded *Lola Versus Powerman* and *Muswell Hillbillies*, the post-war dream was looking quite threadbare indeed. Economic trouble, labour unrest (a dock-workers' strike in 1970, a postal workers' strike in 1971) and the outbreak of violence in Northern Ireland were all contributing to a growing sense of disillusionment with the post-war order, particularly among young people. Ray Davies, who had never really bought into the optimism of the 1960s, must have felt grimly vindicated by the inglorious demise of Swinging London and the confused state of popular culture generally, but what comes through most clearly on the albums of the early 1970s is not *Schadenfreude* but anger. There are still notes of *Village Green*-like escape on these albums, as well as some hints of *Arthur*-like resignation, but there is also a new attitude of defiance, of a willingness to confront quite specific structures of oppression, from the record industry to urban renewal schemes, head-on. The stakes are also much higher in these songs: there is talk of starvation, overpopulation, mental illness, police violence, even nuclear war. The characters find various ways to resist their subjugation by the 'men in black' – made over on *Muswell*

Hillbillies into 'the people in grey' – but mostly what they do is insist, with a very cockney sort of impudence, on their rights to hold on to their own quirky individuality. In place of the compliant, standardized subjects that the Establishment would like to make of them, these characters remain weird, uncooperative and often very funny. As usual with the Kinks, there is a deep pit of despair lurking just beneath the jolly surface, but there is also a degree of anger that hadn't really been heard since the band's early days. 'I was in Singapore once and bumped into Noël Coward,' Davies once told an interviewer. 'He said to me "always keep a smile on your face when singing about anything that makes you angry."'³ Davies mostly takes Coward's advice here, but, far more than on the preceding records, his smile has a way of curling into a snarl.

At a professional level, the dawn of the 1970s was quite a good time for the Kinks. Ray, Rasa and the girls were back living in Fortis Green (now with a recently built extension), bringing an end to their unsatisfying sojourn in outer suburbia. Pete Quaife's painful departure from the group in 1969 was balanced by the final lifting of the American touring ban, which opened the way for two tours with new bassist John Dalton in late 1969 and early 1970. Rave reviews in the underground music press had ensured that the Kinks retained a small but enthusiastic following in America, and that following grew enormously in the summer of 1970 with the smashing success of 'Lola', the group's first worldwide hit since 'Sunny Afternoon'. With an irresistible sing-song chorus and witty lyrics, 'Lola' told a very London kind of story about a naive young man just in from the provinces who visits a Soho club one night and ends up dancing (and maybe doing a bit more) with a cross-dressing clubgoer. Davies has always been cagey about the inspiration for the song, sometimes suggesting that it is based on a wild night that their manager Robert Wace once had in Paris, and sometimes hinting that it is more autobiographical. Whatever its origins, 'Lola' was an ambivalent but

The Kinks perform 'Lola' on *Top of the Pops*, 1970.

ultimately accepting song about sexual deviance, and, according
to Davies, it attracted many drag queens to the Kinks' shows and
became a popular song at gay 'coming out' parties of the period.[4]
It also reminded the world that the Kinks were still in business, as
did the follow-up single, 'Apeman', which was also a hit. This was
a jokey, pseudo-calypso song in which the singer fantasizes about
escaping from the so-called civilized world into a life of primitive
simplicity, a comically extreme version of the rural escapes Davies
had contemplated in earlier songs. Both songs were exceedingly
catchy and also quite amusing, but, as Johnny Rogan points out, for
those very reasons they also 'nailed [the Kinks] in many people's
perceptions as a novelty group'.[5] To revive the Kinks' career under

such a label might have been tempting, but Davies's ambitions were far greater than that.

'Lola' and 'Apeman' both appeared on the LP *Lola Versus Powergoround and the Moneygoround, Part One*, released in November 1970. The whimsical but unwieldy title was somewhat misleading – there would be no Part Two – but it accurately signalled that this was an album pre-eminently about conflict. In one corner stand a scrappy band of misfits led by the loveable Lola. They are mostly naive and a little scared, but they are also full of love, and they happen to resemble the Kinks themselves in one or two particulars. In the other corner is a sort of haunted theme park of capitalist exploitation called the Moneygoround that is ruled by the sinister Powerman, a record executive who uses his vast wealth to enslave the innocent. There is no single narrative running through these songs as there had been on *Arthur*, but the themes are similar. In place of the political and military power structures that trap and brainwash Arthur, the principal villains here are economic: managers, businessmen, union bosses and the like. But unlike Arthur, who sheepishly submits to his fate, the lovers and dreamers who square off against the Powerman and his cronies stand at least a small chance of prevailing. For all its anger, this is, on the whole, a slightly more hopeful album than its predecessor.

Much of the angry mood on *Lola Versus Powerman* is due to the increased prominence of Dave Davies, whose chunky guitar riffs and keening vocals hadn't found much of a place on the last few records. Here Dave has two songs, his first credited album tracks since *Something Else* in 1967, that fully justify his reputation as The Emotional One. The first, 'Strangers', is one of his best, an achingly tender song about finding companionship in love – or love in companionship – and, in both, an antidote to the lies and aggravations of the world. It fits nicely with several of Ray's songs that also present love as a counterforce to power and corruption, but there is a sincerity in the composition, and in Dave's aching vocals, that his brother could never quite achieve. Dave's other song, 'Rats', also elaborates upon and intensifies sentiments found elsewhere on the album. This time the principal sentiment is anger, but whereas Ray's anger generally comes out in sneering sarcasm aimed at carefully selected targets, Dave's is a directionless, all-encompassing sort of rage that takes in the crowding, selfish masses as well as the powerful few. What 'Rats' lacks in nuance it more than makes up for in feeling, providing a passionate counterpoint to Ray's surgical strikes against his own personal enemies.

Ray's enemies are mostly the wire-pullers of the music industry: the publishers, agents, media types and other vampires who, he has come to feel, exist simply to suck the blood of hard-working musicians. These are not subtle songs: while Dave chugs angrily away at his power chords, Ray gives us a morality play that invites us to heckle and jeer at the predators of the music world, whose real-life inspirations he often identifies by name. The Kinks' own managers come in for a kicking on 'The Moneygoround', and on 'Top of the Pops' he mocks the very programme that had frequently hosted his band for televised performances (including twice in 1970) and helped them achieve their early fame. 'Denmark Street' guides us through London's own Tin Pan Alley, where a young hopeful presents his song to a publisher in the hope of making it big. In a tone that anticipates the greedy A&R man of Pink Floyd's hit 'Have a Cigar' (1975), the publisher hates everything about the kid's song but, sensing a hit, offers him a contract anyway, holding out a poisoned chalice of fame and fortune to the innocent hero. The evil genius looming in the background of these songs (though he is never named) is Eddie Kassner, a music publisher with whom Davies had a long-running dispute over the publishing rights to his own songs. The case had been resolved just a month before the album's release with a hefty out-of-court payment by Ray, and on the song 'Powerman' both Ray and Dave lay into Kassner with all the venom that they were unable to express in the courtroom, positioning him as a Bond villain type who rules not through armies and bombs but through money. (Kassner may also have been Ray's target in the song 'King Kong', released as the B-side to 'Plastic Man' in March 1969, which features a similarly greedy tyrant who revels in pointless destruction.)

Against such diabolical forces, the heroes in these songs have only their inner conviction and, in many cases, the support of their lovers. On 'The Contenders', the singer describes how unsuited he is for a normal sort of life – he's cut out neither for street sweeping, political decision making nor fascist dictating – but when he's together with his girl, he thinks they'll probably be just fine. In 'Apeman' the hero fantasizes about playing Tarzan and Jane with his lady love, and on 'Got to Be Free' he promises his baby that they will soon be free 'like the birds and the bees'. The narrator of 'Lola' achieves perhaps the most impressive act of liberation of all by freeing himself from social dictates regarding whom he's allowed to love, which is a much more formidable force than any mere record executive. All of these are atypically poppish sentiments for Davies during this period, and they may simply reflect a bid for more commercial viability (and American radio airplay) after years of dwindling sales, but the frequent references to 'babies' and 'girls' do help to lighten the mood of the record, saving it from becoming an exercise in sheer spite.

Another song that occupies a place on the oppression/freedom continuum is 'This Time Tomorrow', which buckles its narrator into a long-haul flight, presumably across the Atlantic for another American tour, where he broods upon the sprawl of houses below and the unpredictability of what lies ahead. At first it sounds more like a song of entrapment than of freedom, but anybody who has ever taken a long-haul flight knows that those two sensations are, in fact, simultaneous and inextricable from the experience. The singer is being conveyed in a flying metal tube from which he cannot escape and whose course he cannot control, but he is also leaving one place behind and headed for somewhere new, with all the promise that entails. This song is followed by 'A Long Way from Home', which of course is where the narrator of 'This Time Tomorrow' will soon find himself. It describes someone who started from humble beginnings and has now hit the big time. He has money and fancy clothes, but he has become cut off from his roots and is no longer quite sure who he is. Sung to an unnamed 'you', it is in fact a sort of Dejection Ode that Davies is singing to himself, perhaps while holed up in his suburban exile in Borehamwood. It signals a desire to return to his origins both literally (that is, to move back to Fortis Green) and artistically (a notion conveyed by the stripped-down rock sound of the album as a whole). Like travelling in an aeroplane, achieving worldly success can be both liberating and confining; perhaps the ultimate victory of Powerman and his Moneygoround has been to separate the Kinks from the home that they once knew.

While *Lola Versus Powerman* is principally an album about the evils of the record industry and the dangerous temptations of fame, it is also possible to hear it as part of the Kinks' ongoing war against the upper classes. 'That album', Ray Davies told Nick Hasted, 'is fairly accurately about what people give up to conform to the Establishment, the music industry.'[6] The Establishment, of course, was something that young people across the Anglo-American world spent a lot of energy railing against at this time (along with the System, the Man, the Fuzz et al.), but in the context of the British class system, the Establishment had a quite specific meaning. The term was in fact rather new, having first been popularized in the mid 1950s by the journalist Henry Fairlie, who defined it as 'the whole matrix of official and social relations within which power is exercised'. It encompassed not only the heads of Church and State but 'such lesser mortals as the chairman of the Arts Council, the Director-General of the BBC, and even the editor of the *Times Literary Supplement*, not to mention divinities like [the Liberal politician and Churchill crony] Lady Violet Bonham Carter'.[7] A few years later the historian Hugh Thomas defined the Establishment more functionally as 'the assumption of the attributes of a state church by certain powerful institutions and people'.[8] It was, he said, a holdover from the Victorian era, whose 'prejudices, ignorances, and inhibitions' it was designed to protect: like the steam-powered trains that Davies sang about on *Village Green*, for Thomas the Establishment was essentially 'the present-day institutional museum of Britain's past greatness'.[9] Unlike those old smoke-belchers, however, this museum piece was still dragging the whole country along on its antiquated course.

From Davies's perspective, the rulers of the record industry were simply an updated version of the same old Establishment that had always tried to keep the likes of him in his place. In *X-Ray* he recalled, 'My dad always used to say, "If they don't get you one way, they'll get you another way." I guess he knew, but I was determined that they, whoever "they" were, were not going to let me stop doing what I believed in.'[10] During his court appearances against Kassner, he says, he felt disadvantaged simply by virtue of his background and accent, and he resented having to rely on upper-class attorneys to preserve his independence. 'In other words the establishment had grabbed another rebel by the balls and made him kneel before them. I had become classless because of my success, but litigation put me straight back on that cold suburban street surrounded by greyness.'[11] This attitude was consistent with what Richard Hoggart described as the long-standing hostility among the working classes to a group they simply called 'they', a nebulous category that included 'the world of the bosses, whether those bosses are private individuals or, as is increasingly the case today, public officials'. 'They' were policemen, civil servants, teachers, the local council, judges – anybody who held the whip hand over the common man. In working-class vernacular, Hoggart explained,

'They' are 'the people at the top', 'the higher-ups', the people who give you your dole, call you up, tell you to go to war, fine you, made you split up the family in the 'thirties to avoid a reduction in the Means Test allowance, 'get yer in the end', 'aren't really to be trusted', 'talk posh', 'are all twisters really', 'never tell yer owt' (e.g. about a relative in hospital), 'clap yer in the clink', 'will do y' down if they can', 'summons yer', 'are all in a click (clique) together', 'treat y' like muck'.[12]

Working-class attitudes had evolved somewhat since Hoggart recorded these observations in 1957, but mostly they had evolved in the direction of greater working-class self-confidence, rather than increasing trust in 'they'. Indeed, with the expansion of the welfare state and the growing power of big business in the 1960s, 'they' seemed to have a tighter grip on the little guy than ever before.

One of the most moving songs on *Lola Versus Powerman* is not really about the music industry at all, but it is most definitely about 'they'. 'Get Back in the Line' is about the power of a union boss to choose who gets work and who doesn't, and about the helplessness that you feel when you are not among the favoured few. The song was partly inspired by the Kinks' problems with the American Federation of Musicians, but there were several other strands feeding into it. As a teenager, Davies had formed a negative opinion of extreme unionism while working in the layout department of an engineering firm, where, he recalled, his co-workers 'were all militant unionists' who spent their time plotting confrontations with management and making fun of him for working through his tea break.[13] He also drew inspiration from the movie *On the Waterfront* (1954; also an inspiration for the song 'The Contenders'), in which Marlon Brando fights against a corrupt longshoremen's union in New Jersey, and from Fred Davies's humiliating experiences of standing in the dole queue.[14] The song perfectly captures the 'us against them' attitude that Hoggart identified among the urban working classes, the feeling that your fate is being determined by uncaring functionaries who do not see you as fully human. It is a politically awkward song in the same way that *The Happy Family* is a politically awkward film. As a member of the Labour-supporting proletariat, people like Ray Davies and his dad were supposed to be supportive of labour unions, not fuelling Tory fantasies about totalitarian union bosses. Yet in reality there were plenty of working-class people who resented union officials as just another set of interfering authority figures, just another manifestation of 'they'. In his study of Holloway before the Second World War, the historian Jerry White notes a strong anti-union ethos among the very poor that was rooted in 'a resentment of the power wielded over workers by trade union officials who seemed to wax fat on members' contributions'.[15] This same anti-authoritarianism, White says, also prevented fascism from gaining much of a hold in working-class London: whether they came from the Left or the Right, the boss class was never going to garner much support here.

'Get Back in the Line' articulates the idea that, even a quarter-century after the war, for many working-class people it didn't much matter if the elites who controlled their lives wore blue ties or red ties on election night. What mattered was that 'they' still held all the power, that 'they' could still decide whether a person got to work, qualified for the dole or could play music in America. As the young working-class hero of Alan Sillitoe's novel *Saturday Night and Sunday Morning* (1958) reflects,

> They shout at you from soapboxes: 'Vote for me, and this and that,' but it amounts to the same in the end whatever you vote for because it means a government that puts stamps all over your phizzog [physiognomy] until you can't see a hand before you, and what's more makes you buy 'em so's they can keep on doing it. They've got you by the guts, by backbone and skull, until they think you'll come whenever they whistle.[16]

As long as 'they' were in charge, the working classes were never going to control their own destinies.

The Establishment includes much more than just union bosses, judges and record executives, of course, and on the next album Davies adjusted his sights to take in even more of the ruling elite. *Muswell Hillbillies*, released in November 1971, was the Kinks' most political album to date, its cast of villains ranging from policemen and mealy-mouthed politicians to the civil servants who run the welfare state. However, just as *Lola Versus Powerman* had been dominated by Davies's nemeses in the record industry, so on this album one group comes in for particular censure: housing officials. Not much grist for a rock song there, one might think, but at the time these were among the most loathed figures in working-class London. Over the last few years local councils had been implementing massive programmes of slum clearance and urban renewal in working-class neighbourhoods, resettling thousands of poor tenants in tower blocks and housing estates that were often very far from their old homes. Though the intent was essentially benevolent, these schemes constituted about as profound an exercise in social engineering as one could imagine. They reshaped the landscape, reordered the socioeconomic make-up of the cities and drastically altered ordinary people's lives, sometimes for the better but often for the worse. There were other things that working-class people were complaining about in 1971, other examples of how 'they' would always 'get yer in the end', but few were as visible or as problematic as this. Before we get to the songs on *Muswell Hillbillies*, it will help to say a few words about this radical, and sometimes shockingly reckless, experiment in large-scale population transfer.

Local authorities had been demolishing inner-city slums and replacing them with more spacious and sanitary houses since the Victorian era, but the practice really accelerated after the First World War, when Lloyd George's government began promising good houses to former soldiers as a reward for their service. A recession in the early 1920s forced the abandonment of many of these plans, but the interwar years still saw a considerable rise in the number of inner-city neighbourhoods that were condemned as unsafe, along with a corresponding growth in council estates. These estates, mostly low-density affairs on the outskirts of cities and towns, were part of what so exercised the anti-suburb writers whom we examined in the previous chapter: to build miles upon miles of unregulated suburbs in unspoilt countryside was bad enough, but even worse was to fill those suburbs up with former slum-dwellers. After the Second World War, there was a much more determined effort to address the nation's housing shortage through accelerated slum clearances. Much of the demolition work had been done by the German Luftwaffe, so in many cases it was not so much a matter of destroying the old houses as of building new housing estates on the rubble of the old. This was also when the first New Towns were built, either grafted onto the sides of existing villages or newly constructed on empty land, usually just beyond the green belt encircling Greater London.

These post-war housing estates and New Towns were part of Labour's bold new socialist vision for Britain. Through carefully designed social housing and urban planning, it was thought, the sense of common purpose that had brought Britons together during the war could be extended into the peace. It was a time of radical, if sometimes impractical, dreaming. Particularly in the early days, planners were guided by noble intentions that sometimes veered into the realm of the utopian, as in the planned (but never constructed) New Town of Motopia, where residents would live in a concrete grid of modern flats while cars rumbled above their heads on elevated roads, leaving the ground free for pedestrians. 'Caught up in the spirit of socialist euphoria,' writes historian John Burnett,

> many architects and planners saw themselves as social engineers whose principal, and complementary, tasks were to create community and beauty, to reunite the social classes

which the nineteenth century had divided by restoring the town as a natural and desirable organ of civilized life.[17]

New Towns, in particular, were designed to be harmonious, self-contained communities, surrounded by undeveloped green belt, where people would do the majority of their working, shopping, playing and socializing without having to commute somewhere else. There would be big houses for the rich, modest houses for the middling and flats for the less well off, and everything would be linked by good roads, efficient public transportation and shopping and leisure amenities. In a sense, what the planners were trying to accomplish in the New Towns was what Ray Davies would attempt in his imaginary village green: the reconstruction of the small-scale, organic communities that had been destroyed by industrial modernity. This utopian ideal did not turn out quite as envisaged – in time, many New Towns simply became suburbs of London rather than self-contained communities in their own right – but the evidence suggests that most people who lived in them, typically middle- and upper-working-class families, quite liked them.[18]

The post-war village green: a postcard from Stevenage New Town.

Far more problematic were the fates of those further down the social scale who were forced out of inner-city terraces and stacked into blocks of flats. This most loathed form of social housing had its origins in the same idealism that had motivated the New Town planners, but the results were much more mixed. Inspired by the clean, uniform designs and apparently tight-knit communities that British planners had seen in European workers' flats between the wars, high-density blocks seemed to be the perfect antidote to the solipsistic individuality that they felt must be overcome if Britain were to become a truly socialist society.[19] Blocks of flats also took up much less land than areas of semi-detached houses or New Towns, which meant that they would not only be cheaper to build, they would also help to check the 'bungaloid growth' of suburban sprawl. They were a solution that pleased both the idealistic socialist planner and the anti-suburban intellectual (who of course were often one and the same), seeming to offer an ideal environment in which to forge a more cohesive and egalitarian Britain that would not gobble up what remained of the countryside.

The earliest post-war council flats mostly comprised low-rise buildings of four or five storeys, but during the Tory governments of the late 1950s and early 1960s councils began shifting to high-rise towers of fifteen storeys or more. Planners spoke of tilting the Victorian terraced street on its end to create a 'street in the sky', a method that would retain the communal spirit of the inner city while providing people with more modern, comfortable and sanitary accommodation. Demolishing slums and putting people in prefabricated 'system-built' tower blocks was also believed (wrongly, in many cases) to be cheaper than rehabilitating existing houses. By the time a new wave of slum clearance began under Labour in the late 1960s, the tower block had become the default choice of local councils. It was also the choice of building contractors, many of whom cultivated close (and sometimes corrupt) relationships with municipal councillors, profiting mightily from each new street that they tilted on its end.[20]

The trouble was that, until the early 1970s, very few planners stopped to ask people if they actually wanted to live in tower blocks. The people who lived in inner-city slums were among the poorest in Britain, and the decisions to demolish their homes and place them in modern flats were normally taken with only minimal public consultation.[21] In a 1971 documentary called *Where the Houses Used to Be*, a middle-aged woman in the Brutalist Doddington and Rollo estate in Battersea, southwest London, expressed complete bafflement at the thinking that went into her new home.

> I don't know who designs them. I don't know who they design them for. Or if they think that we feel or think any differently than they do . . . If they would've only consulted ordinary people who have to live in these places, what we would like . . . Surely in time somebody will learn to come and ask the ordinary people what they'd like and how they would like them.[22]

It was not that the desires of poor people were not taken into account, precisely, but simply that their desires were thought already to be known. Who wouldn't want to live in a modern flat with running water, indoor lavatories, central heating and stunning vistas over the city? And so, like the 'man in black' in *The Happy Family*, representatives from the local council would simply show up with a compulsory purchase order and a date by which to vacate, and that would be that. Between 1945 and 1968, more than 2.5 million people were rehoused as a result of slum clearance, and very few of them were asked about it beforehand.[23]

As we saw in the previous chapter, there is evidence that people appreciated the upgrade in accommodation that tower blocks seemed to represent, especially at first, but on the whole the new

Where the houses used to be: Doddington and Rollo Estate, Battersea, London (constructed 1967–71).

buildings were quite unpopular. Part of the problem was where they were built. Despite councils' early intentions to build new flats within the inner city, they often ended up selling cleared land to private developers (at hefty profits) and resettling residents in the outskirts. This not only destroyed the social fabric of the street, it made it more difficult and expensive for poor people to get to work or to travel to the city for shopping and entertainment (such amenities as supermarkets and pubs often being in short supply in the satellite towns). Another problem was that people resented the standardization and uniformity of the new estates; the very features that modernist architects hoped would promote social solidarity among the poor were, in fact, detested for the way they suppressed people's individuality. The same Battersea resident whom I quoted above put it this way: in the old terraces, she said,

> You were individuals. You could paint your front door what colour you liked. You could paint your bricks if you wanted

to. You could have what kind of curtains you liked. You were an individual. When you live in a flat you're not. You've got to conform, and really conform, or else you're out.[24]

There were other shortcomings to the high-rise concept. Young children often had nowhere to play other than their own flats and the adjoining corridors, where they frequently provoked complaints from other residents. Lifts required constant maintenance and created nightmares for residents when they broke down. Unsupervised areas such as stairwells and garages succumbed to vandalism by bored teenagers. For these and other reasons, the residents of tower blocks rarely gelled as cohesive social units. The pubs, workplaces and extended families that had been the building blocks of inner-city sociability were simply absent in buildings in which the only place you were likely to see your neighbours was in the local shop (if there was one) or the lift (if it was working). Housewives, stuck at home all day while their husbands went to work, were particularly affected. 'You can't go out on the doorstep and have a chat,' complained one Doddington and Rollo resident. 'There's just no one to chat to. I've been a bag of nerves since we moved here, you know. I've completely changed. I used to be happy-go-lucky; well now I'm not. I'm quite miserable.'[25]

A more serious problem was that many tower blocks were shoddily constructed. By the late 1960s there were more than four hundred tower blocks in Greater London, and many had been built with such haste and economy that they failed to meet basic safety requirements.[26] 'In the first place,' reflected one former planner,

> post-war buildings began to come to pieces: they blew up, collapsed, leaked, burnt out, had their roofs blown off. The spacious new houses and flats that people could not afford to heat suffered appallingly from condensation. In the high flats, the lifts failed and there was no one on hand to repair them ...

People began to look back with regret not only at the styles of
the old architecture but at its comparatively safe technology.[27]

The dangers of cheap building were dramatically demonstrated early
one morning in May 1968 when a new tower block at Ronan Point,
east London, partially collapsed after a resident on the eighteenth
floor struck a match in her kitchen to start the kettle boiling. The
flame sparked a small gas explosion that caused an entire corner of
the building to collapse, killing four people. A subsequent inquiry
found not only that the building failed to meet safety codes, but
that the safety codes themselves were inadequate. Following the
tragedy, the Greater London Council commissioned no more tower
blocks, but it did not halt the building projects already under way.[28]

These massive, state-sponsored population removals were a
re-enactment in real life of the tale told in *The Happy Family*, but on
a much larger scale and usually without the happy ending. 'In effect,'
write historians Alison Ravetz and Richard Turkington, 'the estates
of council flats degenerated into new and in a sense purpose-built
slums, a situation without precedent since some of the worst workers' housing of the industrial revolution.'[29] By 1971, when Ray Davies
turned his jaundiced eye upon the phenomenon, the most sweeping
clearances had largely been completed, but the wounds were still
raw. Of course, as we have seen, slum clearance was not the only
force fragmenting white working-class communities. Affluence and
suburbanization, changing modes of entertainment and socializing,
immigration and emigration – these were all sapping the founda-
tions of the pre-war inner cities in different ways. But unlike the
Arthur Morgans of semi-detached suburbia, the people who were
forced to abandon their old neighbourhoods for malfunctioning
tower blocks often had no choice in the matter. They were victims
not of their own social-climbing ambitions but of arrogant, uncom-
municative officialdom, which was destroying their familiar world
for the sake of goals that were no longer altogether clear.

The Archway Tavern in Holloway.

Muswell Hillbillies perceptively captures this uncertain time. It functions as a sort of return to the old neighbourhood by the globe-trotting Kinks, a momentary drop-in to see how everybody was getting on. 'We'd gone through a phase of expanding through the Sixties,' Davies recalled. '*Muswell Hillbillies* was a return to what we thought we were as people.'[30] The great family parties at 6 Denmark Terrace had long since ceased, but Anne and Fred and the odd Davies sister would still go drinking at the Archway Tavern, a working-class pub in Holloway where an Irish country band sometimes played.

This narrow portal back to the brothers' childhoods provides the setting for the album's jacket art. On the front and back covers, a single photograph shows the Kinks, long-haired and colourfully clad, standing at the bar while working men in caps and jumpers sip pints at the tables. The photo on the inner gatefold shows the band standing in front of a corrugated iron fence surrounding a block of condemned Victorian buildings, a quiet moment amid the ongoing demolition of inner London. The songs on the album are a fusion of Dixieland jazz (courtesy of the three-piece Mike Cotton Sound, who toured with the band at this time) and redneck country, two American styles that had been popular with the older generation and crucial early influences on the Davies brothers. Sloppy, joyous and occasionally maudlin, they are the sounds of smoky dance halls and pub floors covered with sawdust and sour beer. They would fit right in at a Davies family singalong or a Saturday night at the Archway, but they are the very last sounds you would expect to hear blaring from an antiseptic grid of modernist flats.

As on many Kinks albums, the opening track acts as a kind of executive summary of the songs to come. '20th Century Man' is a long letter of complaint to the era in which the singer finds himself, an updating of Noël Coward's 'Twentieth Century Blues' (1931) for the atomic age. But whereas Coward in those post-crash, pre-Hitler days had complained of little more than 'chaos and confusion', now things have gone decidedly off the rails. Technology has created a 'nightmare' of computers and deadly bombs. Civil servants and other welfare-state functionaries are robbing people of their freedom and privacy. Even modern art and literature have become debased. The overall mood is one of betrayal, of a New Jerusalem that, despite the promises of the post-war settlement, is still frustratingly out of reach. Davies says that he 'wrote a little script' for the character in this song. 'He was a person that was holed up. He attached dynamite to all the doors and windows and threatened to blow himself up if they demolished the house. His was the

The changing face of inner London: *Muswell Hillbillies* gatefold.

last house standing in the street.'[31] The song never really indicates that things will go quite this far, but the vocals do become more aggressive as it goes on, from the early lines in which Davies's voice is almost inaudible to the end when he is yelling just a tad uncontrollably, so it is not hard to imagine that the protagonist might have something desperate in mind. This tone of alienation mixed with sub-hysterical desperation will permeate many other songs on the album.

The opening track on Side B, 'Here Come the People in Grey', comes a bit closer to telling the story of Davies's 'little script'. It was inspired by the rehousing of his grandmother, Kate Willmore, in a slum-clearance scheme. As Davies told an interviewer shortly after the album's release, at the age of ninety she was forced out of her 'really nice old house' in Islington and into a block of flats where she no longer had a bath. 'It's just a lack of consideration for people,' he said. 'The government people think they are taking them into a wonderful new world but it's just destroying people.'[32]

The uprooting of Big Granny (as she was universally known) was a traumatic event not just for her but for the entire family. She was the focal point of the family, the wise old counsellor to whom everyone brought their worries and cares. 'She sat in a large chair in the corner of the room like a great dowager', Davies recalled in *X-Ray*, 'and held court over the rest of the family in true matriarchal tradition. Meeting Big Granny was like going to confession, and that's exactly what I did in her presence.'[33] This was the standard role for grandmothers in working-class London. In their study of 1950s Bethnal Green, Willmott and Young describe the grandmother as the 'dominant figure' in the community: 'The local family group, linked together through her bond with her married daughters, was united on her hearth.'[34] To see Big Granny hauled out of her cosy home and installed in a sterile modern flat must have felt like the final destruction not just of a home, but of an entire world.

Davies tells this tale of woe in the first person, opening with a deep tremolo like an old bluesman telling a hard-luck tale from the Mississippi Delta. In the first verse he describes the government's purchase of his home and worries about the far-off flat to which he'll be taken. In the second verse he grows defiant, vowing to run away to live in a tent and to buy a gun to protect himself and his girl from the police. Then he drops the low-voiced lament and becomes strident, pledging to fight a 'one-man revolution' against the 'people in grey' who are trying to take him away. Forms, magistrates and intrusive inspections follow, but the singer remains determined to defeat his oppressors, by hook or by crook – perhaps (although this is unstated) by lining his home with dynamite and threatening to blow himself up. It is possible that the arc of this story was influenced by the final twenty minutes of the *Till Death Us Do Part* film, for which Davies had done the soundtrack in 1969. When Alf Garnett and family are served with a compulsory purchase order for their terrace house in Stepney, the rest of the family comply, but Alf is determined to stay. He rages, prays and dreams that he has been knighted – much to the annoyance of Harold Wilson – but at last the bulldozers and bureaucrats succeed in prying him out of his beloved home, and the film ends with him wandering his new home in a vast, faceless housing estate in search of his displaced family.

Whether this was the inspiration or not, 'Here Come the People in Grey' does accurately reflect a growing mood of opposition to the planners and housing officials who were so ruthlessly rearranging inner London. In the words of historian John Stevenson, 'The headlong rush to build a better world seemed to have run up against not just a minor technical hitch but a host of far more complex and deep-seated problems than originally envisaged . . . The long-standing faith in "experts" and a willingness to trust planners and architects was dwindling rapidly.'[35] While few people went so far as to wage an all-out revolution against the welfare state, a growing grass-roots movement comprising tenants' associations, neighbourhood action committees and conservation groups was finally starting to push back. One particularly combative instance of this, which I briefly mentioned in Chapter Three, was the alliance of cockney traders and renegade planners who banded together to save Covent Garden in the early 1970s. The language used by these campaigners often strikingly resembled the revolutionary rhetoric in 'Here Come the People in Grey'. Here is what Brian Anson, one of the planners who led the campaign, told a Paris magazine about their objectives:

Covent Garden is a traditional struggle between the oppressed and oppressors. It is only marginally different from a war situation, where real weapons are used and where the protagonists actually fight . . . The freedom struggle going on in Ireland this very moment has more in common with the struggle for Covent Garden than people care to admit; the fundamental problem is the same – land, language and culture – but for whom?[36]

Not every campaigner saw things in such absolute terms, but there was definitely a spirit of rebellion in the air. On 3 April 1971 – just four months before *Muswell Hillbillies* was recorded – *The Times* reported on a 'revolt in the cities' in which people across the country were expressing 'a total disaffection with the aims and ideals of Tory and Labour, an ingratitude to planners, and a cynicism about all constitutional processes which will soon be accorded its due place among the most pressing political problems of our age'. Upset about not only slum clearances but the running of motorways through poor neighbourhoods, scorched-earth development plans in commercial districts and the diversion of traffic away from posh streets and into poorer areas (as happened in Granny Davies's own neighbourhood in Islington), people were finding it 'impossible to find any expression within the politics of the established parties for their feelings about the conditions under which they live'.[37]

'Here Come the People in Grey' and other songs on *Muswell Hillbillies* perceptively capture this insurgent attitude, but I think it is a bit of a stretch to hold, as Nick Baxter-Moore does, that Davies's anti-welfare state position here 'was in many ways consistent with the radical, anti-statist neo-conservatism promoted by Margaret Thatcher'.[38] To be sure, many working-class people would eventually channel their disillusionment with 'big government' into votes for Thatcher and her ilk, but it was entirely possible to come at all these problems from the left as well as the right. Brian Anson, the renegade planner who fought for Covent Garden, was not a Thatcherite but a left-wing radical who blamed an unholy (and proto-Thatcherite) alliance of corporate capital and local governments for the destruction of working-class communities. Ray Davies is less easy to pin down on the Left–Right spectrum, but his worries about mechanization, standardization and faceless bureaucracy had more in common with a long-standing anti-rationalist tradition in English thought that encompassed both left and right than it did with puritanical, efficiency-obsessed Thatcherism.

Nevertheless, a sociologist looking for the seeds of Thatcher's eventual assault on the welfare state could do worse than look to '20th Century Man' and 'Here Come the People in Grey' for signs of the popular discontent on which she capitalized.

Most of the other songs on *Muswell Hillbillies* celebrate the survival of human passions and eccentricities in the face of the oppressive modernity embodied by the 'people in grey'. Many of the characters are real people whom Davies knew in his childhood, including members of his own family, whom he often identifies by name as if to insist on their irreplaceable particularity. The hero of 'Uncle Son' was Anne Davies's beloved brother who had died of tuberculosis when Ray and Dave were young. It is one of the most overtly political songs on the album, expressing the notion that for ordinary blokes like Uncle Son (who in real life was a railway worker), it doesn't much matter whether it's Tory or Labour who are in, or what the socialists and ministers are preaching, it only matters whether you're able to do your work and get on with your life. It's his sort, Davies suggests, who will be redeemed if the revolution ever really comes. 'Oklahoma USA' is about his sister Rene, whose death when Ray was thirteen played an important part in shaping his personality and sense of artistic mission. 'Have a Cuppa Tea' is a second song inspired by Big Granny, a woman for whom tea was a panacea for all ills ('the Englishman's opium',[39] George Orwell once called it). According to Davies, 'Holloway Jail', a story-song about a woman who goes to prison to protect her lover, is also based on real people, although it is unclear (apart from one character named Frankie, who might be his uncle Frank) who that might be.[40] There may also be real-life analogues to the manically dieting Fat Flabby Annie of 'Skin and Bone' (possibly Anne Davies herself) and the old man in 'Holiday' (possibly Charlie the gardener from 'Autumn Almanac') who tries and fails to escape his unhappy life with a beach holiday, but their true identities are less important than the fact that, like the others, these are characters who are struggling – not always with much success – to retain a sense of human dignity amid the mechanizing horrors of the age.

Like the character in 'Get Back in the Line', the protagonist of 'Acute Schizophrenia Paranoia Blues' was partly inspired by Davies's father, who suffered from mental health problems late in his life. Among the undeniably paranoid fantasies that the character has – that the milkman is spying on him, that the neighbouring woman works for the KGB – are a few fears that are less obviously delusional, such as his fear that mass demonstrations might provoke a world war, or that the social security office is invading his privacy. These aren't delusions so much as rational concerns arising from the deranged conditions of modern life. In a world in which the government can just show up one day and start knocking your house down, is it really so outlandish to think that 'they' might also be tapping your phone or watching you through the keyhole? Like many other songs on the album, this story is more serious than it first appears. The same goes for 'Alcohol', which was inspired both by Fred Davies's well-known intemperance and by Ray's own growing struggles with drink and depression. It has the sloppy-drunk sound of a Weimar cabaret tune – in concerts Ray performed it while sloshing great quantities of beer across the stage and audience – but the lyrics deal with questions of addiction, infidelity and domestic abuse that cut rather close to the bone. 'Complicated Life' also derives from Davies's experiences with anxiety and depression. It gives us a character who, overwhelmed by life, indulges in a regime of extreme sensory deprivation, deliberately stripping away all distractions, from booze and women to work and food, with disastrous results. Like the others, it is a funny and light-hearted rendering of what was, in fact, quite a serious problem for the man singing the words. As he told *Melody Maker* at the time, 'The songs were also about trying to live, getting up every day and problems like writing letters and paying bills. These are real problems for me, actually getting them done.'[41] As usual, Davies was smiling out of just one side of his mouth.

The song on *Muswell Hillbillies* that most fully combines the autobiographical with the sociological is the final track, 'Muswell Hillbilly'. Taking its cue from the American sitcom *The Beverly Hillbillies*, about a family of Texas yokels who strike it rich and move to California, the song explores the migration of working-class Londoners from the inner-city slums to the suburbs, vaguely echoing the migration of the Davies family from Holloway to East Finchley and Fortis Green in the 1940s. Rosie Rooke, to whom the narrator says goodbye in the first line of the song, was the name of a friend of Anne's from the old neighbourhood. 'She had a very sad life,' Davies said at the time, 'drink and all of that, and she never felt fulfilled as a person . . . Leaving Rosie Rooke behind is like leaving everything behind.'[42] But the analogy with the Davies family is not exact. Whereas Anne and Fred had voluntarily forsaken Holloway for suburban tranquillity in an old and established community, the people in this song have been forcibly cleared out and deposited in tower blocks and New Towns far from their homes, shoved into characterless 'little boxes' that make Arthur Morgan's semi-detached home look like a Shangri-La indeed. But, like the Davies family in their cramped suburban home, the characters in this song are determined to hold on to their old identities. 'They' make one final appearance here, threatening to change the characters' ways of life (right down to their accents) and turn them into zombies, but, the singer insists, they won't kill their 'cockney pride'. This is a joyous and unexpectedly hopeful note on which to end a record that, for all its humour and extravagance, paints a pretty bleak picture of what life was like for the powerless and pushed-around in the London of 1971. It is a reminder that the English working classes have always lived in opposition to the dominant culture being imposed upon them – that, in the words of music scholar Ian Watson, 'the corner-pubs and the "street-families" were defence-mechanisms of the proletariat against the numbing, alienating background of poisonous chimneys, damp and insanitary dwellings and dark dangerous alleys.'[43] If the English working classes could find a way to survive (and even thrive) in such conditions, then surely, these songs suggest, they can do the same in the shiny new housing estates of the distant suburbs.

The scepticism with which both *Lola Versus Powerman* and *Muswell Hillbillies* regard the post-war British Establishment, and their evident pleasure in the anarchic eccentrics who resist it, are not simply the result of Ray Davies's inveterate crankiness, although that certainly plays a role. It also comes from a particular idea of Englishness with which Davies allied himself. Despite their clear American influences – influences which, as we have seen, had long had strong purchase among the English working classes – the songs tap into a deep strand of English thought that goes back centuries and forms a strong component of the national self-understanding. This strand has been called many things over the years – conservatism (with a small c), pragmatism, amateurism, Little Englandism, Anglo-Saxon common sense – but I think it is best described as a distinctly English brand of anti-rationalism, a wariness of all-encompassing social engineering of the sort first attempted in Europe during the French Revolution and embodied in the early 1970s by the planners and bureaucrats of the welfare state. Previous releases had toyed with this theme, but *Lola Versus Powerman* and, especially, *Muswell Hillbillies* offered Davies's fullest articulation to date of this anti-rational outlook, which in this case he happened to share with large segments of the English working classes.

The origins of English hostility to grand, all-encompassing systems can be traced back to the anti-Catholic movements of the sixteenth and seventeenth centuries. Insisting on the sanctity of the individual conscience as against the totalizing power of the Catholic Church, English Puritans and their many offshoots were distant ancestors to the cockney rebels who fought against the grey-clad priesthood of the welfare state. But it is in the eighteenth century, particularly in the intellectual campaign against the French Revolution, that the first great English critique of rationalism can be found. The key figure here was the Whig parliamentarian Edmund Burke, whose *Reflections on the Revolution in France* (1790) predicted catastrophe for the revolution due to its proponents' arrogant disregard for the accumulated wisdom of the ages in favour of an untried programme of rational reform. At first glance, Burke might seem a strange person to designate as the spiritual godfather of a band like the Kinks. An admirer of aristocracies and monarchs and defender of traditional privileges, Burke seems to embody everything that the Davies brothers and their bandmates were fighting against. Yet if we see Burke as an early critic of hyperrational social engineering, then some surprising convergences occur. The danger that Burke saw in the French Revolution was much like the danger Davies saw in the planning department of the local council. In the words of Alan Wolfe, Burke felt that the French National Assembly, 'for all its rhetoric about the rights of man, had come to function as an arbitrary authority lacking any substantial connection with the people it sought to govern on the alleged basis of reason'.[44] To think like Burke is to worry about the possibility that technocratic experts, carried away by the power of their own explanatory models, will impose those models upon society without taking into account the irrational emotions and eccentricities of the people over whom they rule. It is this side of Burke – the side that was hostile to what came to be known as social science and planning – that the Kinks come closest to embodying.

During the nineteenth century, Burkean anti-rationalism became a central component of English national identity, particularly among the governing classes. While other countries (particularly France) seemed to have revolutions every generation or two, England – so the thinking went – muddled along with a series of piecemeal reforms that gradually expanded the franchise, extended civil liberties and reformed abuses. Those with a vested interest in the status quo idealized England as a land in which a carefully balanced constitution and the sturdy common sense of the people obviated any need for dangerous experimentation. In Burke's words, England was a land of ancient and cherished 'prejudices . . . and the longer they have lasted, and the more generally they have prevailed, the more we cherish them'.[45] Take the government, for example: centuries of trial and error had effectively dispersed power among the houses of Parliament, the monarchy, common law, statutory law and customary practice. Burke and his followers argued that this system was suited to the 'sullen resistance to innovation' and 'cold sluggishness' of the English 'national character' – characteristics that, far from being a problem, were in fact a source of the nation's strength.[46] Wrapped up in this idea of Englishness was a deep suspicion of city-based, cosmopolitan intellectuals, who were believed to be too disconnected from the people and the land – too wrapped up in suspect continental theories – to know how to run the country. 'Thus did Englishness', writes Stephen Haseler, 'come to elevate the traditional, the familiar and the practical' over the abstract and theoretical.[47]

This idea of the English people as uniquely ill-suited to rational planning began to come under serious pressure in the early twentieth century. The rise of movements like the socialist-technocratic Fabian Society, the professionalization of the social sciences, the steady secularization of public life and the unique demands of the First World War all helped bring about a new conception of the duties and capabilities of the state. Over time the traditional elite – reared to value well-bred amateurism over too-clever expertise – began making room within their ranks for highly trained technocrats, setting the stage for the expert-driven Labour government of 1945. But national identities are tenacious things, and there remained influential voices, on both the Left and Right, who insisted that England was a land that was, and would always remain, impervious to excessive rationalism. In 1926, in an article for *Harper's Monthly* called 'In

Praise of Muddling Through', the English socialist J. A. Hobson explained half-regretfully that the Englishman's aversion to 'lofty principles, long-laid concerted policies, and the paraphernalia of social science' would prevent the country from ever adopting a fully socialist system. 'We prefer personal liberty (the right to do wrong if you will) not only to sobriety, but to efficiency. Though we are willing to dabble in socialism, as in other isms, any complete rule of life repels us.'[48] This notion was shared by Stanley Baldwin, the Tory prime minister for much of the 1920s and '30s, who was in most ways Hobson's (and Davies's) ideological opposite. In 1924, during a famous speech in which he extolled the virtues of rural England ('the tinkle of hammer on anvil in the country smithy, the corncrake on a dewy morning, the sound of the scythe against the whetstone . . .'), Baldwin claimed that the essence of Englishness lay in the 'diversified individuality' of its people. 'Let us see to it that we never allow our individuality as Englishmen to be steam-rollered,' he said. 'The preservation of the individuality of the Englishman is essential to the preservation of the type of the race, and if our differences are smoothed out and we lose that great gift, we shall lose at the same time our power.'[49] English individuality, in Baldwin's eyes, could be preserved only by adhering to the nation's idiosyncratic but time-tested political and social systems.

A dangerous smoothing-out of differences was precisely what seemed to be going on elsewhere in Europe during much of the twentieth century. As during the French Revolution, first the Bolsheviks and then the Fascists and Nazis had begun building radical new systems on the basis of abstract ideas that took little account of the eccentricities of human nature. Perhaps no Englishman was better at describing the great conflicts of the age as a clash between (Continental) mechanized modernity and (English) quirky individuality than the writer and broadcaster J. B. Priestley. It was Priestley who had immortalized the 'little pleasure-steamers' of Dunkirk as a typically English response to the annihilating horror of Nazism,

Views of rural England at the end of the war. J. B. Priestley, 'A Tribute to Britain', *Picture Post*, 28 April 1945.

an unplanned (and unplannable) instance of English decency and pluck that proved to be the salvation of Western civilization.[50] One particularly resonant example of Priestley's anti-rationalism appeared at the end of the war, when he published a piece in the *Picture Post* that attributed the victory over Nazism to the English people's ability to retain their humanity amid the mechanizing imperatives of modern warfare. 'There have been times', he wrote, 'when we have had to try to behave like robots, but nevertheless we have stayed human all right. We have had to plan and to organise . . . but we did not plan and organise ourselves into spiritless dim-eyed idiocy.'[51] The war machine that Britain was forced to build was characterized not by its ruthless efficiency, Priestley argued, but by its eccentricity. There was always 'a certain wobble' in Britain's war machine, the consequence of the human decency of the people who controlled it and the anti-authoritarian traditions of the nation that created it. 'Lines were drawn, but these lines were rarely quite hard and straight,' he wrote. 'I have no hesitation in declaring that this wobble, this easy play of machine parts, these curving lines, these checks and balances, were a manifestation, even at the last desperate hour, of the British genius for self-government.'[52] Edmund Burke, railing against another outbreak of Continental inhumanity, could hardly have put it better. You could cram the English into straight-edged, machine-made boxes of European rationality all you liked, but you could never get rid of their life-affirming wobble.

This brings us to George Orwell and the title of the present chapter. Like Priestley, Orwell was a socialist whose sympathies nearly always lay with the ordinary, muddle-headed, fundamentally decent common people.[53] Orwell's patriotism, and his opposition to fascism and totalitarianism of all kinds, derived from a deep affection for the ordinary Englishman in all his 'artistic insensibility, gentleness, respect for legality, suspicion of foreigners, sentimentality about animals, hypocrisy, exaggerated class distinctions, and . . . obsession with sport'.[54] Like Priestley, Baldwin, Hobson and Burke, Orwell believed that the English people (as he put it in his wartime essay 'England, Your England') 'feel no need for any philosophy or systematic "world-view."'[55] Instead, they showed an almost religious devotion to outmoded and inefficient ways of doing things, as in their 'spelling system that defies analysis' and their 'system of weights and measures that is intelligible only to the compilers of arithmetic books'.[56] Right up until his death in 1950, Orwell felt that the nation was in desperate need of something like a socialist revolution, but it had to be a decent, gentle, English sort of socialism, not the steamrolling type emanating from Russia or its satellites and imitators. Like everyone else in the modern world, the English would not escape 'being numbered, labelled, conscripted, [and] "coordinated"', but they would always rebel against too much of this sort of thing, and socialism, when it came, would have to be moulded to English civilization, not the other way around.[57]

This outlook was the basis of Orwell's most famous work, *Nineteen Eighty-four* (1949), which is as much a critique of technological modernity as of any particular political creed. The novel's most famous devices – the sinister and devotion-demanding Big Brother, the mass surveillance via telescreen, the endless war with interchangeable enemies – add up to a nightmare vision of the modern world in the age of the atom bomb and the mass media. However, as Davies would later do in *Muswell Hillbillies*, Orwell finds a glimmer of hope in the inveterate irrationality of the English common people. Despite all of the Party's efforts to rewrite history to suit its current needs, the past lives on in the world of the working classes ('the proles'), and it is through them that the novel's hero, Winston Smith, senses the possibility of salvation. The proles have deteriorated from what they once were, drugged into submission by an insipid mass culture (what Priestley once labelled 'Admass') and easily drummed into a jingoistic frenzy when it suits the Party, but on the whole they are left alone to lead their small lives, with their petty cares and sentimental notions derived from old popular songs, in neighbourhoods that closely resemble the working-class districts of London in the 1940s (Orwell wrote parts of the novel in a flat in Canonbury Square, Islington, not far from Big Granny's home in Barnsbury). 'The proles had stayed human,' Winston reflects at one point. 'They had not become hardened inside. They had held on to the primitive emotions which he himself had to relearn by conscious effort.'[58] In contrast with the regimented, cowed and morally bankrupt world of the elite, the proles are anarchic and vital, a last living link to a time when humans were allowed to just be human. Winston's great act of rebellion in the novel is to seek out what in Newspeak is derisively known as 'ownlife' – that is, 'individualism and eccentricity' – by renting a room above a junk shop in the prole quarter, where he and his lover, a fellow dissident named Julia, can live a life of sexual and psychological freedom.[59] One of the novel's most devastating moments comes when their sanctuary is invaded by the Thought Police – their 'ownlife' was never as secure as they believed – but until that moment Orwell holds out the prospect that here, amid the inarticulate but fundamentally decent working classes, Winston and Julia might find their way back to a life that is pleasurable and free.

Ray Davies has spoken often of the influence *Nineteen Eighty-four* has had on him. His parents had not allowed him to watch the 1954 BBC television adaptation starring Peter Cushing, so he had read the book instead, and it made a profound impact.[60] Themes from Orwell's dystopia appear again and again in Davies's work, from the totalitarian movement led by Mr Black in the *Preservation* albums and stage shows to the complex fictional conceit that he employed in his 1994 autobiography *X-Ray*. The most obvious thing Davies seems to have taken from *Nineteen Eighty-four* is its nightmare vision of technological totalitarianism. It is a vision that informs many of the songs on *Muswell Hillbillies*, from the impersonal houses into which people are being shoved to the not-so-paranoid fears of the chap who thinks his milkman might be a spy. But Davies also shares with Orwell a belief that a hopeful future, if it exists, lies with the working classes and the links they retain with the English past. In the junk shop where Winston and Julia hide in *Nineteen Eighty-four*, Winston becomes obsessed with a paperweight in which a delicate English rose is encased in clear glass, a fragment of the past that cannot be erased or rewritten by the Ministry of Truth. The songs on *Muswell Hillbillies*, like many other songs he wrote during his semi-Romantic period, add up to what is, in essence, a junk shop full of such items, portals back to another world that contain within them the possibility of redemption. Like Orwell, Davies is never sure that such redemption is really within reach – or that it is altogether desirable – but he is sure that we cannot hope for salvation if we forget

Ray Davies Unravels
The Muswell Puzzle

"Here come the people in grey/To take me away," sing the Kinks. Did you think it was a fantasy? Not so, says the group's leader.

It's a cold night at the Haymarket—the Manhattan bar where displaced English groups spend a good part of their time pretending they're in London. It's a dark, quiet place and the bartender comes from Liverpool. Ray Davies of the Kinks is sitting in a booth with his head bowed down, reading the *Village Voice*. The dusky amber light falling on his face and hair is reminiscent of the English pub lighting on the cover of the Kinks' new album *Muswell Hillbillies* (RCA).

Spending time with Ray Davies is one way of suspending yourself in time and space. The air around him seems filled with the faces of uncles who died when he was still tiny, working girls who were pretty and young long before he was born, and pop stars who were on the rise when he was first making the charts. This was the fourth time Davies had made himself available in two days. The first three times had been over the telephone; now the previously disembodied voice took on a third dimension.

The dark lining: As we talked, "The House Of The Rising Sun" by the Animals came on the juke box. Raymond Douglas Davies —writer, producer and lead singer since the mid-60's—asked how Eric Burden—another mid-60's veteran—was doing these days. When he had been assured that Eric was doing quite well with War, he seemed satisfied.

Taking paper and a pen Ray started to sketch ("anything that comes to my mind") fat old men, using delicate cartoon-type line drawings. As he hunched over his pen, Ray began to explain how the ghosts that haunt his thoughts had shaped the latest Kinks album:

"I wanted it to be a double album. To start, it's about making people something they're not. I wanted it to be like *Arthur* (Reprise), but I didn't have the time to finish it because I had a lot of things to do this year. I wanted to make little statements about England and what's happened to some of the people."

Ray has taken on a cause lately, and it's crept into most of his music. He explained: "What amazes me is there are new towns like Harlow in England, and in these towns and in Colchester and East Anglia there are all these people who've been taken out of the East End of London and put into these places where they don't really exist as they did before. They're trying to keep things the same as when they lived together in London, but they have to breakdown eventually. You can't just live on memories and things like that."

"People take pictures of each other
Just to prove that they really existed
. . . don't show me no more please"

> *Village Green Preservation Society* (Reprise)

The people in grey: But back to *Muswell Hillbillies:* "it sounds very heavy and serious and it is," Ray warns, "it's just very disturbing to see this happen. They're knocking down all the places in Holloway and Islington and moving all the people off to housing projects in new towns. They say the houses they're tearing down are old and decayed, but they're not really. My Gran used to live in Islington in this really nice old house, and they moved her to a block of flats, and she hasn't got a bath now. She's got a shower because there isn't room for a bath. And like she's ninety years old, she can't even get out of the chair let alone stand in the shower. They haven't taken that into consideration. And they knew she was going to move in because it's a new block and they took her around and showed her where she was gonna live and she didn't have any choice. They didn't think to help her in any way. It's just a lack of consideration for people. The government people think they're taking them into a wonderful new

Photos: Hellmann

The Kinks' 1972 line-up: (L–R) Ray Davies, Mick Avory, Dave Davies, John Dalton and John Gosling. *Circus*, February 1972.

about the past. What makes Davies more of an Orwellian socialist than a Burkean conservative, I think, is precisely his belief that the route to salvation lies through the folk memories and traditions of the humblest among us. It is not through monarchs, aristocrats and churchmen that we will escape the enslaving power of technological modernity. They are every bit as likely to enslave us as the Powermen of the record industry or the men from the council with their compulsory purchase orders. But in the sturdy, quirky, commonsensical and essentially decent English working classes, there may yet be hope.

This is why, to me, *Muswell Hillbillies* is the most complete statement of Ray Davies's artistic vision. Just as *Nineteen Eighty-four* brought together most of the great themes Orwell had been exploring throughout his career, so *Muswell Hillbillies* encapsulated most of the ideas Davies had been exploring in his songs up to that time. The album's baseline is Davies's constitutional unease with the modern world, a predisposition that had characterized the Kinks' music ever since the first jagged chords of 'You Really Got Me' blared through the little green amp in the front room of 6 Denmark Terrace. With the same wry smirk that he had worn from the beginning – part insecurity, part detachment, part indecision – Davies casts a cold eye on the state of the world generally and the state of working-class London in particular. As on *Village Green* and *Arthur*, he is worried about what has happened to the tight-knit community that reared him, pessimistic, as always, but not without hope. He borrows liberally from his own past and that of his family, appropriates musical styles long out of vogue, sings like an old man, sounds jocular when he's actually sad, sounds sad when he's actually uncertain and explores decidedly unfashionable topics like slum clearance and air pollution. In 'Oklahoma USA', he even revisits one of the events that first persuaded him to become a musician, the foundational grief at the loss of a sibling that underlay all of his art. Throughout the album, his sympathy lies unwaveringly with the working classes who doggedly insist on leading their 'ownlife', and if these characters sometimes come across as less than sympathetic, well, that's because they are human beings, with all the weaknesses and limitations that that entails. The enemies that they face are the same enemies the working classes have always faced – 'them', the Establishment, the 'people in grey', the whole sinister panoply of false friends and Big Brothers – and they fight back in the way that they always have: by gritting their teeth and smiling through the pain.

Epilogue

In the summer of 1973, Ray Davies moved away from Fortis Green for good. For the last four years, ever since the Kinks had begun touring America again, his relationship with Rasa had been deteriorating. The usual stresses of touring – the long absences, the loneliness, the temptations to waywardness – were hard enough, but for Davies there was an additional factor. For as long as he could remember, America had existed in his mind as a land of unbounded possibility. Freedom, variety, mystery, sex, sunshine, Hollywood, the open road: for this child of post-war London, with its ration cards and bombsites, its broadcasting monopolies and class prejudices, America was much more than just a lucrative market for his band to capture. It was the ultimate fantasy, a place where he might one day be able to live the kind of life his parents and sisters had dreamed about when they danced to showtunes at the Lyceum or stared longingly at the silver screen. The more time he spent there – and the more fans the Kinks, after their too-long absence, began to acquire there – the more his cosy suburban life in north London came to feel like a prison. He had always resisted the fashionable notion that nothing truly meaningful or exceptional could happen in suburbia. Now, as he approached thirty, with two small children and a wife he had married back when nobody expected this music thing to last, he was having second thoughts.

The divorce was a wrenching one, and it wasn't helped by the fact that the new house he bought, deep in the posh Surrey country-side, didn't suit him any better than the one at Borehamwood had. In July 1973, at the end of a gig supporting Sly and the Family Stone at London's White City, Davies, having drunk too much Dom Pérignon and taken one too many Valiums, announced onstage that he was quitting the Kinks. In typically shambolic Kinks fashion, the house music had been turned on just before he dropped this bombshell, so few people in the crowd heard him. He collapsed shortly there-after and was taken to hospital, and he spent the next few weeks recuperating under the care of his little brother, who was able to put aside his resentment of Ray's growing megalomania long enough to do the sort of thing that brothers do for one another.

The Kinks were not finished – they had more than twenty years ahead of them, in fact – but after the White City meltdown they were never quite the same. First came the musical theatre phase, when Ray's bandmates and label bosses indulged (many would say overindulged) his dream of combining rock concerts with theat-rical narratives to create a new kind of music-hall entertainment for the modern age. Then, in the late 1970s, the Kinks transformed again into a hard-rocking arena band with a rabid following in America but almost no following at all in their native land. That phase lasted into the 1990s, when the band finally broke up, but they have enjoyed a long afterlife, thanks in part to the musicians of the Britpop generation, whose leading figures have pointed to the Kinks, and specifically their oh-so-English songs of the 1960s, as major sources of inspiration. Both Davies brothers continue to write and record new music, much of it quite good, and in recent years Ray has allowed himself to become something of a national treasure, performing 'Waterloo Sunset' at the London Olympics in 2012, writing a hit West End musical based on the Kinks' early days and even receiving a knighthood in 2017. In October 2018, fifty years after it arrived with barely a whisper on the popular music scene,

THE KINKS. Picture by BARRIE WENTZELL

by
Steve
Lake

Kinks: We're not English

"ENGLISH? I don't think of us as an English band at all." Ray Davies is wearing a candy striped bow tie, mid-green baggy cords, and what appear to be bowling shoes. He sips tea through the famous gap that separates his incisors, the little finger of his right hand raised ever so slightly, protruding at about forty five degrees from the teacup's bowl.

It seems a strange comment coming from the man who sang of sunsets over Waterloo, and Carnaby fashion and Muswell Hillbillies, Of Village Green Preservation Societies and autumns (not falls) and steam trains. And, currently, plaster ducks, an almost exclusively English preoccupation.

"I think the fact that we're accepted in America indicates that we're not an English group."

Oh, but that's so obviously an attraction of cultural opposites. They like English people over there . . . we're quaint . . .

"Well, there's Sweden. We can get amazing receptions in Sweden."

No, no one's denying your popularity, Ray. We're simply stating the obvious. That your material is about English life, rather than American life, which is generally the focal point of most rock and roll.

"No, no. I think you're basing your opinion on a certain knowledge of the Kinks' history. I'm not so sure that anybody hearing the Kinks for the first time

into the ground all afternoon, and we won't reach agreement."

RAY DAVIES woke up one morning recently and remembered that the Kinks were a band. A lot of us, I guess, had forgotten that fairly crucial fact. The group have never been exactly what one would term a tight unit.

They've been so loose for so long that a lot of people, self included, weren't exactly sure how many people were officially in the band. I raised an eyebrow at a recent press release that informed us that the Kinks were now a ten piece.

For three years, they've carried a three-man brass section at all gigs, and vartly last year added a couple of girlie vocalists for good measure.

"I guess we still think of

variably focuses on the brothers Davies, Ray and Dave. As if to amend this fact, five Kinks fill an upstairs office at RCA today. Ray reclines in an upholstered armchair in the middle of the room, while the other four, guitarist Dave, long-serving drummer Mick Avory, bassist John Dalton, and keyboard man John Gosling decorate a shelf placed just above waist level along one wall. Their balance is precarious: already a large portion of the shelf has collapsed, neatly demolishing a rather attractive light arrangement designed to project from beneath.

But where were we? Right. The Kinks as band rather than mere vehicle for the grand concepts of Raymond Douglas Davies.

view or otherwise. "I think we'll get an outside producer in for our next album, 'cos I'm sure that over the years it must've created a bit of a gulf.

"Like, the fact that I go into the box (studio control booth) sometimes, which means I'm not a hundred per cent involved in the actual creation of the music.

"Y'know, I've been so involved in writing long stories like 'Starmaker' and 'Preservation' — I'd really like to just do some albums of songs, unrelated songs.

"It's not generally acknowledged, but ALL of the Kinks' RCA albums were conceived only as soundtracks — "Muswell Hillbillies" and "Everybody's In Showbiz — Everybody's A Star" included. All of them are designed to have visual accompaniment.

New worlds to conquer. *Melody Maker*, 19 April 1975.

the rerelease of *The Kinks Are the Village Green Preservation Society* entered the British album charts for the first time (at #47), and Sir Raymond had begun talking about a stage show based on the album and an impending reunion of the surviving members.

Each of the Kinks' later phases, particularly the musical theatre phase, could be subjected to the kind of historically informed criticism that I have attempted here. But I have chosen to end this book in the early 1970s because this was when the umbilical connection between the Kinks and their north London roots was finally cut. The album that came after *Muswell Hillbillies*, 1972's *Everybody's in Show-Biz*, follows the gaze of its predecessor across the Atlantic to tell some amusing and occasionally moving stories about life on the road, but it is predominately an album about America, for America. The only glimmer of north London is the feeling you get that the lads singing and playing these songs are very much fish out of water, simultaneously fascinated and disgusted by the country in which they are now spending so much of their time. The musical theatre albums that came next are undoubtedly English in topic and syntax, but they mostly rehearse themes that Davies had already explored on earlier (and stronger) albums, and the variety of Englishness they peddle has the whiff of the theme park about it, as if the Kinks are consciously pandering to the Anglophile fantasies of their American fans. The songs of the later 1970s to the 1990s are often English songs, and sometimes London songs, but – with a few exceptions, such as their last major hit, 'Come Dancing', in 1982 – they are much more often about the new worlds that the Kinks were entering than the world from which they came.

A sense of place, and the associated search for home, would always play a role in Davies's songwriting, but his engagement with the world of his childhood – not just as he remembered it, but as he actually experienced it during the supercharged 1960s – would never again be as deep as it was when he could look into his own back garden and write a song like 'Autumn Almanac'. Back in 1967 he had vowed, in the voice of his father's friend Charlie, never to leave the street on which he had been born. But eventually he did leave it, and his songs, inevitably, changed. How Charlie fared in the tumultuous times that followed is anybody's guess.

References

Introduction: A Face in the Crowd

1 George Melly, *Revolt into Style: The Pop Arts* (Garden City, NY, 1971), p. 99.
2 The biographical works that I have found especially useful are Dave Davies, *Kink: An Autobiography* (New York, 1996); Ray Davies, *X-Ray: The Unauthorized Autobiography* (London, 1994); Ray Davies, *Americana: The Kinks, the Riff, the Road: The Story* (New York, 2013); Nick Hasted, *You Really Got Me: The Story of the Kinks* (London, 2013); Doug Hinman, *The Kinks: All Day and All of the Night* (San Francisco, CA, 2004); Thomas M. Kitts, *Ray Davies: Not Like Everybody Else* (New York and London, 2008); Andy Miller, *The Kinks Are the Village Green Preservation Society*, 33¹/₃ series (New York, 2003); Johnny Rogan, *Ray Davies: A Complicated Life* (London, 2016); and Jon Savage, *The Kinks: The Official Biography* (London, 1984).
3 Quoted in John Berger, *Landscapes: John Berger on Art*, ed. Tom Overton (London, 2016), p. 48.
4 Especially fine examples of this academic work include Carey Fleiner, *The Kinks: A Thoroughly English Phenomenon* (Lanham, MD, 2017); Keith Gildart, 'From "Dead End Streets" to "Shangri Las": Negotiating Social Class and Post-war Politics with Ray Davies and the Kinks', *Contemporary British History*, XXVI/3 (2012), pp. 273–98; Thomas M. Kitts and Michael J. Kraus, eds, *Living on a Thin Line: Crossing Aesthetic Borders with the Kinks* (Rumford, RI, 2002); and contributions by Nick Baxter-Moore and Michael J. Kraus to a special Kinks issue of *Popular Music and Society*, XXIX/2 (2006).
5 David Dalton, 'The Kinks: Remembrance of Kinks Past', *Gadfly* (March 1999), available at www.rocksbackpages.com, accessed 15 June 2018.
6 William Empson, *Seven Types of Ambiguity*, 3rd edn (Norfolk, CT, 1953), pp. 192–3.

7 Simon Frith, *Performing Rites: On the Value of Popular Music* (Cambridge, MA, 1996), p. 182.

8 Ray Davies interviewed by Keith Altham, 'Ray Davies Quitting Kinks?', *New Musical Express*, 20 May 1967, p. 9.

9 Ray Davies interviewed by Jonathan Cott, 'Afternoon Tea with Ray Davies', *Rolling Stone*, 26 November 1970, pp. 30–31: p. 30.

10 D. Davies, *Kink*, p. 107.

11 Cott, 'Afternoon Tea', p. 31.

12 Ray Davies interviewed in *New Musical Express*, 20 February 1971.

13 R. Davies, *X-Ray*, p. 163.

14 Nik Cohn, *Awopbopaloobop Alopbamboom: The Golden Age of Rock* (New York, 1996), p. 166.

15 R. Davies, *X-Ray*, p. 329.

16 Ibid., p. 144.

17 Andy Miller, liner notes for the Kinks, *The Kinks Are the Village Green Preservation Society*, Special Deluxe Edition (Sanctuary Records, 2004).

18 Daniel Rachel, *The Art of Noise: Conversations with Great Songwriters* (New York, 2013), p. 8.

19 Ibid., p. 14.

20 Ray Davies interviewed by Chris Ingham, 'Ten Questions for Ray Davies', *Mojo* (April 1997), available at www.rocksbackpages.com, accessed 15 June 2018.

21 Frith, *Performing Rites*, p. 171.

22 Ray Davies interviewed by Johnny Black, 'Ray Davies: Sadness and a Kind of Fame', *Sunday Times* (18 March 1984), available at www.rocksbackpages.com, accessed 15 June 2018. On the construction of personas in Davies's songs, see Matthew Gelbart, 'Persona and Voice in the Kinks' Songs of the Late 1960s', *Journal of the Royal Musical Association*, CXXVIII/2 (2003), pp. 200–241.

23 Janet Maslin, 'Something Else by the Kinks', in *Stranded: Rock and Roll for a Desert Island*, ed. Greil Marcus (New York, 1979), pp. 100–107: p. 102.

24 R. Davies, *X-Ray*, p. 338.

1 The North London Post-war Affluent Society Blues

1 Johnny Rogan, *Ray Davies: A Complicated Life* (London, 2016), pp. 51–3; Ray Davies, *X-Ray: The Unauthorized Autobiography* (London, 1994), pp. 64–5; Dave Davies, *Kink: An Autobiography* (New York, 1996), p. 16.

2 Jean Delire, dir., *Low Light and Blue Smoke: Big Bill Blues* (Kaleidoscope, 1956).

3 R. Davies *X-Ray*, p. 69; Julien Temple, dir., *Ray Davies: Imaginary Man* (BBC One, 2010). Dave has also said that Broonzy was 'a big, big influence, because of the grit'. Dave Davies interviewed by Richie Unterberger, 'Dave Davies: Face to Face', *Ugly Things*, 38 (2014), pp. 5–21: p. 6.

4 Ray Davies interviewed by Will Hodgkinson, 'Home Entertainment', www.guardian.com, 17 May 2002.

5 *The Davies Diaries*, ep. 3, BBC Radio 2, 23 November 2000.

6 Quoted in Rogan, *Ray Davies*, p. 91.

7 Ray Davies interviewed by Pat Gilbert, 'The Story of My Life', *Mojo* (March 2017).

8 Ray Davies, *Americana: The Kinks, the Riff, the Road: The Story* (New York, 2013), p. 34.

9 Rogan, *Ray Davies*, p. 11.

10 Peter Willmott and Michael Young, *Family and Class in a London Suburb* (London, 1960), p. vii.

11 Quoted in Rogan, *Ray Davies*, p. 169.

12 Peter Willmott and Michael Young, *Family and Kinship in East London* (London, 1957), p. xviii.

13 Richard Hoggart, *The Uses of Literacy: Changing Patterns in English Mass Culture* (Fair Lawn, NJ, 1957), p. 32.

14 R. Davies, *Americana*, pp. 38–9; Rogan, *Ray Davies*, pp. 23–4.

15 Temple, dir., *Ray Davies: Imaginary Man*.

16 Rogan, *Ray Davies*, p. 59.

17 Oliver Double, *Britain Had Talent: A History of Variety Theatre* (London, 2012), pp. 82–3.

18 Roberta Freund Schwartz, *How Britain Got the Blues: The Transformation and Reception of American Blues Style in the United Kingdom* (Aldershot, 2007), pp. 2–3.

19 Double, *Britain Had Talent*, p. 63.

20 John Chilton, *The Song of the Hawk: The Life and Recordings of Coleman Hawkins* (Ann Arbor, MI, 1990), pp. 150–51.

21 Stuart Nicholson, *Ella Fitzgerald: A Biography of the First Lady of Jazz* (New York, 2004), pp. 113–14.

22 Double, *Britain Had Talent*, p. 63.

23 Schwartz, *How Britain Got the Blues*, pp. 9–11.

24 On the impact of American rock 'n' roll among working-class British teens, see David Simonelli, *Working Class Heroes: Rock Music and British Society in the 1960s and 1970s* (Lanham, MD, 2013), pp. 6–17.

25 Data from Paul Addison, *No Turning Back: The Peacetime Revolutions of Post-war Britain* (New York, 2010), p. 177; and Steve Humphries and John Taylor, *The Making of Modern London: 1945–1985* (London, 1986), p. 94.

26 Addison, *No Turning Back*, p. 177.

27 Rogan, *Ray Davies*, pp. 52–3. In Dave's memory it was his mother who lent him the £7 for a down payment on the guitar, but in any case such an extravagant purchase was only possible thanks to cheaper consumer goods and the availability of hire-purchase options. See Nick Hasted, *You Really Got Me: The Story of the Kinks* (London, 2013), p. 11.

28 Edward Royle, 'Trends in Post-war British Social History', in *Understanding Post-war British Society*, ed. James Obelkevich and Peter Catterall (London, 1994), pp. 9–18: p. 13.

29 Colin MacInnes, *England, Half English* (New York, 1961), p. 47.

30 Rogan, *Ray Davies*, p. 129; Doug Hinman, *The Kinks: All Day and All of the Night* (San Francisco, CA, 2004), p. 10; Hasted, *You Really Got Me*, p. 16.

31 Schwartz, *How Britain Got the Blues*, p. 28.

32 Ibid., p. 45.

33 Nik Cohn, *Awopbopaloobop Alopbamboom: The Golden Age of Rock* (New York, 1996), p. 16.

34 Schwartz, *How Britain Got the Blues*, p. 65.

35 Ibid., p. 66.

36 Billy Bragg, *Roots, Radicals and Rockers: How Skiffle Changed the World* (London, 2017), p. 389; Rogan, *Ray Davies*, p. 129.

37 Schwartz, *How Britain Got the Blues*, p. 89.

38 Ibid., p. 39.

39 Ibid., p. 77.

40 Ibid., p. 40.

41 Quoted in Simon Frith, *Sound Effects: Youth, Leisure, and the Politics of Rock'n'Roll* (New York, 1981), pp. 19–20.

42 Quoted in Schwartz, *How Britain Got the Blues*, p. 74.

43 Ibid.

44 Frith, *Sound Effects*, p. 20.

45 'Big Bill Blues', as it was sometimes called, first appeared on *This Wonderful World* on 15 September 1958. It proved so popular that it was included on many additional episodes of the programme, including twice more in 1958. Programme listing, John Grierson Collection, GB 559 G, University of Stirling, G8.1.1.

46 Statement by Humphrey Lyttleton on Bill Broonzy,
   11 September 1958, John Grierson Collection, G8.6.015.
47 R. Davies, *X-Ray*, p. 146.
48 Temple, dir., *Ray Davies: Imaginary Man*.
49 Hinman, *The Kinks*, p. 6.
50 Rogan, *Ray Davies*, p. 50.
51 R. Davies, *X-Ray*, p. 64.
52 Unterberger, 'Dave Davies', p. 6.
53 Rogan, *Ray Davies*, pp. 50, 137.
54 '12-page special! We choose the Top 12 best Kinks songs for Q's
   Classic Songwriter to pick apart for your delectation', *Q Magazine*,
   29 November 2016, available at www.pressreader.com, accessed
   19 January 2018.
55 Quoted in Hasted, *You Really Got Me*, p. 24.
56 Quoted in Brian Harrison, *Seeking a Role: The United Kingdom,
   1951-1970* (Oxford, 2009), p. 477.

2 The Kinks vs Swinging London

1 Dave Davies, *Kink: An Autobiography* (New York, 1996), p. 41.
2 Such speculation has generally centred on Robert Wace, one of the
   band's two managers, but Davies has also said that it was inspired by
   a snobbish hotel guest in Torquay who once invited him to play golf,
   inadvertently stoking Davies's fear that he was losing his working-
   class roots. On Davies's affection for Terry-Thomas, see Jon Savage,
   'Ray Davies: The Jon Savage Interviews', *Ugly Things*, 30 (2010),
   pp. 9–26: p. 15.
3 Charles Dickens, *The Old Curiosity Shop* (Oxford, 1951), pp. 1–2.
4 Charles Dickens, *The Uncommercial Traveller, and Additional Christmas
   Stories* (Boston, MA, 1877), p. 65.
5 Ray Davies, *X-Ray: The Unauthorized Autobiography* (London, 1994),
   p. 53.
6 Ray Davies, *Americana: The Kinks, the Riff, the Road: The Story*
   (New York, 2013), p. 71.
7 John Killham, 'Pickwick: Dickens and the Art of Fiction', in *Dickens
   and the Twentieth Century*, ed. John Gross and Gabriel Pearson
   (London, 1962), pp. 35–47: p. 47.
8 D. Davies, *Kink*, p. 48.
9 Quoted in Johnny Rogan, *Ray Davies: A Complicated Life*
   (London, 2016), p. 258.
10 D. Davies, *Kink*, p. 101.

11 Patsy Puttnam quoted in Shawn Levy, *Ready, Steady, Go! The Smashing Rise and Giddy Fall of Swinging London* (New York, 2002), p. 275.
12 R. Davies, *X-Ray*, p. 239.
13 Quoted in Rogan, *Ray Davies*, p. 223.
14 Richie Unterberger, 'Dave Davies: Face to Face', *Ugly Things*, 38 (2014), pp. 5–21: p. 7.
15 Doug Hinman, *The Kinks: All Day and All of the Night* (San Francisco, CA, 2004), pp. 59–60.
16 R. Davies, *Americana*, p. 49.
17 Andy Miller, liner notes for the Kinks, *The Kinks Are the Village Green Preservation Society*, Special Deluxe Edition (Sanctuary Records, 2004).
18 Julien Temple, dir., *Ray Davies: Imaginary Man* (BBC One, 2010).
19 Simon Frith, *Sound Effects: Youth, Leisure, and the Politics of Rock'n'Roll* (New York, 1981); David Simonelli, *Working Class Heroes: Rock Music and British Society in the 1960s and 1970s* (Lanham, MD, 2013).
20 R. Davies, *X-Ray*, pp. 350–51.
21 Ray Davies interviewed by Keith Altham, 'New Sounding Kinks', *New Musical Express*, 24 December 1965, available at www.rocksbackpages.com, accessed 20 May 2018.
22 Quoted in Rogan, *Ray Davies*, p. 248.
23 R. Davies, *X-Ray*, pp. 311–12.
24 'You Can Walk Across It on the Grass', *Time*, LXXXVII/15 (1966), pp. 38–45.
25 On the use of humour in the Kinks' music, see Carey Fleiner, *The Kinks: A Thoroughly English Phenomenon* (Lanham, MD, 2017), pp. 61–81.
26 Rogan, *Ray Davies*, p. 256.
27 Quoted in Jon Savage, *The Kinks: The Official Biography* (London, 1984), pp. 64–5.
28 Ray Davies interviewed by Jon Savage, 'Ray Davies', p. 17.
29 D. Davies, *Kink*, p. 89.
30 Rogan, *Ray Davies*, pp. 74, 143.
31 Ray Davies interviewed by Keith Altham, 'Kinks Don't Mind "Formby Quartet" Tag', *New Musical Express*, 18 March 1966, available at www.rocksbackpages.com, accessed 15 June 2018.
32 Rogan, *Ray Davies*, p. 257; Hinman, *The Kinks*, p. 111.
33 *The Davies Diaries*, ep. 3, BBC Radio 2, 30 November 2000.
34 Hinman, *The Kinks*, pp. 84–5.

35 Quoted in Savage, *The Kinks*, p. 96.
36 Henry Fairlie, 'Britain Seems Willing to Sink Giggling into the Sea', *New York Times Magazine*, 12 June 1966.
37 See for example Anthony Hartley, *A State of England* (London, 1963), Paul Einzig, *Decline and Fall? Britain's Crisis in the Sixties* (London, 1969), and the series of books titled *What's Wrong with Britain?*, published by Penguin prior to the 1964 general election.
38 Piri Halasz, 'Transition from Mystery into History: How the Internet Revived My Faith in "Swinging London"', *Independent Scholar*, 1 (December 2015), pp. 3–19.
39 D. Davies, *Kink*, p. 100.
40 Judith R. Walkowitz, *City of Dreadful Delight: Narratives of Sexual Danger in Late-Victorian London* (Chicago, IL, 1992).
41 William Wycherley, *The Country Wife*, in [*The Plays of*] *William Wycherley*, ed. W. C. Ward (London, 1893), pp. 333, 359.
42 Laura J. Rosenthal, 'Staging London in the Restoration and Eighteenth Century', in *The Cambridge Companion to the Literature of London*, ed. Lawrence Manley (Cambridge, 2011), pp. 85–101: p. 87.
43 Savage, *The Kinks*, p. 81.
44 'A Girl Comes to London', *Special Enquiry*, series 5, produced by Anthony de Lotbinière (British Broadcasting Corporation, 24 October 1956).
45 Quoted in Levy, *Ready, Steady, Go!*, p. 27.
46 Ibid., p. 20.
47 Arthur Marwick, 'Class', in *A Companion to Contemporary Britain, 1939–2000*, ed. Paul Addison and Harriet Jones (Oxford, 2005), pp. 76–92: p. 83.
48 Paul Addison, *No Turning Back: The Peacetime Revolutions of Post-war Britain* (Oxford, 2010), pp. 183–5.
49 Benjamin Disraeli, *Sybil; or, The Two Nations*, vol. I (London, 1845), p. 149.
50 Addison, *No Turning Back*, p. 181.
51 R. Davies, *X-Ray*, p. 284.
52 Ray Davies interviewed by Will Hodgkinson, 'The Conversation: America, You Really Got Me', *The Times: Saturday Review*, 28 September 2013, p. 8.
53 Paul Williams, 'The Kinks: Face to Face', *Crawdaddy*, March 1967, available at www.rocksbackpages.com, accessed 28 May 2018.
54 Savage, *The Kinks*, p. 71.
55 R. Davies, *X-Ray*, p. 285. Davies's own party-political loyalties have long been a matter of uncertainty. While he has often stressed his

socialist roots and his hatred of extremism on the left or right, he has also given mixed signals about which political party he supports. In his 2013 memoir *Americana* (p. 9), he says that he 'was never swayed to become conservative or Tory' and 'remained a staunch Labour supporter even in the mid-1990s'. However, four years later he told *The Quietus* that he had 'never voted' because he hadn't 'found a political party that adequately expresses how I feel about the world'. Ray Davies interviewed by Patrick Clarke, 'Amended Legacy: The Kinks' Ray Davies Interviewed', www.thequietus.com, 11 April 2017. Keith Gildart has identified three distinct strands of political engagement in Davies's songs, which sometimes appear separately and sometimes simultaneously: 'Patriotic Conservative', 'Orwellian Socialist' and 'Working-class Populist'. See Keith Gildart, 'From "Dead End Streets" to "Shangri Las": Negotiating Social Class and Post-war Politics with Ray Davies and the Kinks', *Contemporary British History*, XXVI/3 (2012), pp. 273–98.

56 Rogan, *Ray Davies*, p. 283.

57 This is the interpretation preferred by Thomas Kitts. See Thomas M. Kitts, *Ray Davies: Not Like Everybody Else* (New York and London, 2008), p. 73.

3 Ready, Steady, Stop! (or, Rock Music as Historic Preservation)

1 Johnny Rogan, *Ray Davies: A Complicated Life* (London, 2016), p. 347.

2 *The Davies Diaries*, ep. 5, BBC Radio 2, 21 December 2000.

3 Julien Temple, dir., *Ray Davies: Imaginary Man* (BBC One, 2010).

4 Doug Hinman, *The Kinks: All Day and All of the Night* (San Francisco, CA, 2004), pp. 92, 110–18.

5 On the affinities between Davies and the English Romantic tradition, see Michael J. Kraus, 'The Greatest Rock Star of the 19th Century: Ray Davies, Romanticism, and the Art of Being English', *Popular Music and Society*, XXIX/2 (2006), pp. 201–12; and Thomas M. Kitts, *Ray Davies: Not Like Everybody Else* (New York and London, 2008), pp. 82–101, 115–16.

6 Nik Cohn, *Awopbopaloobop Alopbamboom: The Golden Age of Rock* (New York, 1996), p. 166.

7 Edward Royle, 'Trends in Post-war British Social History', in *Understanding Post-war British Society*, ed. James Obelkevich and Peter Catterall (London, 1994), pp. 9–18: p. 9.

8 Dave Davies, *Kink: An Autobiography* (New York, 1996), p. 106.

9 Peter Willmott and Michael Young, *Family and Kinship in East London* (London, 1957), p. 10.

10 Ferdynand Zweig, *The Worker in an Affluent Society: Family Life and Industry* (New York, 1961), pp. 23–30.

11 Ibid., p. 107.

12 Anthony Sampson, *The New Anatomy of Britain* (London, 1971), p. 441.

13 Dick Hebdige, *Subculture: The Meaning of Style* (London, 1979), p. 74. See also Simon Frith, *Sound Effects: Youth, Leisure, and the Politics of Rock'n'Roll* (New York, 1981), p. 263.

14 Joe Boyd, *White Bicycles: Making Music in the 1960s* (London, 2005), p. 66.

15 Brian Harrison, *Seeking a Role: The United Kingdom, 1951–1970* (Oxford, 2009), p. 136.

16 J. H. Westergaard, 'Sociology: The Myth of Classlessness', in *Ideology in Social Science: Readings in Critical Social Theory*, ed. Robin Blackburn (New York, 1972), pp. 119–63: p. 146.

17 Jerry White, *The Worst Street in North London: Campbell Bunk, Islington, between the Wars* (London, 1986), p. 82.

18 Paul Addison, *No Turning Back: The Peacetime Revolutions of Post-war Britain* (Oxford, 2010), pp. 234–5.

19 Quoted in Dominic Sandbrook, *The Great British Dream Factory: The Strange History of Our National Imagination* (London, 2015), p. 292.

20 Ibid., pp. 290, 301.

21 Quoted in Owen Hatherley, *The Ministry of Nostalgia* (London, 2016), p. 1.

22 Louis MacNeice, 'Autumn Journal', Canto III, in Louis MacNeice, *Collected Poems*, ed. Peter McDonald (London, 2007), pp. 101–64: p. 105.

23 '12-page special! We choose the Top 12 best Kinks songs for Q's Classic Songwriter to pick apart for your delectation', Q *Magazine*, www.pressreader.com, 29 November 2016.

24 Ibid.

25 '*Eye to Eye* Presents: The More We Are Together', written and produced by Stephen Hearst, BBC Television, 7 March 1958.

26 See for example Elizabeth Field, 'Food and Drink Imagery in the Kinks' Music, 1965–94', in *Food in the Arts: Proceedings of the Oxford Symposium on Food and Cookery, 1998*, ed. Harlan Walker (Totnes, 1999), pp. 73–83; and Ray Davies, *X-Ray* (London, 1994), p. 79.

27 Quoted in Field, 'Food', p. 75.

28 Ibid.

29 Sandbrook, *The Great British Dream Factory*, p. 301.
30 For a thoughtful examination of Davies's incorporation of music-hall sounds and techniques, see Patricia Gordon Sullivan, '"Let's Have a Go at It": The British Music Hall and the Kinks', in *Living on a Thin Line: Crossing Aesthetic Borders with the Kinks*, ed. Thomas M. Kitts and Michael J. Kraus (Rumford, RI, 2002), pp. 80–99.
31 Ray Davies interviewed by Keith Altham, 'Kinks Don't Mind "Formby Quartet" Tag', *New Musical Express*, 18 March 1966, available at www.rocksbackpages.com, accessed 15 June 2018.
32 Richard Hoggart, *The Uses of Literacy: Changing Patterns in English Mass Culture* (Fair Lawn, NJ, 1957), p. 130.
33 Quoted in Hinman, *Kinks*, p. 121.
34 Temple, dir., *Ray Davies: Imaginary Man*.
35 For an excellent analysis that identifies many literary resonances in addition to those mentioned here, see Andy Miller, *The Kinks Are the Village Green Preservation Society*, 33¹⁄₃ series (New York, 2003).
36 Ray Davies interviewed by Jonathan Cott, 'Afternoon Tea with Ray Davies', *Rolling Stone*, 26 November 1970, pp. 30–31: p. 31.
37 Dylan Thomas, *Under Milk Wood: A Play for Voices* (New York, 1954), p. 3.
38 Raymond Williams, *The Country and the City* (New York, 1973), p. 165.
39 Quoted in Jon Savage, *The Kinks: The Official Biography* (London, 1984), p. 101.
40 *Davies Diaries*, ep. 5.
41 Savage, *The Kinks*, p. 102. See also David Simonelli, *Working Class Heroes: Rock Music and British Society in the 1960s and 1970s* (Lanham, MD, 2013), p. 150.
42 Michael Mooradian Lupro, 'Preserving the Old Ways, Protecting the New: Post-war British Urban Planning in *The Kinks Are the Village Green Preservation Society*', *Popular Music and Society*, XXIX/2 (2006), pp. 189–200: p. 197. See also Raphael Costambeys-Kempczynski, 'Preservation Society', in *Preserving the Sixties: Britain and the 'Decade of Protest'*, ed. Trevor Harris and Monia O'Brien Castro (New York, 2014), pp. 173–91; Savage, *The Kinks*, pp. 101–2; Irene Morra, *Britishness, Popular Music, and National Identity: The Making of Modern Britain* (New York, 2014), pp. 164–6; and Nick Baxter-Moore, '"This Is Where I Belong": Identity, Social Class, and the Nostalgic Englishness of Ray Davies and the Kinks', *Popular Music and Society*, XXIX/2 (2006), pp. 145–65.
43 Quoted in Daniel Rachel, *The Art of Noise: Conversations with Great Songwriters* (New York, 2013), p. 9.

44 For a subtle analysis of Davies's engagement with nostalgia, which argues that his interest is more in recovering a lost home than in revelling in a romanticized English past, see Carey Fleiner, *The Kinks: A Thoroughly English Phenomenon* (Lanham, MD, 2017), pp. 121–40.

45 My argument complements that of Barry Faulk that *Village Green* represented a modernist move by Davies to fashion himself into a 'rock auteur'. However, where Faulk explicitly downplays the 'content' of the album in order to focus on its sonic forms, I focus on the lyrical devices and musical appropriations that give the album its distinctly Pop art qualities. Barry J. Faulk, *British Rock Modernism, 1967–1977: The Story of Music Hall in Rock* (London and New York, 2010), pp. 105–27.

46 George Melly, *Revolt into Style: The Pop Arts* (Garden City, NY, 1971), p. 15.

47 See Ariel Dorfman and Armand Mattelart, *How to Read Donald Duck: Imperialist Ideology in the Disney Comic* (New York, 1991).

48 Ray Davies interviewed by Keith Altham, 'The Kinks: Kinks Have Problems', *New Musical Express*, 3 December 1966, www.rocksbackpages.com, accessed 28 May 2018.

49 Lawrence Alloway, 'The Long Front of Culture', *Cambridge Opinion*, 17 (1959), p. 25.

50 Robert Hewison, *Too Much: Art and Society in the Sixties, 1960–75* (London, 1986), p. 46.

51 Melly, *Revolt into Style*, p. 14.

52 Ray Davies, *X-Ray*, p. 79. On the influence of art school on Davies, see Thomas M. Kitts, *Ray Davies: Not Like Everybody Else* (New York and London, 2008), pp. 22–8.

53 Harrison, *Seeking a Role*, p. 401.

54 Years later Peter Blake recognized the affinities between his work and that of the Kinks. As a guest on the BBC radio programme *My Top Twelve* in 1983, he said that 'he liked the Kinks because he shared Ray Davies's obsession with an imagery taken from everyday elements of British culture – London sunsets, the village green, the taxman, the commuter, the followers of fashion'. Simon Frith and Howard Horne, *Art into Pop* (London, 1987), p. 56.

55 Ibid., p. 107.

56 Jocelyn Brooke, *Ronald Firbank and John Betjeman* (London, 1962), p. 40.

57 John Betjeman, 'Inexpensive Progress', in *Collected Poems*, 4th edn (London, 1988), pp. 286–7.

58 John Betjeman, 'The Town Clerk's Views', ibid., pp. 144–7.

59 Brooke, *Ronald Firbank*, p. 41.

60 Rogan, *Ray Davies*, p. 375.

61 John Betjeman, 'Conclusion' (*Town Tours* series, West of England Programme, 24 June 1937), in John Betjeman, *Trains and Buttered Toast: Selected Radio Talks*, ed. Stephen Games (London, 2006), pp. 82–6: p. 83.

62 Christopher Inwood, *A History of London* (New York, 1998), p. 847.

63 Philip Larkin, 'Going, Going' (1972), www.poeticous.com, accessed 3 August 2018.

64 R. Davies, *X-Ray*, p. 312.

65 John Betjeman, 'Coming Home, or England Revisited' (BBC Home Service, 29 February 1943), in *Trains and Buttered Toast*, ed. Games, pp. 134–9: pp. 138–9.

66 Quoted in Harrison, *Seeking a Role*, p. 149.

67 Paul Readman, 'Preserving the English Landscape, *c.* 1870–1914', *Cultural and Social History*, v/2 (2008), pp. 197–218: p. 200.

68 John Pendlebury, *Conservation in the Age of Consensus* (Abingdon, 2009), p. 39.

69 C.E.M. Joad, *The Horrors of the Countryside* (London, 1931), p. 16.

70 Readman, 'Preserving the English Landscape', p. 210.

71 Brian Bailey, *The English Village Green* (London, 1985), pp. 32–52.

72 John Clare, 'Remembrances', in *Clare: Selected Poems and Prose*, ed. Eric Robinson and Geoffrey Summerfield (Oxford, 1966), pp. 193–6.

73 John Clare, 'The Village Minstrel', quoted in Williams, *The Country*, p. 136.

74 Inwood, *History*, pp. 883–4.

75 Brian Anson, *I'll Fight You for It! Behind the Struggle for Covent Garden* (London, 1981), p. xv.

76 Quoted in Nick Hasted, *You Really Got Me: The Story of the Kinks* (London, 2013), p. 129.

4 The Glory of Being Boring

1 Quoted in Johnny Rogan, *Ray Davies: A Complicated Life* (London, 2016), p. 371.

2 Ibid., p. 374; Thomas Kitts, *Ray Davies: Not Like Everybody Else* (New York and London, 2008), p. 127.

3 Alan A. Jackson, *Semi-detached London: Suburban Development, Life and Transport, 1900–1939*, 2nd edn (Didcot, 1991), pp. 137–8. See also Mark Clapson, *Invincible Green Suburbs, Brave New Towns:*

Social Change and Urban Dispersal in Postwar England (Manchester, 1998), pp. 121–55.

4 Simon Rycroft, *A Cultural Geography of London, 1950–1974* (Farnham, 2011), p. 43.

5 Julian Mitchell, *The White Father* (New York, 1964), p. 295.

6 Anthony Sampson, *Anatomy of Britain* (New York, 1962), p. 633.

7 Ray Davies, *X-Ray: The Unauthorized Autobiography* (London, 1994), p. 52.

8 Quoted in Rogan, *Ray Davies*, p. 48.

9 R. Davies, *X-Ray*, p. 366.

10 Doug Hinman, *The Kinks: All Day and All of the Night* (San Francisco, CA, 2004), pp. 132–3.

11 This interpretation is the opposite of the position recently advanced by Irene Morra, who sees *Arthur* as a 'reactionary' album that repeats 'long-standing clichés of a simple, ignorant, and dutiful working class' and reinforces 'class stereotypes from an establishment position'. Such an interpretation ignores the multivocal nature of the album and the ambivalence that has always informed Davies's writing. Irene Morra, *Britishness, Popular Music, and National Identity: The Making of Modern Britain* (New York, 2014), p. 168.

12 T. E. Kebbel, ed., *Selected Speeches of the Late Right Honourable the Earl of Beaconsfield*, vol. II (London, 1882), pp. 527–8.

13 Dave Davies, *Kink: An Autobiography* (New York, 1996), p. 119.

14 Ferdynand Zweig, *The Worker in an Affluent Society: Family Life and Industry* (New York, 1961), p. 106.

15 Richard Hoggart, *The Uses of Literacy: Changing Patterns in English Mass Culture* (Fair Lawn, NJ, 1957), p. 130.

16 Quoted in Peter Scott, *The Making of the Modern British Home: The Suburban Semi and Family Life between the Wars* (Oxford, 2013), p. 63.

17 Clapson, *Invincible Green Suburbs*, pp. 24–5.

18 Lynne Hapgood, *Margins of Desire: The Suburbs in Fiction and Culture, 1880–1925* (Manchester, 2005), p. 190.

19 George and Weedon Grossmith, *The Diary of a Nobody* (New York, 1892).

20 C.F.G. Masterman, *The Condition of England* (London, 1909), pp. 76–7.

21 Hapgood, *Margins of Desire*, pp. 60–89, 195.

22 Edward Thomas, *Heart of England* (London, 1906), p. 1.

23 Ibid., p. 3.

24 David Matless, *Landscape and Englishness* (London, 2016), p. 59.

25 T.W.H. Crosland, *The Suburbans* (London, 1905), p. 50.

26 Todd Kuchta, *Semi-detached Empire: Suburbia and the Colonization of Britain, 1880 to the Present* (Charlottesville, VA, 2010), p. 7.

27 Elliott Evans Mills, *The Decline and Fall of the British Empire* (Oxford, 1905), p. 2.

28 John Betjeman, 'Swindon' (*Town Tours* series, West of England Programme, 8 May 1937), in John Betjeman, *Trains and Buttered Toast: Selected Radio Talks*, ed. Stephen Games (London, 2006), pp. 67–71: p. 69.

29 C.E.M. Joad, *The Horrors of the Countryside* (London, 1931), p. 22.

30 John Betjeman, 'Slough', in *Collected Poems*, 4th edn (London, 1988), pp. 20–21.

31 W. H. Auden, 'Letter to Lord Byron', in *Letters from Iceland* (London, 1937), p. 54.

32 George Orwell, *Coming Up for Air* (London, 1939), p. 10.

33 Some 25 per cent of urban workers moved to suburban housing of various sorts between the wars. Scott, *The Making*, p. 10.

34 Ian Nairn, 'Subtopia', *Architectural Review*, CXVII/702 (1955), pp. 364–71: p. 366.

35 Ibid., p. 367.

36 *A City Crowned with Green*, produced by Nancy Thomas, BBC One, 12 June 1964.

37 Ray Davies interviewed by Jonathan Cott, 'Afternoon Tea with Ray Davies', *Rolling Stone*, 26 November 1970, pp. 30–31: p. 31.

38 Nick Hasted, *You Really Got Me: The Story of the Kinks* (London, 2013), p. 144.

39 D. Davies, *Kink*, pp. 118–19.

40 Arnold Bennett, *A Man from the North* (London, 1898), pp. 100–101. This passage is partially quoted in John Carey, *The Intellectuals and the Masses: Pride and Prejudice among the Literary Intelligentsia, 1880–1939* (New York, 1992), p. 161.

41 Hapgood, *Margins of Desire*, p. 220.

42 Quoted ibid., p. 178.

43 Quoted in Ged Pope, *Reading London's Suburbs: From Charles Dickens to Zadie Smith* (Basingstoke, 2015), p. 57.

44 Charles Dickens, *Great Expectations* (New York, 2001), p. 186. In 1927 the architect E. M. Trowbridge brought Dickens's fantasy to life by designing a semi-detached castle, complete with battlements and round towers, in Kingsbury, Middlesex. John Betjeman visited it in his *Metro-Land* documentary (BBC One, 1973).

45 Hapgood, *Margins of Desire*, p. 40.

46 R. C. Sherriff, *Greengates* (New York, 1936), p. 174.

47 John Betjeman, 'Some Comments in Wartime' (BBC Home Service, 4 July 1940), in *Trains and Buttered Toast*, ed. Games, pp. 129–33: p. 131.

48 J. M. Richards, *The Castles on the Ground: The Anatomy of Suburbia*, 2nd edn (London, 1973), p. 17.

49 Ibid., p. 20.

50 Ibid., p. 36.

51 Ibid., p. 55.

52 Quoted ibid., pp. 256–7.

53 Zweig, *The Worker*, p. 207.

54 John Burnett, *A Social History of Housing, 1815–1985*, 2nd edn (London, 1986), pp. 236–7.

55 Jackson, *Semi-detached London*, p. 137.

56 Jerry White, *The Worst Street in North London: Campbell Bunk, Islington, between the Wars* (London, 1986), p. 160.

57 *Somewhere Decent to Live*, directed by Ronald E. Haddock, Greater London Council, 1967, London Metropolitan Archives, GLC/DG/PRB/11/03/001.

5 Muswell Hillbillies vs Big Brother

1 Muriel Box, dir., *The Happy Family* (London Independent Producers, 1952).

2 Quoted in Lionel Esher, *A Broken Wave: The Rebuilding of England, 1940–1980* (London, 1981), p. 49.

3 Ray Davies interviewed by Alex Bellotti, 'Ray Davies Likes to Keep Accent on Authenticity', *Ham and High Etcetera*, www.hamhigh. co.uk, 28 June 2013.

4 Julien Temple, dir., *Ray Davies: Imaginary Man* (BBC One, 2010). Although 'Lola's' sexual politics might seem a little retrograde by twenty-first-century standards, its spirit was directly opposed to the violent homophobia that characterized much working-class youth culture at the time, which often took the form of violent 'queer-bashings' by skinhead gangs.

5 Johnny Rogan, *Ray Davies: A Complicated Life* (London, 2016), p. 402.

6 Quoted in Nick Hasted, *You Really Got Me: The Story of the Kinks* (London, 2013), p. 160.

7 Henry Fairlie, 'Political Commentary', *The Spectator*, 21 September 1955, pp. 379–80: p. 380.

8 Hugh Thomas, 'The Establishment and Society', in *The Establishment*, ed. Hugh Thomas (London, 1959), pp. 9–20: p. 20.

9 Ibid., p. 15.

10 Ray Davies, *X-Ray: The Unauthorized Autobiography* (London, 1994), p. 342.

11 Ibid.

12 Richard Hoggart, *The Uses of Literacy: Changing Patterns in English Mass Culture* (Fair Lawn, NJ, 1957), p. 62.

13 Davies, *X-Ray*, pp. 53–4.

14 Jon Savage, *The Kinks: The Official Biography* (London, 1984), p. 117; R. Davies, *X-Ray*, p. 73.

15 Jerry White, *The Worst Street in North London: Campbell Bunk, Islington, between the Wars* (London, 1986), p. 108.

16 Alan Sillitoe, *Saturday Night and Sunday Morning* (New York, 1992), p. 221.

17 John Burnett, *A Social History of Housing, 1815–1985*, 2nd edn (London, 1986), p. 292.

18 Ibid., p. 190.

19 Peter Scott, *The Making of the Modern British Home: The Suburban Semi and Family Life between the Wars* (Oxford, 2013), p. 238.

20 Ibid., p. 239.

21 Christopher Inwood, *A History of London* (New York, 1998), p. 846.

22 Carlos Pasini, dir., *Where the Houses Used to Be* (Thames Television, 1971).

23 John Stevenson, 'The Jerusalem that Failed? The Rebuilding of Post-war Britain', in *Britain since 1945*, ed. Terry Gourvish and Alan O'Day (Basingstoke, 1991), pp. 89–110: p. 101.

24 Pasini, dir., *Where the Houses Used to Be*.

25 Ibid.

26 Steve Humphries and John Taylor, *The Making of Modern London, 1945–1985* (London, 1986), pp. 156–7.

27 Esher, *A Broken Wave*, p. 80.

28 Humphries and Taylor, *Making of Modern London*, p. 158.

29 Alison Ravetz and Richard Turkington, *The Place of Home: English Domestic Environments, 1914–2000* (London, 1995), p. 59.

30 Ray Davies interviewed by Daniel Rachel, *The Art of Noise: Conversations with Great Songwriters* (New York, 2013), p. 19.

31 Ibid., p. 21. He also told this story to Nick Hasted (*You Really Got Me*, p. 173).

32 Ray Davies interviewed by Janis Schacht, 'Ray Davies Unravels the Muswell Puzzle', *Circus*, February 1972, p. 2.

33 R. Davies, *X-Ray*, p. 297.

34 Peter Willmott and Michael Young, *Family and Class in a London Suburb* (London, 1960), p. 61.

35 Stevenson, 'The Jerusalem that Failed?', p. 105.

36 Quoted in Brian Anson, *I'll Fight You for It! Behind the Struggle for Covent Garden* (London, 1981), p. 93.

37 David Wiggins, 'Revolt in the Cities', *The Times: Saturday Review* (3 April 1971), p. 19.

38 Nick Baxter-Moore, '"This Is Where I Belong": Identity, Social Class, and the Nostalgic Englishness of Ray Davies and the Kinks', *Popular Music and Society*, xxix/2 (2006), pp. 145–65. A similar argument appears in Keith Gildart, *Images of England through Popular Music: Class, Youth, and Rock 'n' Roll, 1955–1976* (Basingstoke, 2013), p. 144.

39 George Orwell, *The Road to Wigan Pier* (New York, 1958), p. 96.

40 Rachel, *Art of Noise*, p. 21.

41 Ray Davies interviewed by Chris Charlesworth, 'The Kinks: Muswell Hillbillies', *Melody Maker*, 25 December 1971, available at www.rocksbackpages.com, accessed 15 June 2018.

42 Quoted in Schacht, 'Ray Davies', p. 4.

43 Ian Watson, *Song and Democratic Culture in Britain: An Approach to Popular Culture in Social Movements* (London, 1983), p. 84.

44 Alan Wolfe, 'Democracy, Social Science, and Rationality: Reflections on Burke's *Reflections on the Revolution in France*', in Edmund Burke, *Reflections on the Revolution in France*, ed. Frank M. Turner (New Haven, CT, 2003), pp. 268–90: p. 276.

45 Edmund Burke, *Reflections on the Revolution in France* (London, 1910), p. 84.

46 Ibid., p. 83.

47 Stephen Haseler, *The English Tribe: Identity, Nation and Europe* (Basingstoke, 1996), p. 21.

48 J. A. Hobson, 'In Praise of Muddling Through: A Study of English Policy', *Harper's Monthly Magazine* (July 1926), pp. 177–84: p. 180.

49 Stanley Baldwin, 'England: At the Annual Dinner of the Royal Society of St George, at the Hotel Cecil, 6th May, 1924', in *On England and Other Addresses* (London, 1926), pp. 1–9.

50 J. B. Priestley, *Postscripts* (London, 1940), pp. 2–3.

51 J. B. Priestley, 'A Tribute to Britain', *Picture Post* (28 April 1945), pp. 14–17: pp. 15–16.

52 Ibid., p. 17.

53 The affinities between Priestley and Orwell have frequently been noted by scholars. See Peter Mandler, *The English National Character: The History of an Idea from Edmund Burke to Tony Blair* (New Haven, CT, 2006), p. 189; David Matless, *Landscape and Englishness* (London, 2016), pp. 270–71; and Haseler, *The English Tribe*, pp. 60–61.

54 George Orwell, *The English People* (New York, 1974), p. 8.
55 George Orwell, 'England, Your England', in *Facing Unpleasant Facts: Narrative Essays*, ed. James Packer (Boston, MA, and New York, 2009), pp. 109–38: p. 112.
56 Ibid.
57 Ibid., p. 113.
58 George Orwell, *Nineteen Eighty-four* (New York, 1949), p. 165.
59 Ibid., p. 82.
60 Temple, dir., *Ray Davies: Imaginary Man*.

Select Bibliography

Print

Addison, Paul, *No Turning Back: The Peacetime Revolutions of Post-war Britain* (Oxford, 2010)

Anson, Brian, *I'll Fight You for It! Behind the Struggle for Covent Garden* (London, 1981)

Baxter-Moore, Nick, '"This Is Where I Belong": Identity, Social Class, and the Nostalgic Englishness of Ray Davies and the Kinks', *Popular Music and Society*, XXIX/2 (2006), pp. 145–65

Betjeman, John, *Collected Poems*, 4th edn (London, 1988)

—, *Trains and Buttered Toast: Selected Radio Talks*, ed. Stephen Games (London, 2006)

Burke, Edmund, *Reflections on the Revolution in France* (London, 1910)

Burnett, John, *A Social History of Housing, 1815–1985*, 2nd edn (London, 1986)

Clapson, Mark, *Invincible Green Suburbs, Brave New Towns: Social Change and Urban Dispersal in Postwar England* (Manchester, 1998)

Cohn, Nik, *Awopbopaloobop Alopbamboom: The Golden Age of Rock* (New York, 1996)

Cott, Jonathan, 'Afternoon Tea with Ray Davies', *Rolling Stone*, 26 November 1970, pp. 30–31

Davies, Dave, *Kink: An Autobiography* (New York, 1996)

Davies, Ray, *Americana: The Kinks, the Riff, the Road: The Story* (New York, 2013)

—, *X-Ray* (London, 1994)

Double, Oliver, *Britain Had Talent: A History of Variety Theatre* (London, 2012)

Esher, Lionel, *A Broken Wave: The Rebuilding of England, 1940–1980* (London, 1981)

Fleiner, Carey, *The Kinks: A Thoroughly English Phenomenon* (Lanham, MD, 2017)

Frith, Simon, *Performing Rites: On the Value of Popular Music*
 (Cambridge, MA, 1996)
—, *Sound Effects: Youth, Leisure, and the Politics of Rock'n'Roll*
 (New York, 1981)
—, and Howard Horne, *Art into Pop* (London, 1987)
Gildart, Keith, 'From "Dead End Streets" to "Shangri Las": Negotiating
 Social Class and Post-war Politics with Ray Davies and the Kinks',
 Contemporary British History, XXVI/3 (2012), pp. 273–98
Grossmith, George and Weedon, *The Diary of a Nobody* (New York, 1892)
Hapgood, Lynne, *Margins of Desire: The Suburbs in Fiction and Culture,*
 1880–1925 (Manchester, 2005)
Harrison, Brian, *Seeking a Role: The United Kingdom, 1951–1970*
 (Oxford, 2009)
Haseler, Stephen, *The English Tribe: Identity, Nation and Europe*
 (Basingstoke, 1996)
Hasted, Nick, *You Really Got Me: The Story of the Kinks* (London, 2013)
Hinman, Doug, *The Kinks: All Day and All of the Night* (San Francisco,
 CA, 2004)
Hoggart, Richard, *The Uses of Literacy: Changing Patterns in English*
 Mass Culture (Fair Lawn, NJ, 1957)
Humphries, Steve, and John Taylor, *The Making of Modern London:*
 1945–1985 (London, 1986)
Inwood, Christopher, *A History of London* (New York, 1998)
Jackson, Alan A., *Semi-detached London: Suburban Development, Life*
 and Transport, 1900–1939, 2nd edn (Didcot, 1991)
Joad, C.E.M., *The Horrors of the Countryside* (London, 1931)
Kitts, Thomas M., *Ray Davies: Not Like Everybody Else* (New York and
 London, 2008)
—, and Michael J. Kraus, eds, *Living on a Thin Line: Crossing Aesthetic*
 Borders with the Kinks (Rumford, RI, 2002)
Kraus, Michael J., 'The Greatest Rock Star of the 19th Century: Ray
 Davies, Romanticism, and the Art of Being English', *Popular Music*
 and Society, XXIX/2 (2006), pp. 201–12
Levy, Shawn, *Ready, Steady, Go! The Smashing Rise and Giddy Fall*
 of Swinging London (New York, 2002)
Matless, David, *Landscape and Englishness* (London, 2016)
Melly, George, *Revolt into Style: The Pop Arts* (Garden City,
 NY, 1971)
Miller, Andy, *The Kinks Are the Village Green Preservation Society*, 33^1/$_3$
 series (New York, 2003)
Mitchell, Julian, *The White Father* (New York, 1964)

Morra, Irene, *Britishness, Popular Music, and National Identity: The Making of Modern Britain* (New York, 2014)

Orwell, George, *Coming Up for Air* (London, 1939)

—, *Nineteen Eighty-four* (New York, 1949)

Pope, Ged, *Reading London's Suburbs: From Charles Dickens to Zadie Smith* (Basingstoke, 2015)

Rachel, Daniel, *The Art of Noise: Conversations with Great Songwriters* (New York, 2013)

Readman, Paul, 'Preserving the English Landscape, *c.* 1870–1914', *Cultural and Social History*, v/2 (2008), pp. 197–218

Richards, J. M. *The Castles on the Ground: The Anatomy of Suburbia* (London, 1946)

Rogan, Johnny, *Ray Davies: A Complicated Life* (London, 2016)

Savage, Jon, *The Kinks: The Official Biography* (London, 1984)

Schwartz, Roberta Freund, *How Britain Got the Blues: The Transformation and Reception of American Blues Style in the United Kingdom* (Aldershot, 2007)

Scott, Peter, *The Making of the Modern British Home: The Suburban Semi and Family Life between the Wars* (Oxford, 2013)

Sillitoe, Alan, *Saturday Night and Sunday Morning* (New York, 1992)

Stevenson, John, 'The Jerusalem that Failed? The Rebuilding of Post-war Britain', in *Britain since 1945*, ed. Terry Gourvish and Alan O'Day (Basingstoke, 1991), pp. 89–110

Thomas, Dylan, *Under Milk Wood: A Play for Voices* (New York, 1954)

White, Jerry, *The Worst Street in North London: Campbell Bunk, Islington, between the Wars* (London, 1986)

Williams, Raymond, *The Country and the City* (New York, 1973)

Willmott, Peter, and Michael Young, *Family and Class in a London Suburb* (London, 1960)

—, *Family and Kinship in East London* (London, 1957)

Zweig, Ferdynand, *The Worker in an Affluent Society: Family Life and Industry* (New York, 1961)

Film and Television

A City Crowned with Green, produced by Nancy Thomas (BBC One, 12 June 1964)

'*Eye to Eye* Presents: The More We Are Together', written and produced by Stephen Hearst (BBC Television, 7 March 1958)

'A Girl Comes to London', *Special Enquiry*, series 5, produced by Anthony de Lotbinière (BBC Television, 24 October 1956)

The Happy Family, directed by Muriel Box (London Independent
  Producers, 1952)
Low Light and Blue Smoke: Big Bill Blues, directed by Jean Delire
  (Kaleidoscope, 1956)
Ray Davies: Imaginary Man, directed by Julien Temple (BBC One, 2010)
Where the Houses Used to Be, directed by Carlos Pasini (Thames
  Television, 1971)

Select Discography

Singles and EPs

'Long Tall Sally' / 'I Took My Baby Home', Pye (UK) / Cameo (U.S.), 1964

'You Still Want Me' / 'You Do Something to Me', Pye (UK), 1964

'You Really Got Me' / 'It's Alright', Pye (UK) / Reprise (U.S.), 1964

'All Day and All of the Night' / 'I Gotta Move', Pye (UK) / Reprise (U.S.), 1964

Kinksize Session EP, Pye (UK), 1964

'Tired of Waiting for You' / 'Come on Now', Pye (UK) / Reprise (U.S.), 1965

'Ev'rybody's Gonna Be Happy' / 'Who'll Be the Next in Line', Pye (UK) / Reprise (U.S., A/B sides reversed), 1965

'Set Me Free' / 'I Need You', Pye (UK) / Reprise (U.S.), 1965

'See My Friends' / 'Never Met a Girl like You Before', Pye (UK) / Reprise (U.S.), 1965

Kwyet Kinks EP, Pye (UK), 1965

'Till the End of the Day' / 'Where Have All the Good Times Gone', Pye (UK) / Reprise (U.S.), 1965 (UK) / 1966 (U.S.)

'Dedicated Follower of Fashion' / 'Sittin' on My Sofa', Pye (UK) / Reprise (U.S.), 1966

'Sunny Afternoon' / 'I'm Not Like Everybody Else', Pye (UK) / Reprise (U.S.), 1966

'Dead End Street' / 'Big Black Smoke', Pye (UK) / Reprise (U.S.), 1966

'Mister Pleasant' / 'Harry Rag', Reprise (U.S.), 1967

'Waterloo Sunset' / 'Act Nice and Gentle' (UK) / 'Two Sisters' (U.S.), Pye (UK) / Reprise (U.S.), 1967

'Death of a Clown' / 'Love Me Till the Sun Shines', Pye (UK) / Reprise (U.S.), 1967

'Autumn Almanac' / 'Mister Pleasant' (UK) / 'David Watts' (U.S.), Pye (UK) / Reprise (U.S.), 1967

'Wonderboy' / 'Polly', Pye (UK) / Reprise (U.S.), 1968

'Days' / 'She's Got Everything', Pye (UK) / Reprise (U.S.), 1968

'Starstruck' / 'Picture Book', Reprise (U.S.), 1969

'Plastic Man' / 'King Kong', Pye (UK), 1969

'Drivin'' / 'Mindless Child of Motherhood', Pye (UK), 1969

'Shangri-La' / 'This Man He Weeps Tonight', Pye (UK), 1969

'Victoria' / 'Mr Churchill Says' (UK) / 'Brainwashed' (U.S.), Pye (UK) /
    Reprise (U.S.), 1969

'Lola' / 'Berkeley Mews' (UK) / 'Mindless Child of Motherhood' (U.S.),
    Pye (UK) / Reprise (U.S.), 1970

'Apeman' / 'Rats', Pye (UK) / Reprise (U.S.), 1970

'20th Century Man' / 'Skin and Bone', RCA Victor (U.S.), 1971

'Supersonic Rocketship' / 'You Don't Know My Name', RCA Victor
    (UK/U.S.), 1972

'Celluloid Heroes' / 'Sitting in My Hotel', RCA Victor (UK/U.S.), 1972

'One of the Survivors' / 'Scrapheap City', RCA Victor (U.S.), 1973

'Sitting in the Midday Sun' / 'One of the Survivors' (UK) / 'Sweet Lady
    Genevieve' (U.S.), RCA Victor (UK/U.S.), 1973

'Sweet Lady Genevieve' / 'Sitting in My Hotel', RCA Victor (UK), 1973

'Money Talks' / 'Here Comes Flash', RCA Victor (U.S.), 1974

'Mirror of Love' / 'He's Evil', RCA Victor (UK/U.S.), 1974

'Holiday Romance' / 'Shepherds of the Nation', RCA Victor (UK), 1974

'Preservation' / 'Salvation Road', RCA Victor (U.S.), 1974

'Starmaker' / 'Ordinary People', RCA Victor (U.S.), 1974

'Ducks on the Wall' / 'Rush Hour Blues', RCA Victor (UK), 1975

'You Can't Stop the Music' / 'Have Another Drink', RCA Victor (UK), 1975

'I'm in Disgrace' / 'The Hard Way', RCA Victor (U.S.), 1976

'No More Looking Back' / 'Jack the Idiot Dunce' / 'The Hard Way', RCA
    Victor (UK), 1976

'Sleepwalker' / 'Full Moon', Arista (UK/U.S.), 1977

'Juke Box Music' / 'Sleepless Night' (UK) / 'Life Goes On' (U.S.),
    Arista (UK/U.S.), 1977

'Father Christmas' / 'Prince of the Punks', Arista (UK/U.S.), 1977

'A Rock 'n'Roll Fantasy / 'Artificial Light' (UK) / 'Live Life' (U.S.),
    Arista (UK/U.S.), 1978

'Live Life' / 'In a Foreign Land' (UK) / 'Black Messiah' (U.S.),
    Arista (UK/U.S.), 1978

'Black Messiah / 'Misfits', Arista (UK), 1978

'(Wish I Could Fly Like) Superman' / 'Low Budget', Arista (UK/U.S.), 1979

'A Gallon of Gas' / 'Low Budget', Arista (U.S.), 1979

'Catch Me Now I'm Falling' / 'Low Budget', Arista (U.S.), 1979

'Moving Pictures' / 'In a Space', Arista (UK), 1979
'Pressure' / 'National Health', Arista (UK), 1979
The Kinks Live EP, Arista (UK), 1980
'Destroyer' / 'Back to Front', Arista (U.S.), 1981
'Predictable' / 'Back to Front', Arista (UK), 1981
'Better Things' / 'Yo-Yo', Arista (U.S.), 1981
'Come Dancing' / 'Noise', Arista (UK/U.S.), 1982 (UK) / 1983 (U.S.)
'Don't Forget to Dance' / 'Bernadette', Arista (UK/U.S.), 1983
State of Confusion EP, Arista (UK), 1984
'Good Day' / 'Too Hot' / 'Don't Forget to Dance', Arista (UK), 1984
'Do It Again' / 'Guilty', Arista (UK/U.S.), 1984
'Summer's Gone' / 'Going Solo', Arista (U.S.), 1985
'Rock 'n' Roll Cities' / 'Welcome to Sleazy Town', MCA (U.S.), 1986
 'Lost and Found' / 'Killing Time', London (UK) / MCA (U.S.), 1987
'How Are You' / 'Working at the Factory', MCA (U.S.), 1987
'Down All the Days (Till 1992)' / 'You Really Got Me' live / 'Entertainment',
    London (UK), 1989
'How Do I Get Close' / 'Down All the Days (Till 1992)', London (UK),
    1990
'Did Ya' / 'I Gotta Move' live / 'Days' 2nd version / 'New World' / 'Look
    Through Any Doorway', Columbia (U.S.), 1991
'Scattered' / 'Hatred (A Duet)' / 'Days' 2nd version, Columbia (UK), 1993
'Only a Dream' / 'Somebody Stole My Car' / 'Babies', Columbia (UK),
    1993
Waterloo Sunset '94 EP, Konk/Grapevine (UK), 1994

Albums

Kinks, Pye (UK) / Reprise (U.S.), 1964
Kinda Kinks, Pye (UK) / Reprise (U.S.), 1965
Kinks-Size, Reprise (U.S.), 1965
Kinks Kinkdom, Reprise (U.S.), 1965
The Kink Kontroversy, Pye (UK) / Reprise (U.S.), 1965 (UK) / 1966 (U.S.)
The Kinks Greatest Hits, Reprise (U.S.), 1966
Face to Face, Pye (UK) / Reprise (U.S.), 1966
Something Else by The Kinks, Pye (UK) / Reprise (U.S.), 1967 (UK) / 1968 (U.S.)
The Kinks Live at Kelvin Hall, Pye (UK) / Reprise (U.S.), 1968 (UK) / 1967 (U.S.)
The Kinks Are the Village Green Preservation Society, Pye (UK) / Reprise
    (U.S.), 1968 (UK) / 1969 (U.S.)
Arthur (or, The Decline and Fall of the British Empire), Pye (UK) / Reprise
    (U.S.), 1969

The Kinks, Pye (UK), 1970

Lola Versus Powerman and the Moneygoround, Part One, Pye (UK) /
    Reprise (U.S.), 1970

Percy, Pye (UK), 1971

Muswell Hillbillies, RCA Victor (UK/U.S.), 1971

Everybody's in Show-Biz – Everybody's a Star, RCA Victor (UK/U.S.), 1972

Preservation Act 1, RCA Victor (UK/U.S.), 1973

The Great Lost Kinks Album, Reprise (U.S.), 1973

Preservation Act 2, RCA Victor (UK/U.S.), 1974

(The Kinks Present) A Soap Opera, RCA Victor (UK/U.S.), 1975

(The Kinks Present) Schoolboys in Disgrace, RCA Victor (UK/U.S.),
    1976 (UK) / 1975 (U.S.)

Sleepwalker, Arista (UK/U.S.), 1977

Misfits, Arista (UK/U.S.), 1978

Low Budget, Arista (UK/U.S.), 1979

One for the Road, Arista (UK/U.S.), 1980

Give the People What they Want, Arista (UK/U.S.), 1982 (UK) / 1981 (U.S.)

State of Confusion, Arista (UK/U.S.), 1983

Word of Mouth, Arista (UK/U.S.), 1984

Think Visual, London (UK) / MCA (U.S.), 1986

The Road, London (UK) / MCA (U.S.), 1988

UK Jive, London (UK) / MCA (U.S.), 1989

Phobia, Columbia (UK/U.S.), 1993

To the Bone, Konk (U.S.) / Guardian (UK), 1994 (UK) / 1996 (U.S.)

Acknowledgements

The origins of this book lie in my classrooms at Middle Tennessee State University. Several years ago I began introducing 'musical interludes' during my class on Britain in the twentieth century – a brief pause to allow me to catch my breath and my students to check their phones – and as I began searching online for songs to play, I kept coming upon tracks from the Kinks' 1969 album *Arthur (or, The Decline and Fall of the British Empire)*. I don't know how the students felt about it, but it made me extremely happy to be able to break up a lecture on the Second World War with 'Mr Churchill Says', or a discussion of interwar suburbia with 'Shangri-La' (I also played songs from the actual periods under discussion, of course). I had known about and admired the Kinks for years, but somehow this album had passed me by. Now I began digging deeper, and the deeper I dug the more I came to appreciate the ways their music encapsulated not just the youth culture of the 1960s, but the British working-class experience of the twentieth century generally. So my first thanks must go to my students, who, even if they didn't always share my enthusiasm, never asked me to stop playing these songs in class.

Additional thanks go to the many people who helped me figure out how to write about twentieth-century British music and culture. My usual academic stomping grounds are nineteenth-century Ireland and the British Empire, so I have relied quite a bit on the experience of others to bring me up to speed. Among those who have helped this project along are Nick Bray, Katie Burnett, Carey Fleiner, Linda Kutner, Andy Miller and Bob Riesman. Thanks also to Rosanna Al-Mulla at the University of Stirling Archives and Special Collections for sending me information related to Big Bill Broonzy's appearances on British television (and saving me a trip to Scotland); Greg Reish and the Center for Popular Music at Middle Tennessee State University for the opportunity to test out some of my early ideas before a live audience; the Summer of Love conference at

Northeastern University's San Francisco campus in July 2017 for allowing me to stage a miniature British Invasion; the staff of the London Metropolitan Archives; and the volunteer staff at the Elstree & Borehamwood Museum, especially Simon Gee and members of the museum's Facebook group, who provided some fascinating anecdotes about Ray Davies's brief time in their town. Thanks also to the History Department and Office of International Affairs at Middle Tennessee State University, both of which funded portions of the travel necessary to write this book. Many thanks are also due to John Scanlan, who encouraged me to develop this book out of was originally a very different project, and who has patiently handled my pestering enquiries ever since.

My deepest appreciation, as always, goes to my wife Kate, who took on a heroic amount of child-distracting and stress-absorbing while I immersed myself in Daviesland. The phrase 'labour of love' has a treacly sound to it that I don't much care for, but it describes my attitude towards this book fairly well. About fifteen years ago my little brother, Joseph Paul Doyle, burned me a copy of the two-disc Kinks compilation *The Ultimate Collection*. He wanted to show me that there was much more to the Kinks than just the early singles that we knew from the classic-rock radio stations in our home town, a judgement with which I (of course) immediately agreed. My brother died in an accident in July 2010, and after that I promised myself that I would live the sort of full, adventurous life that he didn't have enough time to lead. This book, about two brothers who often fought but also made some phenomenal music together, is submitted in partial fulfilment of that promise.

Photo Acknowledgements

The author and the publishers wish to express their thanks to the below sources of illustrative material and/or permission to reproduce it.

Alamy: pp. 9 (Tracksimages.com), 16, 21, 22, 58 (Pictorial Press Ltd); author's collection: pp. 6, 19, 28, 37, 61, 62, 105, 149, 181, 189, 200, 204–5, 210 ; author's photographs: pp. 30, 36, 41, 66, 123, 133, 184, 187; Getty images: p. 25 (Andrew Maclear/Redferns); Imperial War Museums: p. 108; © Tate, London 2018: p. 107 (© The Estate of L. S. Lowry. All Rights Reserved, DACS/ARS 2019); © TfL from the London Transport Museum collection: p. 160; © Board of Trustees, National Gallery of Art, Washington, DC: p. 119; Youtube: pp. 33, 106, 171.

Index

Page numbers in *italics* refer to illustrations